D0260982

LANCASHIRE COUNTY LIBRARY

3011813788637 4

YETI

Also by Graham Hoyland

Last Hours on Everest
Walking Through Spring

YETI

An Abominable History

Graham Hoyland

WILLIAM
COLLINS

William Collins
An imprint of HarperCollins*Publishers*
1 London Bridge Street
London SE1 9GF

WilliamCollinsBooks.com

First published in the United Kingdom by William Collins in 2018

23 22 21 20 19 18
11 10 9 8 7 6 5 4 3 2 1

Text © Graham Hoyland, 2018
Photographs © individual copyright holders

The author asserts his moral right to be identified as the author of this work.
All rights reserved. No parts of this publication may be reproduced, stored in a
retrieval system or transmitted, in any form or by any means, electronic, mechanical,
photocopying, recording or otherwise, without the prior permission of the publishers.
A catalogue record for this book is available from the British Library.

All reasonable efforts have been made by the author and publishers to trace
the copyright owners of the material quoted in this book and of any images
reproduced in this book. In the event that the author or publishers are notified of
any mistakes or omissions by copyright owners after publication, the author and
publishers will endeavour to rectify the position accordingly for any subsequent printing.

HB ISBN 978-0-00-827949-3
TPB ISBN 978-0-00-827950-9

Typeset in Birka by Palimpsest Book Production Ltd, Falkirk, Stirlingshire
Printed and bound by CPI Group (UK) Ltd, Croydon CR0 4YY

MIX
Paper from
responsible sources
FSC
www.fsc.org FSC™ C007454

This book is produced from independently certified FSC™ paper
to ensure responsible forest management.
For more information visit: **www.harpercollins.co.uk/green**

LANCASHIRE COUNTY LIBRARY	
3011813788637 4	
Askews & Holts	08-Jan-2019
001.944 HOY	£20.00
NST	

To the seekers after truth

Introduction

October 2016

The footprints in the snow were large, bigger than a human's, with clearly defined toes. There was no sign of claw-marks. These prints looked as though they had been made only minutes before we arrived. I shivered and glanced around the deserted valley. We were the first Westerners ever to see this place, and we really hadn't meant to come here.

Our expedition was in trouble. We had been trying to reach Gangkar Punsum, the world's highest unclimbed mountain. This lies on the Tibetan border in Bhutan, the Himalayan kingdom to the east of Kathmandu which is rarely visited by Westerners. The weather had been the worst in living memory, with rain or snow on every single day since leaving Thimpu, the capital. On day three, our packhorses were attacked by wild bees, and then our leader had suffered a back injury and was now lying in a crude shelter in the jungle four days behind, tended by our doctor. Our problem was that the high pass we had just crossed was now closed to our yaks by heavy snow. We couldn't retreat that way, and the passes towards the mountain were closed too. We were trapped, and the 25 yaks only carried supplies for three weeks. We had to get out before winter set in. As the five remaining Westerners, we could have attempted to re-cross the pass, leaving the yaks behind, but as acting leader I was unhappy about splitting the party even further. We had to stay with our tents and food. We also had a whole yak-herder family with us, including a young mother nursing an 8-month-old baby, so it was clear that we had to sink or swim together.

I asked our yak-herder Namgay Tsering for advice, and it was then that he told me of a lost valley that might provide a route back to civilisation, with two higher but easier passes that the yaks could just about manage in the snowy conditions. So the next morning we set off, guided by Pem Dem, the 20-year-old mother, with her baby Thinley. The yaks were being gathered up and loaded and would follow up behind us. After a few hours, we walked up into the Lost Valley and Pem Dem sat down in the swirling snow to breastfeed her baby. It was only then that I noticed the solitary yak standing in the snow a few yards away. It seemed distressed. These animals are sometimes abandoned by the yak-herders when they are too old to carry heavy loads. This poor creature bellowed when it scented our baggage yaks coming up the valley behind. The significance of this animal was soon to be revealed.

Mother Pem Dem and son Thinley: the witnesses.

After feeding her baby, Pem Dem slung him onto her back again and we set off towards the Wangchum La pass at the head of the valley. We were all anxious about tackling this: at 16,400 feet it was the highest we had climbed so far, some 650 feet higher than Mont Blanc. It had never before been seen or crossed by Westerners. A few minutes later, just as the first bunch of baggage yaks stampeded past us, I spotted Sonam, our deaf-mute kitchen boy, pointing at the snow to the left of our path.

There they were: two footprints, spaced quite far apart, larger than human size. The left one was very clear, and my flesh crawled as I saw how the toes had curled into the snow for grip. The prints were larger than my own size-ten feet. My mind raced. I had to record this evidence and establish its authenticity in around twenty minutes. Any longer and I would be endangering our party. While I filmed the footprints and took a snow sample, Predrag Jovanovic, our resident particle physicist, scouted ahead and behind the prints, which crossed our path at right angles, away from the solitary yak. He reported that in one direction the baggage yaks had obliterated all traces, and in the other our own footprints had done the same.

Had we disturbed a stalking creature? Was some large predator lurking behind one of the huge boulders that were scattered around the Lost Valley? I stood up and uneasily gazed up at the large boulders on the snow-covered hillside above me. Was there something up there that I couldn't see but the old yak could smell? I crouched down again and took scrapings of dirty snow within the footprints for DNA testing. I didn't want to try to remove the whole footprint, as there was a chance that we might have to retreat from the pass. In that case we could camp, re-examine the print and scout around for further signs.

I knew that anyone hearing our story would assume these footprints had been faked, and this was foremost in my mind too, and so I hastened forwards to the rest of the party. Had they seen the prints? Had they seen anyone bending down? The answer was a flat no. Everyone was too intent on getting to the pass, and anyway I had everyone in view just in front of me. No one had even hesitated. We set off again. I was frustrated that I had no time to record the prints in more detail, but at least I was fairly sure that there was no fakery: Pem Dem was too busy with her baby and with route-finding, and I was watching everyone else closely for signs of fatigue. Sonam, although obviously an intelligent and helpful man, was impossible to question, being deaf and unable to speak.

In the event we crossed the Wangchum La, becoming the first Westerners to do so and leaving the Lost Valley behind us. We then camped below the Saga La, climbed it the next day and were eventually reunited with our leader who was now recovered. Later in the expedition, two of us stood on the summit of a previously unclimbed mountain and gazed over hundreds of square miles of country previously unseen by Western eyes. There was plenty of terrain here for the snow leopards whose tracks we saw regularly, so why not a larger predator? We saw blue sheep and musk deer, so there was surely enough prey.

So, what was the creature? Was it a bear? The absence of claw-marks suggested otherwise. Could it therefore be the mythical beast that is spoken of all along the Himalayas: the Abominable Snowman, or yeti? Is the yeti really living in the unexplored wilderness of North Bhutan?

I decided to find out what I could about the strange world of mythical beasts: the cryptids.

CHAPTER ONE

A surprising discovery. . .Attenborough, a believer. . .Tintin in Tibet. . .the Third Eye. . .upon that mountain. . .a hero of Mount Everest. . .a wild goose chase. . .a lost camera. . .his shroud the snow.

When I gazed at those yeti footprints in the Lost Valley, I felt a mixture of fear and bewilderment. It was only later that I felt a connection to those who had gone before. For nearly a century, Western explorers had been coming back from the heights with reports of man-like beasts in the Himalayas. They began with stories of strange footprints, then told of the violent deaths of their pack animals, killed with one savage blow. Their Sherpas told them that yetis were seven feet tall, covered with brownish hair. Their feet faced backwards, which made them confusing to track. The males had a long fringe of hair over their eyes and the females had pendulous breasts which they slung over their shoulders when they ran. Your only hope of escaping from a yeti was to quickly determine which sex it was and then run downhill if it was a male, who would be blinded by his fringe, or run uphill if it was a female, who would be impeded by her breasts. Sometimes lonely males would kidnap Sherpa women and keep them in their caves, breeding strange children.

I decided to look back through the years and try to disentangle myth from reality, cryptozoology from science. In thirty years of climbing in these mountains, why had I only seen footprints? Why had no one managed to capture one of these fabled beasts? Where did they live, and could I find any solid proof of the yeti? Furthermore, was there any evidence for Bigfoot, the yeti's American cousin?

Mountaineering as a sport has collected a great literature around it in a way that, say, football or table tennis have not, so this book will take us through some of the most gripping accounts of the Abominable Snowman ever written. Cryptozoology itself has given us great fiction too, such as Arthur Conan Doyle's *The Lost World* and Hollywood's *Jurassic Park*. Somewhere in these pages lies the truth about these beasts and the dangers contained within them. This is a detective story, and like the best detective stories it starts with a discovery and a mystery.

We humans have only identified about two million of the estimated 10 million living species on our planet, and new species have been discovered in modern times that scientists had previously refused to accept. The gorilla was a legendary creature seen in the fifth century BCE by Hanno the Navigator, who described 'a savage people, the greater part of whom were women, whose bodies were hairy, and who our interpreters called Gorillae. We pursued but could take none of the males; they all escaped to the top of precipices, which they mounted with ease, and threw down stones.' The name was derived from Ancient Greek Γόριλλαι (*gorillai*), meaning 'tribe of hairy women'. An Andrew Battel of Leigh, Essex, traded in the Kingdom of Congo during the 1590s and described 'a kind of Great Apes, if they might be so termed, of the height of a man but twice as bigge in features of their limes with strength proportionable, hairie all over, otherwise altogether like men

2

and women in the whole bodily shape'. This was a good description of the gorilla, but the animal was regarded as mythical until 1902 when Captain Robert von Beringe shot and recovered two mountain gorilla specimens in the course of an expedition to establish the boundaries of German East Africa. When standing on two legs, they look remarkably like the speculative pictures of the yeti I have seen.

Then there was the 'African unicorn', the okapi, which was only discovered in 1901. It turned out to be a relative of the giraffe. Even giraffes themselves were regarded as fabulous until the mid-nineteenth century. A hairy pig thought to be extinct since the Pleistocene, the Chacoan peccary, was found trotting around happily in Argentina as late as 1971. Live giant pandas weren't seen in Europe until 1916, and the existence of the Komodo dragon was disbelieved until 1926. So there were plenty of precedents for legendary animals such as the yeti eventually being accepted by scientists once they had been found (and then shot) by Westerners.

Sir David Attenborough is convinced. 'I believe the Abominable Snowman may be real,' said the TV naturalist. 'There are footprints that stretch for hundreds of miles and we know that in the 1930s a German fossil was found with these huge molars that were four or five times the size of human molars. They had to be the molars of a large ape, one that was huge, about 10 or 12 feet tall. It was immense. And it is not impossible that it might exist. If you have walked the Himalayas, there are these immense rhododendron forests that go on for hundreds of square miles which could hold the yeti. If there are some still alive and you walked near their habitat, you can bet that these creatures may be aware of you, but you wouldn't be aware of them.'*

The New Scientist magazine, reporting on a photograph of a yeti footprint, was confident that the creature existed. Like Attenborough, the writer concluded that it could be a giant

* Radio Times, 10 September 2013.

ape: 'The Abominable Snowman might well be a huge, heavily-built bipedal primate similar to the fossil *Gigantopithecus*. . . the Snowman must be taken seriously.'*

And what about the North American cousin of the yeti, the Bigfoot? 'I'm sure that they exist,' said the celebrated primatologist Jane Goodall on NPR radio. 'I've talked to so many Native Americans, who've all described the same sounds, two who've seen them.'†

There was good reason to believe, therefore, that I had been close to a large primate unknown to science. Had I disturbed the beginning of a stalking manoeuvre which would have led to the violent death of the solitary yak? The predator would have to have been big enough to take on a yak bull, with jaws and teeth powerful enough to kill it. Or would it despatch the animal with one savage blow, and then turn towards me?

When I was a child, all I knew about the Abominable Snowman was what I had read in *Tintin in Tibet*, drawn by the Belgian cartoonist Hergé and published in 1959. Tintin has a dream in which he sees his Chinese friend Chang lying in plane wreckage. Tintin, Captain Haddock and Snowy the dog travel to Kathmandu, then trek to Tibet. After various adventures they encounter the terrifying yeti, or *migou*, and their porters run away. Eventually Chang is found in the yeti's cave, having been nursed back to health by the beast. They all return to civilisation without a proper encounter with the animal, who watches them depart with apparent sadness. In the last frame, Chang says: 'You know, I hope they never succeed in finding him. They'd treat him like some

* 'It Seems To Me,' *New Scientist*, 12 May 1960, p. 1218.

† Interview on National Public Radio's *Science Friday*, 27 September 2002.

wild animal. I tell you, Tintin, from the way he took care of me, I couldn't help wondering if deep down, he hadn't a human soul.'

The drawings in the book were inspired by reports from the Golden Age of Himalayan climbing, then in full swing. Kathmandu is represented as it was in the 1950s, with no cars or even bicycles, just porters, and the city's streets are so empty they are covered with red pimento peppers drying in the sun. I was entranced by the drawings of the mountains and in particular by the idea of a giant man-beast with a coconut-shaped head. How wonderful it would be if there existed a huge, orange, hairy creature, living in the high mountains, unknown to science! How marvellous it would be to contact him, to learn his language and protect him and his furry family! No doubt he would look just like the yeti in *Tintin in Tibet*, and would be a giant, cuddly, missing link.

Tintin Yeti

However, as with most children's books there was a darker adult subtext. During composition, Hergé (Georges Remi) was in the throes of a mental breakdown caused by the real-isation that he had fallen out of love with his wife Germaine, whom he had married in 1932, and fallen into love with Fanny

Vlamink, a colourist who worked with him at the Studios Hergé. Fanny was 28 years his junior and a master of the colouring technique that he felt he had never quite come to grips with. Hergé's breakdown included nightmares about the colour white:

> At the time, I was going through a time of real crisis and my dreams were nearly always white dreams. And they were extremely distressing. . . At a particular moment, in an immaculately white alcove, a white skeleton appeared that tried to catch me. And then instantly everything around me became white.*

Hergé, a Catholic, went to see a Jungian psychoanalyst who interpreted his dreams as a search for purity and tried to persuade him to abandon his work. He ignored the advice and persisted with *Tintin in Tibet*, which eventually became his favourite work. The book's plates contain large areas of the colour white depicting the snowy Himalayas (Tibet, of course, is largely an orangey-brown high-altitude desert). The mountain above the Tibetan monastery is called the White Goddess. And Tintin's companion is a white dog named Snowy. Hergé himself stated that the story 'must be a solo voyage of redemption' from the 'whiteness of guilt'.†

Of course, these interpretations can be taken too far: Tintin's other companion is the alcoholic sea-captain Archibald Haddock. His name came from 'a sad English fish' cooked by the long-suffering Germaine.

It is worth noting that the front cover of *Tintin in Tibet* does not incorporate an image of the yeti, just his footprints. In the picture, Tharkey, the loyal Sherpa (another Western archetype), looks matter-of-fact, as if to him the yeti is an accepted phenom-

* Interview with Numa Sadoul, 1975.

† H. Thompson, *Tintin: Hergé and his Creation* (Hodder & Stoughton, 1991).

enon, but Tintin and Captain Haddock look astounded by the size of the footprints in the snow.

Tintin in Tibet

As a child during the 1960s, I became interested in Tibet and Buddhism. One book that went around my school in Rutland was *The Third Eye*, an autobiography by the Tibetan lama Lobsang Rampa. It is a gripping read. Born to a wealthy Lhasa aristocrat, he has a hole bored in his skull to reveal a third eye with which he discerns the auras of those around the Dalai Lama, and thus understands their true motives. He sees the British ambassador Sir Charles Alfred Bell as naive but unthreatening, but warns the Dalai Lama that the Chinese diplomats are a real threat to Tibet's independence and that he must prepare for war and invasion. He practises levitation and clairvoyance.

Tuesday Lobsang Rampa (to give him his full name) also

describes an encounter with a yeti. 'We looked at each other, both of us frozen with fright for a period which seemed ageless. It was pointing a hand at me and making a curious mewing noise like a kitten. The head had no frontal lobes but seemed to slope back almost directly from the heavy brows. The chin receded greatly and the teeth were large and prominent. As I looked and perhaps jumped with fright, the yeti screeched, turned and leaped away.'*

The Third Eye was immensely popular and became a best-seller. There were follow-ups: *Doctor from Lhasa* and *The Rampa Story*. I, for one, was absolutely gripped and couldn't wait to get my hands on the next T. Lobsang Rampa book. After all, boys reading this stuff were considered cool.

Unfortunately for us, T. Lobsang Rampa was in fact Cyril Hoskins, a plumber's son from Plympton, Devon. Cyril didn't possess a passport, hadn't ever been to Tibet and couldn't even read or speak the language. The whole series of books had been faked.

Hoskins had been uncovered by the real Tibetologist and climber, the great Heinrich Harrer, who had become suspicious of one of the books. Before the Second World War, Harrer had been attempting to climb the mountain Nanga Parbat in British India when he was captured and interned in a prisoner of war camp. Being Harrer, he managed to escape, cross the border into Tibet and become the young Dalai Lama's personal tutor. He was the real thing: a mountaineering hero. On reading *The Third Eye*, he became suspicious of certain details. There was the description of a tropical oasis on the Tibetan plateau,

* Dr T. Lobsang Rampa, *The Third Eye* (Secker & Warburg, 1956).

something which does not and cannot exist. The plateau itself was described as being at an altitude of 24,000 feet instead of around 14,000 feet. There were other discrepancies, such as Lobsang Rampa's claim that the Tibetan apprentices had to memorise every page of the Kangyur Buddhist Sutras. These were not even read by students.

Harrer and other Tibetan scholars became convinced that the book was fiction, so they hired Clifford Burgess, a private detective from Liverpool, to investigate Lobsang Rampa. He revealed Cyril Hoskins, and the whole inglorious story of fakery was exposed on 3 February 1958 in the *Daily Express* under the headline: 'The Full Truth About The Bogus Lama.' It turned out that Hoskins had got the idea for *The Third Eye* by reading books such as Harrer's *Seven Years in Tibet* in the London libraries.* T. Lobsang Rampa lived to write again, however, producing books such as *Living with the Lama* and *My Visit to Venus*.

The significance of this tale is not the fact of the hoax but the amount of credence attached to it. I swallowed the story whole. So did my school friends and most adult readers. *The Third Eye* inspired many who later became Tibetologists, and in many ways T. Lobsang Rampa helped to start New Age culture. We *wanted* to believe in him. And we wanted to believe in his yeti.

I learned more about the yeti during nine expeditions to Mount Everest in my search for the English climber George Mallory. I lived for a total of two years on that mountain. As a boy, I had heard stories about my Uncle Hunch who had made the very first climb of the mountain with his friend Mallory. I

---

* Lobsang Rampa's story is recounted in Geoff Tibballs, *The World's Greatest Hoaxes* (Barnes & Noble, 2006), pp. 27–29.

remember standing on the lawn outside Verlands House in Painswick, aged twelve, and looking up at Hunch: the legendary Howard Somervell (who was actually a cousin, not an uncle). By then he was a stout old man in his eighties, but with a youthful twinkle in his eye. He knew he was starting a hare in front of this young boy.

Somervell was a remarkable polymath: a double first at Cambridge, a talented artist (his pictures of Everest are still on the walls of the Alpine Club in London) and an accomplished musician (he transcribed the music he heard in Tibet into Western notation). He had worked as a surgeon during the Somme offensive in the First World War, and during that apocalyptic battle he had to operate in a field hospital with a mile-long queue of litters carrying the broken and dying youth of Britain. During a rest from surgery, he sat and watched a young soldier lying asleep on the grass. It slowly dawned on him that the boy was dead, and it seems that it was this particular trauma that prompted him to throw away a successful career as a London surgeon and become a medical missionary in India instead.

Before all that, he was one of the foremost Alpinists in England. He was invited to join the 1922 Mount Everest expedition and took part in the first serious attempt to climb the mountain with his friend Mallory, and his oxygen-free height record with fellow climber Edward Norton in 1924 stood for over fifty years. He even won an Olympic gold medal. He was one of the extraordinary Everesters, from the land of the yeti.

Of course, I was only interested in the amazing story he was telling me. 'Norton and I had a last-ditch attempt to climb Mount Everest, and we got higher than any man had ever been before. I really couldn't breathe properly and on the way down my throat blocked up completely. I sat down to die, but as one last try I pressed my chest hard [and here the old man pushed his chest to demonstrate to me] and up came the blockage. We got down safely. We met Mallory at the North Col on his way up. He said to me that he had forgotten his camera, and I lent him mine. So if my camera was ever found, you could prove that Mallory got to the top.' It was a throwaway comment, which he probably made a hundred times in the course of telling this story, but this time it found its mark.

So I spent much of the rest of my life learning to be a mountaineer and then hunting for the camera on Mount Everest. This search would also lead me to the yeti. Many times, I cursed myself for chasing Uncle Hunch's wild goose, but on the way we found George Mallory's body. Poor Mallory. His shroud was the snow.*

* G. Hoyland, *Last Hours on Everest* (William Collins, 2013).

CHAPTER TWO

*When men and mountains meet. . .campfire stories. . .the
Abdominal Snowman. . .the 1921 Reconnaissance of Mount
Everest. . .a remarkable man. . .more footprints. . .The Valley of
the Flowers.*

'Great things are done when men and mountains meet' wrote
William Blake. He might have added that there would be some
great tales, too. On one Mallory filming expedition, I climbed
with the actor Brian Blessed to around 25,000 feet on the North
Ridge of Mount Everest. His generous stomach and his
bellowing of stories around the campfire earned him the nickname of *Abdominal* Snowman. The Sherpas were fascinated by
him and swore that he actually was a yeti. They would giggle
explosively and roll on the snow with laughter at his antics.
Sherpa people generally have a good sense of fun, and I noticed
that whenever a yeti was mentioned this would often provoke
a smile, a laugh – but occasionally an uneasy look.

In the course of thirty or so trips to the Himalayas, I heard
many tales about the beast from Sherpas and they were clearly
believers. There are very similar stories from local villagers all
along the Himalayas, from Arunachal Pradesh to Ladakh, and
even though the names changed they seemed to be talking about

three kinds of yeti. First, and largest, is the terrifying *dzu-teh*, who stands eight feet tall when he is on his back legs; however, he prefers to walk on all fours. He can kill a yak with one swipe of his claws. There is the smaller *chu-the* or *thelma*, a little reddish-coloured child-sized creature who walks on two legs and has long arms. He is seen in the forests of Sikkim and Nepal. Then there is the *meh-teh*, who is most like a man and has orangey-red fur on his body. He attacks humans and is the one most often depicted on monastery wall paintings. *Yeh-teh* or yeti is a mutation of his name. He looks most like the *Tintin in Tibet* yeti.

Some of the Sherpas I climbed with had stories about family yaks being attacked, and yak-herders terrorised by a creature

The Meh-Teh, the Dzu-Teh and the Chu-Teh.

A drawing of the three yetis by Lama Kapa Kalden of Khumjung, 1954.

that sounds like the enormous *dzu-teh*. In 1986 in Namche Bazaar, capital of the Sherpa Khumbu region, I met Sonam Hisha Sherpa. Twenty years previously, he had been grazing his yak/cow crosses, the *dzo*, high on a pasture. During the night, he heard loud whistling and bellowing while he cowered with fright in a cave with his companions. They were sure they were going to be killed by the *dzu-teh* after it had finished with their livestock. In the morning, Sonam and his men found that two *dzo* had been killed and eaten. There was no meat or bones remaining: only blood, dung and intestines.

So what was the truth about the yeti? After my own Bhutanese yeti finding, I decided to follow the footprints back in recorded history and see what stood up to scrutiny. In this book, we'll follow the Westerners' yeti tracks first and see if they lead us to the original Himalayan yeti. On the way, we will meet some of the most remarkable men in exploration history.

The earliest Western account of a wild man in the Himalayas dates from 1832 and is given by Brian Houghton Hodgson, the Court of Nepal's first British Resident, and the first Englishman permitted to visit this forbidden land. Hodgson had to contend with the hotbed that was (and still is) Nepalese politics. He was particularly interested in the natural history and ethnography of the region, and so his report carries some weight. He recorded that his native hunters had been frightened by a 'wild man':*

Religion has introduced the Bandar [rhesus macaque] monkey into the central region, where it seems to flourish, half domesticated, in the neighbourhood of temples, in

---

* *Journal of the Asiatic Society of Calcutta, India,* 1832.

the populous valley of Nepal proper [this is still the case]. My shooters were once alarmed in the Kachár by the apparition of a 'wild man', possibly an ourang, but I doubt their accuracy. They mistook the creature for a càcodemon or rakshas (demons), and fled from it instead of shooting it. It moved, they said, erectly, was covered with long dark hair, and had no tail.

It has to be noted that Hodgson didn't see the wild man of Nepal himself, and he doubted the story. We can go back further in history for stories about wild men. Alexander the Great set out to conquer Persia and India in 326 BC, penetrating nearly as far as Kashmir. He heard about strange wild men of the snows, who were described as something like the satyrs, the lustful Greek gods with the body of a man but the horns, legs and feet of an animal. Alexander demanded to have one of them brought to him, but the local villagers said the creature could not survive at low altitude (rather a good excuse). Later, Pliny the Elder wrote in his *Naturalis Historia*: 'In the land of the satyrs, in the mountains that lie to the east of India, live creatures that are extremely swift, as they can run on both four feet and on two. They have bodies like men, and because of their speed can only be caught when they are ill or old.' He went on to describe monstrous races of peoples such as the cynocephali or dog-heads, the sciapodae, whose single foot was so huge it could act as a sunshade, and the mouthless astomi, who lived on scents alone. By comparison, his yeti sounds quite plausible. 'When I have observed nature she has always induced me to deem no statement about her incredible.'

Septimius Severus was the only Roman emperor to be born in Libya, Africa, and he lived in York between 208 and 211 BC. His head priest, Claudius Aelianus, wrote *De Natura Animalium* (*On the Nature of Animals*), a book of facts and fables about the animal kingdom designed to illustrate human morals. I like to imagine the Roman emperor reading it to take his mind off his final illness during the Yorkshire drizzle. In his book, Aelianus describes an animal similar to the yeti:

> If one enters the mountains of neighbouring India, one comes upon lush, overgrown valleys . . . animals that look like Satyrs roam these valleys. They are covered with shaggy hair and have a long horse's tail. When left to themselves, they stay in the forest and eat tree sprouts. But when they hear the dim of approaching hunters and the barking of dogs, they run with incredible speed to hide in mountain caves. For they are masters at mountain climbing. They also repel approaching humans by hurling stones down at them.

The first sighting of yeti footprints by a Westerner was made by the English soldier and explorer Major Laurence Waddell. He was a Professor of Tibetan Culture and a Professor of Chemistry, a surgeon and an archaeologist, and he had roamed Tibet in disguise. He is thought by some to be the real-life precursor of the film character Indiana Jones.* One of his theories included a belief that the beginning of all civilisation dated from the Aryan Sumerians who were blond Nordics with blue eyes. These theories were later picked up by the German Nazis and led to their expedition to Tibet in 1938–39. While exploring in northeast Sikkim in 1889, Waddell's party came across a set of large footprints which his servants said were made by the yeti, a beast that was highly dangerous and fed on humans:

* C. Preston, *The Rise of Man in the Gardens of Sumeria: A Biography of L. A. Waddell* (Sussex Academic Press, 2009).

Some large footprints in the snow led across our track and away up to the higher peaks. These were alleged to be the trail of the hairy wild men who are believed to live amongst the eternal snows, along with the mythical white lions, whose roar is reputed to be heard during storms [perhaps these were avalanches]. The belief in these creatures is universal amongst Tibetans. None, however, of the many Tibetans who I have interrogated on this subject could ever give me an authentic case. On the most superficial investigation, it always resolved into something heard tell of. These so-called hairy wild men are evidently the great yellow snow-bear (*Ursus isabellinus*) which is highly carnivorous and often kills yaks. Yet, although most of the Tibetans know this bear sufficiently to give it a wide berth, they live in such an atmosphere of superstition that they are always ready to find extraordinary and supernatural explanations of uncommon events.*

Note that Major Waddell did not believe in the story of wild men, and identified the creature as a bear. It should also be noted that *Ursus isabellinus* comes in many colours: sometimes yellow, sometimes sandy, brown or blackish. Crucially for our story, Waddell was the first modern European to report the existence of the yeti legend. In so doing, he was the first in a long line of British explorers whose words on the yeti were misrepresented and whose conclusions were deleted.

The next explorer to march across our stage is Lt-Col. Charles Howard-Bury, leader of the 1921 Everest reconnaissance

* L. A. Waddell, *Among the Himalayas* (Andesite Press, 2015).

expedition, who saw something strange when he was crossing the Lhakpa' La at 21,000 feet.

Howard-Bury was another of the extraordinary Everesters. He was wealthy and moved easily in high society. He had a most colourful life, growing up in a haunted gothic castle at Charleville, County Offaly, Ireland. Then, in 1905, he stained his skin with walnut juice and travelled into Tibet without permission, being ticked off by the viceroy of India, Lord Curzon, on his return (Tibet must have been crowded with heavily stained Englishmen at that time). He bought a bear cub, named it Agu and took it home to Ireland where it grew into a seven-foot adult. So he was familiar with bear prints. He was taken prisoner during the First World War by the Germans and staged an escape with other officers. He never married and lived with the Shakespearean actor Rex Beaumont, whom he had met, aged 57, when Beaumont was 26. Together they restored Belvedere House, Westmeath, Ireland, and also built a villa in Tunis. Here they entertained colourful notables such as Sacheverell Sitwell, Dame Freya Stark and the professional pederast André Gide.

Was Howard-Bury prone to the telling of tall stories? Fellow Everester George Mallory didn't much like him but thought not. The story he brought back seemed entirely plausible to fellow members of the Alpine Club. He was a careful observer of nature and a plant hunter (*Primula buryana* is named after him). After the Mallory research, I found it hard to disentangle truth from wishful thinking, but I felt that it was important to note what Howard-Bury himself observed and then see how the newspapers reported the story. Howard-Bury's diary notes for 22 September 1921 read: 'We distinguished hare and fox tracks; but one mark, like that of a human foot, was most puzzling. The coolies assured me that it was the track of a wild, hairy man, and that these men were occasionally to be found in the wildest and most inaccessible mountains.'

Later, he expanded the story: he reported that the party (including Mallory, who also saw the tracks) was camped at

20,000 feet and set off at 4am in bright moonlight to make their crossing of the pass. On the way, they saw the footprints, which 'were probably caused by a large loping grey wolf, which in the soft snow formed double tracks rather like those of a bare-footed man'. However, the porters 'at once volunteered that the tracks must be that of "The Wild Man of the Snows", to which they gave the name *metoh kangmi*'.

Howard-Bury himself did not believe these stories. He had sent a newspaper article home by telegraph, and, as Bill Tilman so delightfully put it in his famous yeti Appendix B to *Mount Everest 1938*: 'In order to dissociate himself from such an extravagant and laughable belief he put no less than three exclamation marks after the statement (the Wild Men of the Snows!!!); but the telegraph system makes no allowance for subtleties and the finer points of literature, the savings sign were omitted, and the news was accorded very full value at home.'*

The Times of London ran the story under the lurid headline of 'Tibetan Tales of Hairy Murderers'. As a result, a journalist for *The Statesman* in Calcutta, Henry Newman, who wrote under the telling pseudonym 'Kim', interviewed the porters on their return to Darjeeling. It is rare that you can spot the actual beginning of a legend, but here is the moment of birth of the Western yeti:

I fell into conversation with some of the porters, and to my surprise and delight another Tibetan who was present gave me a full description of the wild men, how their feet were turned backwards to enable them to climb easily and how their hair was so long and matted that, when going downhill, it fell over their eyes . . . When I asked him what name was applied to these men, he said '*metoh kangmi*': kangmi means 'snow men' and the word 'metoh' I translated as 'abominable'.

* H.W. Tilman, *Mount Everest 1938* (Cambridge University Press, 1948).

This was a mis-translation. Howard-Bury had already offered 'man-bear' as the translation. Later we will see that what 'another Tibetan' probably said was *meh-teh,* which was a fabled creature familiar to any Sherpa or Tibetan who had heard the stories on his mother's knee, or who had looked up at the frescoes in a Buddhist monastery. What the porters were describing was perfectly familiar to them in their own terms: 'man-bear'. Tilman recounted in his Appendix B how Newman wrote a letter long afterwards in *The Times,* a paper with a long and profitable relationship with the Abominable Snowman and Mount Everest. 'The whole story seemed such a joyous creation, that I sent it to one or two newspapers. Later I was told I had not quite got the force of the word *"metch",* which did not mean "abominable" quite so much as filthy or disgusting, some-body wearing filthy tattered clothing. The Tibetan word means something like that, but it is much more emphatic, just as a Tibetan is more dirty than anyone else.'

In fact, Newman, Tilman or his publisher had got the spelling wrong: the letters TCH cannot be rendered in Tibetan, and what Newman probably should have written was 'metoh', meaning man-bear and certainly not 'abominable'. The word that the Sherpas use to refer to the creature is actually *yeh-teh,* or yeti, which is perhaps a corruption of *meh-teh,* again 'man-bear'.

It may seem that I am making a meal of this, but whether by accident or by design Newman had 'improved' the story to invent a name that was not a true translation of what the porters had actually said, but instead was destined to send a frisson of horror through *The Times* readers of the Home Counties. This was such a powerful new myth that it may have helped the eventual climbing of Mount Everest.

Newman had gleaned the fascinating fact that the wild men had their feet turned backwards to enable them to climb easily, which is an odd detail as climbers in those pre-war days used to reverse up very steep ice slopes when wearing their flexible crampons. Newman's pseudonym 'Kim' suggests that he was an admirer of Rudyard Kipling's character, the boy-spy, and so the Western yeti also began his long and peculiar association with the intelligence services, eventually reaching as far as MI5 and the CIA. As for Newman's exaggeration of the name Abominable Snowman, perhaps he was gilding a dog's ear, but whatever his reason the name stuck.

Thus began the long-running Western legend of the Abominable Snowman/yeti. And all because of the absence of three exclamation marks!!! Another newspaper picked up the first report and embellished it in January 1922, claiming that Howard-Bury's party had discovered 'a race of wild men living among the perpetual snows'. There was a quote from one William Hugh Knight, who the writer claimed was 'one of the best known explorers of Tibet', and a member of 'the British Royal Societies club' who said that he had 'seen one of the wild men from a fairly close distance sometime previously; he hadn't reported it before, but felt that due to the statement about manlike footprints that was made by Howard-Bury's party, he was now compelled to add his own evidence to the growing pile'.

Knight said that the wild man was '. . .a little under six feet high, almost stark naked in that bitter cold: it was the month of November. He was kind of pale yellow all over, about the colour of a Chinaman, a shock of matted hair on his head, little hair on his face, highly-splayed feet, and large, formidable hands. His muscular development in the arms, thighs, legs, back, and chest was terrific. He had in his hand what seemed to be some form of primitive bow.' The article went on to claim that the porters had seen the creatures moving around on the snow slopes above them.

The only problem is that William Hugh Knight wasn't one of the best-known explorers of Tibet, and the British Royal Societies club didn't exist. However, there was a Captain William

Henry Knight, who had obtained six months' leave to explore Kashmir and Ladakh over sixty years earlier, in 1860, and wrote the *Diary of a Pedestrian in Cashmere and Thibet,** but nothing in his book resembles the reported description. It would seem that the journalist had plucked the name of a long-dead real Tibetan explorer, changed the name slightly, invented an explorer's club and made up the quote.† This was indeed part of a growing pile: a pile of lies. Incidentally, note that at this stage the wild man is recognisably human: he is partly clothed, he has little hair on his face and he carries a bow. It is only later that he becomes more like the furry ape of legend.

Howard-Bury was well aware of the sensation his report had caused. In his book about the expedition, *Mount Everest: The Reconnaissance, 1921,* he wrote: 'We were able to pick out tracks of hares and foxes, but one that at first looked like a human foot puzzled us considerably. Our coolies at once jumped to the conclusion that this must be "The Wild Man of the Snows", to which they gave the name of *metoh kangmi*, "the abominable snowman" who interested the newspapers so much. On my return to civilised countries I read with interest delightful accounts of the ways and customs of this wild man who we were supposed to have met.'‡

What was needed now, of course, was a sighting, and so along it came. In 1925 the British-Greek photographer N. A. Tombazi was on a British Geological Expedition near the Zemu glacier, when he spotted a yeti-like figure between 200 and 300 yards away. He reported: 'Unquestionably, the figure in outline was exactly like a human being, walking upright and

---

* W. H. Knight, *Diary of a Pedestrian in Cashmere and Thibet* (Cosimo, 2005).

† For an excellent analysis of this, see http://anomalyinfo.com/stories/pre-1922-william-hugh-knights-yeti-sighting.

‡ C. Howard-Bury, G. Leigh-Mallory and A. F. R. Wollaston, *Mount Everest: The Reconnaissance, 1921* (Blumenfeld Press, 2009).

stopping occasionally to uproot or pull at some dwarf rhodo-dendron bushes. It showed up dark against the snow and as far as I could make out, wore no clothes. Within the next minute or so it had moved into some thick scrub and was lost to view.'

Later, Tombazi and his companions descended to the spot and saw footprints 'similar in shape to those of a man, but only six to seven inches long by four inches wide . . . The prints were undoubtedly those of a biped.'* Tombazi did not believe in the Abominable Snowman and thought what he had seen was a wandering pilgrim. One wonders why he bothered to report the sighting at all, but this suggests that thoughts of mysterious bipedal beasts were beginning to enter the minds of Himalayan explorers.

Undaunted by this conclusion, writers of books about Mount Everest, fuelled by George Mallory and Andrew Irvine's myste-rious disappearance near the summit in 1924, embroidered the tale even further. In 1937, Stanley Snaith produced a pot-boiler, *At Grips with Everest,* covering the five Everest expeditions to date, filled with speech-day guff about how Everest was 'spirit-ually within our Empire'. He described how the Abominable Snowman's footprints were made by 'a naked foot: large, splayed, a mark where the toes had gripped the ground where the heel had rested.'† This is not what Howard-Bury reported, but from then on these tracks were made by a man-like monster.

The Case of the Abominable Snowman was a whodunit written in 1941 by one of our poets laureate, Cecil Day-Lewis, using the pen-name Nicholas Blake. Although not featuring the yeti but instead a corpse discovered inside a melting snowman, it indi-cated that the term had entered the public mind.

Our next book which exaggerated and distorted the Howard-

* N. A. Tombazi, *Account of a Photographic Expedition to the Southern Glaciers of Kangchenjunga in the Sikkim Himalaya* (Bombay, 1925).

† S. Snaith, *At Grips with Everest* (The Percy Press, 1937).

Bury and Waddell reports was *Abominable Snowmen* by Ivan T. Sanderson. According to Sanderson, in 1920 (the wrong date) the Everest team led by Howard-Bury were under the Lhapka-La [*sic*] at 17,000 feet (the wrong altitude) watching 'a number of dark forms moving about on a snowfield far above'. (They didn't.) They hastened upwards and found footprints a size 'three times those of normal humans'. (No!) Ivan T. Sanderson then states that the porters used the term yeti (and no, they didn't).

Furthermore, Sanderson completely misrepresented Major Waddell's report, making up details about bare feet making the footprints and completely omitting Waddell's conclusion that they were made by a bear. *Abominable Snowmen* became the starting point for many subsequent yeti writers. But Sanderson listed both Howard-Bury's and Waddell's books in his bibliography and thus knew that neither of the expedition leaders believed their porters' interpretation. But why spoil a good story?

If the first Western sightings of yeti prints were exaggerated and distorted, did this necessarily mean that all subsequent sightings were unreliable? As a BBC producer, I sometimes felt the temptation to embroider stories, but I can honestly say that in thirty years with the Corporation I saw little fakery. The temptation was always there, though.

Let me give an example. A good friend of mine was shooting a documentary series for an un-named TV company about a certain tribe in a certain country. It was horribly hot, and the director was loud, sweltering and increasingly angry that the local men he was filming on a hunting trip couldn't even find and kill a rabbit. The budget was fast running out and he had a mortgage to pay. Aware, no doubt, that his next gig depended on a kill, he phoned a game park in a neighbouring country and ordered a small antelope to be shot and airlifted in. The resulting film shows a clip of grainy footage of a similar animal running away, and then cuts to a spear sticking out of the bullet hole in the corpse. The audience were shown this as a representation of truth and were deceived. The director got another job and his executive producer was satisfied. The problem is this: it was a lie.

As a rule, though, newspapers seem to be worse than TV, and the Internet is worse still. The rise of US President Donald Trump was accompanied by the rise of the so-called false news sites, where there are no editorial controls over content, and the only driver is the number of dollars racked up by click-bait.

I decided to check a few more of the famous yeti sightings and try to get to the bottom of them. Was the beast going to disappear before my eyes?

Our next account of the yeti, from 1937, is to be found in *The Valley of the Flowers*,* by the English mountaineer, Frank Smythe. He was the first climber to make a living by writing books about his expeditions, unlike the Alpine Club set who were often independently wealthy. Smythe's particular genius was the way in which he brought the wonder and pleasure of mountaineering to a wider public. However, in person he was famously grumpy, a condition which a companion wryly noted 'decreased with altitude'. He initiated a furious volley of letters in *The Times* after his encounter with the yeti.

In *The Valley of the Flowers*, he wrote a chapter dedicated to the Abominable Snowman. This is worth quoting at length as it gives a flavour of Smythe's writing style with his love of flowers, his gentle humour and his scientific approach to the subject of the yeti. It also contains all the classic ingredients of a yeti hunt: the exotic location, the find, the puzzlement and fear, the tracking and the deductions. His conclusions led to a public rebuttal, which would have consequences later.

---

* F. Smythe, *The Valley of the Flowers* (Hodder & Stoughton, 1938).

Smythe was with a small party of Sherpas in an unexplored valley parallel to the Bhyundar valley, now in the state of Uttarakhand, northern India:

On July 16th I left the base camp, taking with me Wangdi, Pasang and Nurbu with light equipment and provisions for five days. The past week had seen many more flowers come into bloom, prominent among which was the *pedicularis*. This plant goes by the unpleasant popular name of lousewort, from the Latin *pediculus*, a louse, as one of the species, *Pedicularis palustris*, was said to infect sheep with a lousy disease; but it would be difficult to associate the beautiful *pedicularis* of the Bhyundar Valley with any disease, particularly the *Pedicularis siphonantjia* with its light purple blooms. . .

Next morning we were away in excellent weather. Being lightly laden, I was well ahead of the men. On approaching the pass, I was surprised to notice some tracks in the snow, which I first took to be those of a man, though we had seen no traces of shepherds. But when I came up to the tracks I saw the imprint of a huge naked foot, apparently of a biped, and in stride closely resembling my own tracks.

What was it? I was very interested, and at once proceeded to take some photographs. I was engaged in this work when the porters joined me. It was at once evident when they saw the tracks that they were frightened. Wangdi was the first to speak.

'Bad Manshi!' he said, and then 'Mirka!' And in case I still did not understand, 'Kang Admi' (Snowman).

I had already anticipated such a reply and to reassure him and the other two, for I had no wish for my expedition to end prematurely, I said it must be a bear or snow leopard. But Wangdi would have none of this and explained at length how the tracks could not possibly be those of a bear, snow leopard, wolf or any other animal. Had he not

26

seen many such tracks in the past? It was the Snowman, and he looked uneasily about him . . .

Presently the men plucked up courage and assisted me. They were unanimous that the Snowman walked with his toes behind him and that the impressions at the heel were in reality the front toes. I was soon able to disprove this to my own satisfaction by discovering a place where the beast had jumped down from some rocks, making deep impressions where he had landed, and slithering a little in the snow . . .

Superstition, however, knows no logic, and my explanation produced no effect whatsoever on Wangdi.

At length, having taken all the photographs I wanted on the pass, I asked the men to accompany me and follow up the tracks. They were very averse to this at first, but eventually agreed, as they said, following their own 'logic', that the Snowman had come from, not gone, in that direction. From the pass the tracks followed a broad, slightly ascending snow-ridge and, except for one divergence, took an almost straight line. After some 300 yards they turned off the ridge and descended a steep rock-face fully 1,000 feet high seamed with snow gullies. Through my monocular glass I was able to follow them down to a small but considerably crevassed glacier, descending towards the Bhyundar valley and down this to the lowermost limit of the new snow. I was much impressed by the difficulties overcome and the intelligence displayed in overcoming them. In order to descend the face, the beast had made a series of intricate traverses and had zigzagged down a series of ridges and gullies. His track down the glacier was masterly, and from our perch I could see every detail and how cunningly he had avoided concealed snow-covered crevasses. An expert mountaineer could not have made a better route and to have accomplished it without an ice-axe would have been both difficult and dangerous, whilst the unroped descent of a crevassed snow-covered glacier must be accounted as unjustifiable. Obviously the 'Snowman' was well qualified for membership of the Himalayan Club.

My examination in this direction completed, we returned to the pass, and I decided to follow the track in the reverse direction. The man, however, said that this was the direction in which the Snowman was going, and if we overtook him, and even so much as set eyes upon him, we should all drop dead in our tracks, or come to an otherwise bad end. They were so scared at the prospect that I felt it was unfair to force them to accompany me, though I believe that Wangdi, at least, would have done so had I asked him.

The tracks, to begin with, traversed along the side of a rough rock-ridge below the minor point we had ascended when we first visited the pass. I followed them for a short distance along the snow to one side of the rocks, then they turned upwards into the mouth of a small cave under some slabs. I was puzzled to account for the fact that, whereas tracks appeared to come out of the cave, there were none going into it. I had already proved to my own satisfaction the absurdity of the porters' contention that the Snowman walked with his toes behind him; still, I was now alone and cut off from sight of the porters by a mist that had suddenly formed, and I could not altogether repress a ridiculous feeling that perhaps they were right after all; such is the power of superstition high up in the lonely Himalayas. I am ashamed to admit that I stood at a distance from the cave and threw a lump of rock into it before venturing further. Nothing happened, so I went up to the mouth of the cave and looked inside; naturally there was nothing there. I then saw that the single track was explained by the beast having climbed down a steep rock and jumped into the snow at the mouth of the cave. I lost the track among the rocks, so climbed up to the little summit we had previously visited. The mist was now dense and I waited fully a quarter of an hour for it to clear. It was a curious experience seated there with no other human being within sight, and some queer thoughts passed through my mind. Was there really a Snowman? If so, would I encounter him? If I did, an ice-axe would be a poor substitute for a rifle, but Wangdi had said that even to see a Snowman was to die. Evidently he killed you by some miraculous hypnotism; then presumably gobbled you up. It was a fairy-tale come to life . . . Meditating on this strange affair, I returned to the porters, who were unfeignedly glad to see me, for they had assumed that I was walking to my death.

This, the classic sighting of bear tracks masquerading as yeti prints, is worth deconstructing. All the usual features are present: the shock of the initial sighting, the puzzlement, the backwards-facing feet, the fear of the Sherpas and the curiosity of the Sahib. As John Napier explains in his seminal study *Bigfoot: The Yeti and Sasquatch in Myth and Reality*,* bears are a good candidate for the makers of yeti footprints for several reasons. First, like humans, bears are plantigrade; that is, the anatomy of their walking leg is such that the sole of the foot takes the weight. Their toes and metatarsals are flat on the ground. So they make footprints that look like those of a huge human (or yeti). The other options are digitigrade, walking on the toes with the heel and wrist permanently raised, like dogs and cats, and unguligrade, walking on the nail or nails of the toes (what we call the hoof) with the heel/wrist and the digits permanently raised. So horses are running on their toenails.

Secondly, when bears are walking slowly their hindfeet land just behind the impression made by their forefeet, and when

---

* J. Napier, *Bigfoot: The Yeti and Sasquatch in Myth and Reality* (E. P. Dutton, 1973).

they are walking fast their hindfeet land just *beyond* the impression of the forefeet. And – here's the important bit – at an intermediate speed the two footprints join together, sometimes with the toes of the forefeet appearing to be . . . reversed toes. To make this clear, the oft-repeated story of toes at the *rear* of the yeti footprint could be explained by medium-speed bears.

At an amble, the bear footprints follow one another more in a line, rather like those of a fashion model on a catwalk (well, a bit like that). This just might explain the footprints in a line seen by some witnesses. But there is another possible explanation for those linear sightings. Bears can also walk on their hindlegs for short distances and will stand on their hindlegs to fight with the claws on their front paws, to reach fruit from high branches, or to climb trees. These behaviours will result in human-looking bipedal footprints.

As for the 'elephant' footprints noted later by Shipton et al., when overnight temperatures are low an icy crust forms on the snow. This icy crust is 2 to 3 inches deep and can support the weight of a man. Mountaineers know this, so they get up just after midnight for an 'Alpine start' and move fast across the surface of the snow. Your crampons barely scratch the snow and it is a delight to climb at this time of the morning and watch the sun rise on the peaks around you. Later in the day, the crust melts and gives way when walked on, to the despair of the knackered climber, whose every step now plunges deep into the snow. At either side of the footprint, a roughly triangular area of snow caves in and the resulting shape is rhomboidal. If melting is now added, gigantic elephant-like tracks are the result.

Let's get back to Frank Smythe:

On returning to the base camp some days later, the porters made a statement. It was witnessed by Oliver and runs as follows:

'We, Wangdi Nurbu, Nurbu Bhotia and Pasang Urgen, porters employed by Mr F. S. Smythe, were accompanying Mr Smythe on July 17th over a glacier pass north of the Bhyundar Valley when we saw on the pass tracks which we knew to be those of a Mirka or jungli Admi (wild man). We have often seen bear, snow leopard and other animal tracks, but we swear that these tracks were none of these, but were the tracks of a Mirka.

'We told Mr Smythe that these were the tracks of a Mirka and we saw him take photographs and make measurements. We have never seen a Mirka because anyone who sees one dies or is killed, but there are pictures of the tracks, which are the same as we have seen, in Tibetan monasteries.'

My photographs were developed by Kodak Ltd of Bombay under conditions that precluded any subsequent accusation of faking and, together with my measurements and observations, were sent to my literary agent, Mr Leonard P. Moore, who was instrumental in having them examined by Professor Julian Huxley, Secretary of the Zoological Society, Mr Martin A. G. Hinton, Keeper of Zoology at the Natural History Museum, and Mr R. I. Pocock. The conclusion reached by these experts was that the tracks were made by a bear. At first, due to a misunderstanding as to the exact locality in which the tracks had been seen, the bear was said to be *Ursus arctos pruinosus*, but subsequently it was decided that it was *Ursus arctos isabellinus,* which is distributed throughout the western and central Himalayas. The tracks agreed in size and character with that animal and there is no reason to suppose that they could have been made by anything else. This bear sometimes grows as large as, or larger than, a grizzly, and there is a well-grown specimen in the Natural History Museum. It also varies in colour from brown to silvergrey.

The fact that the tracks appeared to have been made by a biped is explained by the fact that the bear, like all bears, puts its rear foot at the rear end of the impression left by its front foot. Only the side toes would show, and this explains the Tibetans' belief that the curious indentations, in reality superimposed by the rear foot, are the front toes of a Snowman who walks with his toes behind him. This also explains the size of the spoor, which when melted out by the sun would appear enormous. Mr Eric Shipton describes some tracks he saw near the peak of Nanda Ghunti in Garhwal as resembling those of a young elephant. So also would the tracks I saw when the sun had melted them away at the edges . . .

The Snowman is reputed to be large, fierce, and carnivorous; the large ones eat yaks and the small ones men. He is sometimes white, and sometimes black or brown. About the female, the most definite account I have heard is that she is only slightly less fierce than the male, but is hampered in her movements by exceptionally large pendulous breasts, which she must per force sling over her shoulders when walking or running.

Of recent years considerable force has been lent to the legend by Europeans having seen strange tracks in the snow, sometimes far above the permanent snow-line, apparently of a biped. Such tracks had in all cases been spoiled or partially spoiled by the sun, but if such tracks were made by bears, then it is obvious that bears very seldom wander on to the upper snows, otherwise fresh tracks unmelted by the sun would have been observed by travellers. The movements of animals are incalculable, and there seems no logical explanation as to why a bear should venture far from its haunts of woodland and pasture. There is one point in connection with this which may have an important bearing on the tracks we saw, which I have omitted previously in order to bring it in at this juncture. On the way up the Bhyundar Valley from the base camp, I saw a bear about 200 yards distant on the northern slopes of the valley. It bolted immediately, and so quickly that I did not catch more than a glimpse of it, and disappeared into a small cave under an overhanging crag. When the men, who were behind, came up with me, I suggested that we should try to coax it into the open, in order that I could photograph it, so the men threw stones into the cave while I stood by with my camera. But the bear was not to be scared out so easily, and as I had no rifle it was not advisable to approach near to the cave. It is possible that we so scared this bear that the same evening it made up the hillside some 4,000 feet to the pass. There are two objections to this theory: firstly, that it appeared to be the ordinary small black bear, and too small to make tracks of the size we saw, and, secondly, that the tracks ascended the glacier fully a mile to the east of the point where we saw the bear. We may, however, have unwittingly disturbed another and larger bear during our ascent to our camp. At all events, it is logical to assume that an animal would not venture so far from its native haunts without some strong motive to impel it. One last and very interesting point – The Sikh surveyor who I had met in the Bhyundar Valley was reported by the Postmaster of Joshimath as having seen a huge white bear in the neighbourhood of the Bhyundar Valley.

It seems possible that the Snowman legend originated through certain traders who saw bears when crossing the passes over the Himalayas and carried their stories into Tibet, where they became magnified and distorted by the people of that superstitious country which, though Buddhist in theory, has never emancipated itself from ancient nature and devil worship. Whether or not bears exist on the Tibetan side of the Himalayas I cannot say.

It is probable that they do in comparatively low and densely forested valleys such as the Kharta and Kharma Valleys east of Mount Everest, and it may be that they are distributed more widely than is at present known.

After my return to England I wrote an article, which was published by *The Times*, in which I narrated my experiences and put forward my conclusions, which were based, of course, on the identifications of the zoological experts. I must confess that this article was provocative, not to say dogmatic, but until it was published I had no idea that the Abominable Snowman, as he is popularly known, is as much beloved by the great British public as the sea-serpent and the Loch Ness monster. Indeed, in debunking what had become an institution, I roused a hornet's nest about my ears. . .*

There is a great deal to draw from Frank Smythe's account.† His observations are comprehensive and his conclusions are clear: he decided that the tracks he saw were made by a bear. But did that mean that *all* footprints in snow were made by bears? He admits to his *Times* article being provocative and dogmatic, and in time this would have repercussions. The British public, however, were having none of it. Their appetite was for more mystery. And soon enough, along came some more clues.

* Smythe, op. cit.

† T. Smythe, *My Father, Frank: Unresting Spirit of Everest* (Baton Wicks Publications, 2013).

CHAPTER THREE

Nazi SS Operation Tibet. . .shooting your wife is wrong. . .Abominable Snowmen of Everest. . .Shipton and Tilman. . .the last explorers. . .a Blank on the Map. . .Appendix B. . .a one-legged, carnivorous bird. . .the Ascent of Rum Doodle.

In his book *My Quest for the Yeti*, the mountaineer Reinhold Messner reproduces a letter sent to him by the German explorer Ernst Schäfer which refers to footprints seen by Smythe and Shipton:

> In 1933–35, the British mountaineers Frank Smythe and Eric Shipton discovered the first 'yeti footprints', and published the pictures they took in *The London Illustrated News* and in *Paris Match* [Schäfer seemed unaware of the earlier Howard-Bury report]. This created a sensation. The 'Abominable Snowman' aroused the interest of journalists and opened up financial resources for numerous Everest expeditions. In 1938, after I had uncovered the whole sham in my publications with Senckenberg in Frankfurt and established the yeti's real identity with the pictures and pelts of Tibetan bears, Smythe and Shipton came to me

on their knees, begging me not to publish my findings in the English-speaking press. The secret had to be kept at all costs – 'Or else the press won't give us the money we need for our next Everest expedition.'*

Can this be true? Could Smythe and Shipton really have been so cynical? If so, this would cast doubt on the yeti's most iconic footprint, discovered later by Shipton in 1951. This case will take some unravelling, but it is an interesting journey to Mount Everest and beyond.

At the time of his alleged meeting with Smythe and Shipton, the 28-year-old Ernst Schäfer was a swashbuckling German explorer and ornithologist who had already been on two expeditions to China and Tibet under the leadership of Brooke Dolan, the son of a wealthy American industrialist. Schäfer had worked on these trips as a scientist and wrote a successful book about the second expedition which had made his name in Germany.† He could have emigrated to America and had a gilded career, but he sold out to the Nazis, as did hundreds of other young academics, seeing opportunities ahead. And then the Nazis demonstrated exactly what happens when criminals get hold of a modern industrial state, using fake science to justify their actions.

Schäfer's colleague in 1938 was the anthropologist Bruno Beger, who was fascinated by the idea that the Aryans, ancestors of the Nordics, could still be found in a lost civilisation somewhere in Tibet. His proposal to the expedition was 'to study the current racial-anthropological situation through measurements, trait research, photography and moulds. . . and to collect material about the proportion, origins, significance and development of the Nordic race in this region'.

Nordic culture was all the rage in the 1930s, as was the pseu-

---

* R. Messner, *My Quest for the Yeti* (St Martin's Press, 2000), ch 8.

† E. Schäfer, *Dach der Erde* (Verlag Paul Parey, 1938).

do-science of eugenics. Tolkien used the *Völsunga* saga translated by William Morris of the Arts and Crafts movement in his *The Lord of the Rings*, as did Wagner in his *Ring of the Nibelung* cycle of operas. The eponymous ring would grant magical domination over the whole world. Wagner's ideas were much lauded by Hitler and the Nazi hierarchy, and these Nordic myths fed the strange beliefs held by Hitler and his Reich Minister of the Interior, Heinrich Himmler, who was the founder of the German SS.

Schäfer's third expedition was under Himmler's personal patronage and he was promoted to SS-Sturmbannführer, a Nazi party rank approximating to major. Rather like the alpinist Heinrich Harrer, Schäfer claimed after the war that he had joined the SS to advance his career, but in fact he colluded in the hunt for evidence to support these Nazi folk myths. The expedition would search for proof of Aryan supremacy and also serve as a cover for offensive operations against British India during the coming war. Schäfer eventually would regret his alliance with the top Nazis: 'He was to later call his alliance with Himmler his biggest mistake. But he was an opportunist who had a tremendous craving for recognition.'*

Himmler was obsessed by the belief in Aryan and Nordic racial superiority over lesser races (some of these ideas may have originated with Major Waddell, whom we met earlier, in Chapter Two). He believed in the Welteislehre, or Glacial Cosmogony, which held that the planets and moon were made of ice and that the solar system had evolved out of a cosmic collision of an icy star with our sun. This theory contradicted Albert Einstein's 'Jewish' theory of relativity. Somehow, the Aryan race was bred out of an ice storm, evolved in the Arctic or Tibet, and founded a civilisation on the lost continent of Atlantis. Himmler, a failed chicken farmer, was fascinated by eugenics and wanted to breed back to 'racially pure and healthy' Aryans.

* P. Meier-Hüsing, *Nazis in Tibet: Das Rätsel um die SS-Expedition Ernst Schäfer* (Theiss, 2017).

For this he needed to know where the original stock originated.

The discovery of the Tarim mummies at Lop Nor in Central Asia by explorers such as Sven Hedin, Albert von Le Coq and Sir Aurel Stein lent credence to the idea that the Aryans came from Tibet. These corpses looked German or Irish and they were buried with sun symbols and woven twill cloth like that found in Austria. One found after the Nazi era even had greying reddish-brown hair framing high cheekbones, an aquiline nose, full lips and a ginger beard, and he was wearing a red twill tunic and leggings with a pattern resembling tartan. Was the homeland of the Indo-Germans therefore located somewhere in Tibet? Had there been an Aryan civilisation there, now lost? Was the Abominable Snowman racially related to Germans, and somehow branched off from our ancestors and still living in the ice of the Himalayas? These and other mystical ideas swirled around in the heads of the Welteislehre adherents such as Heinrich Himmler and Adolf Hitler, who said the Aryan type was 'the Prometheus of mankind from whose bright fore-head the divine spark of genius has sprung'.

To support his theories, Himmler founded the SS Ahnenerbe (Ancestral Heritage Society), an institute which mounted eight Indiana Jones-style expeditions worldwide to uncover the archaeological and cultural history of the Aryan race. The Ahnenerbe became a magnet for dubious individuals with bizarre ideas. One senior figure was interested in finding out whether Tibetan women hid magical stones in their vaginas. Others believed that ancient Nordic folk myths might act as an antidote to the disturbing new world of industrialisation, cities and consumerism. The Ahnenerbe also attracted ambi-tious young scientists like Schäfer who felt they needed a leg up the academic career ladder, despite the number of Jews whom the Nazis had removed from the universities.

Himmler's ideas verged on the delusional. He instructed his scientists to look for evidence of 'the thunderbolt, Thor's hammer', which he believed to be 'an early, highly developed form of war weapon of our forefathers'. This notion is eerily prescient of the atomic bomb which the Nazis' *Uranprojekt* was racing to build. It would be the magic ring which would give them mastery over the whole world. Himmler himself wore a Mjölnir pendant in the shape of Thor's hammer.

The Ahnenerbe's expeditions were calculated to promote the racial theories of the Nazis, and so the participating scientists had to allow the ideology in order to overcome any scientific objectivity. For a serious scientist such as Schäfer, this might have involved a certain amount of double-think. Ahnenerbe's researchers travelled to Finland and Sweden to examine Bronze Age carvings and study folk customs; during the war they removed the Bayeux Tapestry to examine it for Aryan clues; they raced to Poland to appropriate the Veit Stoss altarpiece, and to the Crimea for Gothic artefacts; and, in this case, sent Schäfer to Tibet to find evidence of early Aryans' conquest of Asia. And while they were at it, they might as well cause trouble for the British in India.

On his 1938–39 Tibet expedition, Schäfer's first task was to research passes from which to mount guerrilla attacks on British India, and his second assignment was to find the blue-eyed, blond-haired lost tribe of Aryans living in Tibet. Just before the team left Germany in 1938, the *Völkischer Beobachter* newspaper ran an article on the expedition which alerted British officials to its intentions. They knew war was coming and refused Schäfer's team entry to India. Himmler then wrote to Admiral Barry Domvile who happened to be both a Nazi supporter and former head of British naval intelligence, and Domvile gave Himmler's letter to British Prime Minister Neville Chamberlain. He then allowed the SS team to enter Sikkim, a region of northern India bordering Tibet (Domvile was interned during the war for his pro-Nazi inclinations).

Just before departure to Tibet, Schäfer had shot his wife Hertha in a bizarre duck-hunting accident. He said a sudden wave had unbalanced him and caused him to discharge the weapon into his spouse of only four months. The two servants with them did what they could, but she was dead by the time they got her home.

Schäfer had his own agenda in Tibet and considered Glacial Cosmogony as pseudo-scientific. His instincts were right, as this theory is now considered completely unscientific and another example of how easily large numbers of humans can be fooled. However, he went along with Himmler's demands in order to be able to mount the expedition. In effect, he was doing precisely what he had accused Smythe and Shipton of: compromising with the truth to facilitate another trip.

The expedition did not go well. After obstructions from the British authorities in India, the party camped on the border between Sikkim and Tibet. After making contact with locals, Tibet's council of ministers permitted Schäfer, the self-described 'master of a hundred sciences', to visit the forbidden capital of Lhasa. His team were told that they could not bring scientific equipment with them or kill any animals or birds, but both conditions were ignored. They decorated their mules with Nazi swastikas and shot every wild creature that came within range. They collected a staggering 3,500 birds, 2,000 eggs, 400 skulls and the pelts of countless mammals, reptiles, amphibians, several thousand butterflies, grasshoppers, 2,000 ethnological objects, minerals, maps and 40,000 black-and-white photographs which still reside in German museums and research institutes.

Schäfer was proud of being 'the second white man to shoot a Giant Panda' and he liked to smear the blood of his animal victims on his face. As we have seen, on the expedition with him was Bruno Beger, the anthropologist who later helped to select Jewish victims from Auschwitz for a skeleton collection. He measured the skulls of the Tibetan people they met with callipers and took plaster casts.* The first attempt at making a mask failed when the

---

* See http://img.mp.sohu.com/upload/20170511/e792ca7ad0bd-4d549eed0b55de25e99e_th.png.

Tibetan subject had a seizure and nearly choked to death.

Schäfer decided to commemorate his wife Hertha by firing a symbolic shot from his rifle, a curious idea considering the circumstances of her death. However, he forgot to remove the cleaning rod from the barrel and the breech exploded, knocking him off his feet and burning his face with the explosion.

On the positive side, Schäfer refused to take the stories of wild men seriously. He became testy with his porters, who day and night discussed the yeti, and so he started faking large footsteps outside their tents in the snow. In this he was to start a long tradition in yeti fakery. He was quite sure the stories arose from the Himalayan brown bear, and described the adventure that proved his theory:

On the morning of the second day, a wild-looking Wata [local tribesman] with a rascally face comes to me and tells the fantastic story of a snowman that haunts the tall mountains. This is the same mythical creature about which Himalaya explorers always like to write because it envelops the unconquered peaks of the mountain chains with the nimbus of mystery. It is supposed to be as tall as a yak, hairy like a bear, and walk on two legs like a man, but its soles are said to point backward so that one can never track its trail. At night it is supposed to roam, descend deep into the valleys, devastate the livestock of the native people, and tear apart men whom it then carries up to its mountain home near the glaciers.

After I listen calmly to this bloody tale, I convey to the Wata that he does not have to make up such a tall tale; however, if he could bring me to the cave of such a 'snowman', and if the monster is actually in its lair, then the empty tin can in my tent, which appears to be the object of his great pleasure, would be his reward. But should he have lied to his lord, added Wang [his Tibetan foreman], he could expect a beating with the riding crop. Smiling, with many bows, the lad bids his leave with the promise to return early the next morning and report to me. Wang is also of the opinion that there are snowmen and draws for me the face of the mystery animal in the darkest colours, just like he has heard about it from the elders of his native tribe countless times: devils and evil spirits wreak havoc up there day and night in order to kill men. 'But Wang,' I scoffed, 'how can you as my senior companion believe in such fairy tales?' Wang explained that these forces were manifest all around them. After all, 'the same evil demons already tried to menace us many times as we traverse the wild steppes. They also sent us the violent snowstorms that fell on our weak little group like supernatural forces and at night wanted to rip apart our tents with crude fists as if they had rotten canvas before them.' I insisted 'that this snowman is nothing other than a bear, perhaps a "Mashinng", a really large one; but with our "big gun", I will easily shoot him dead before he even leaves the cave!'

The Wata returned within the day with a witness who had, while searching for lost sheep, found a cave in which 'he beheld for the first time with his own eyes the yellow head of a snowman.'

Following his guides to the den of the yeti, I shot it at point-blank range when it emerged, roaring angrily, from its nap and it was indeed a Himalayan brown bear.[*]

On their return home to Germany, Reichsführer-SS Himmler greeted Schäfer and his expedition members on the tarmac at Tempelhof Airport in Berlin, where he presented Schäfer with the SS skull ring and dagger of honour. However, it

[*] D. Loxton and D. R. Prothero, *Abominable Science! Origins of the Yeti, Nessie, and Other Famous Cryptids* (Columbia University Press, 2013).

ended badly for them all. Himmler's puny physique, poor eyesight and digestive problems hardly made him the figurehead for a super-race. He was a pedant, a sadist, probably the most brutal mass murderer in history and the architect of the Holocaust. He was, in short, the middle manager from hell. He committed suicide in custody using a hidden cyanide pill.

Schäfer returned from Tibet with his 7,000 plant specimens with the intention of developing hardy strains of cereals for the newly conquered regions of Eastern Europe. He also brought back a poorly faked yeti specimen with a lower jaw made of clay with teeth jammed into it. His scientific reputation after the war was damaged by his association with Himmler, which perhaps explains why his rebuttal of the yeti story didn't gain ground. The expedition cameraman who filmed the Tibet expedition afterwards worked at Dachau, recording prisoners made hypothermic in freezing water or suffocating in decompression chambers. These experiments on living human subjects were used to solve high-altitude and pilot-survival problems for the Luftwaffe.

Bruno Beger was soon busy selecting Jewish prisoners at Auschwitz and recording their skeletons and skulls for an anatomical institute in Strasbourg. Although convicted by a German court long after the war as an accessory to 86 murders, he was given the minimum sentence of three years in prison, which he never served. Author Heather Pringle tells how she tracked him down, aged ninety. Beger was unrepentant: he still thought that the Jews were a 'mongrel race', and he still believed in the racial science of the 1930s.* Towards the end of their collaboration, Beger wrote to Schäfer, describing a 'tall, healthy child of nature' he had been experimenting on. 'He could have been a Tibetan. His manner of speaking, his movements and

---

* H. Pringle, *The Master Plan: Himmler's Scholars and the Holocaust* (Hachette Books, 2006).

the way he introduced himself were simply ravishing; in a word, from the Asian heartland.' And then this child of nature was killed and dissected, another victim of the mindset that enabled Nazi science to regard fellow humans as objects to be experimented upon.

Schäfer had plans for a further expedition to Tibet during the war, ostensibly to harass the British forces in India. These hopes came to nothing. He wrote several books on Tibet, and may have had something to do with the Iron Man statue, a Buddhist figurine which mysteriously appeared in Germany sometime after 1939. This is beautifully carved from a piece of meteorite and featured an anticlockwise Buddhist swastika. This space Buddha was about as close as the Nazis got to their dreams of Glacial Cosmogony.

In this context, then, Schäfer's letter to Messner is puzzling. He himself was convinced that the native porter's stories about the yeti were simply sightings of Himalayan bears. And Frank Smythe had by then published articles and a book setting out his own reasons for the same conclusion. Shipton was another kettle of fish. I believe Schäfer had the wrong name: he meant Shipton and *Tilman*, a British climber and explorer with a more ambiguous attitude towards the yeti.

It could be argued that Schäfer had an axe to grind. He can hardly have been expected to be a British sympathiser. However, his conviction that the yeti was in fact a bear and his careful unravelling of the 'hoax' in his books suggests that he took a serious and scientific approach towards the truth. He quite rightly objected to what he regarded as a mischievous fable being used to fund Mount Everest expeditions. In the case of Shipton and Tilman, it is also just possible that he had misinterpreted the British humorous tendency.*

Besides, if Schäfer had captured a live yeti and taken him

---

* C. Hale, *Himmler's Crusade: The True Story of the 1938 Nazi Expedition to Tibet* (Bantam Press, 2003).

back to Nazi Germany, what would have become of the poor creature?

Somervell and Norton's near-success on Mount Everest in 1924, coming to within 1,000 feet of the summit without oxygen sets, misled those who followed. Time and time again, the British sent expensive expeditions out to Tibet, and time and time again they were repulsed at around the same altitude. But the combination of the world's highest mountain and now a mysterious man-beast was to prove irresistible for the British press and public alike. Pressure mounted on the Mount Everest Committee to make another attempt. So, in 1938, the inimitable Bill Tilman, the 'last explorer', was invited to lead a lightweight, somewhat cheaper, expedition to Everest, with a £2,360 budget instead of the £10,000 that the 1936 expedition had squandered: about £110,000 versus £500,000 in today's money.

Tilman was certainly the greatest explorer and adventurer of the twentieth century. He won the Royal Geographical Society's Founder's Medal in 1952, but his career also encompassed military service in both world wars: he won the Military Cross twice in the first conflict and led a band of underground Albanian Resistance fighters for the British Special Services in the Second World War. In between the wars, he worked as a planter in Africa where he met his long-term climbing companion Eric Shipton. He was the first to climb the Indian mountain Nanda Devi, the highest peak then climbed, and he led the 1938 Everest expedition. He evolved a lightweight, living-off-the-land style of exploration which is now much admired by other adventurers but which was difficult for his companions, who were expected to eat lentils and pemmican at high altitude. After the Second World War, he undertook a little spying in the Karakoram and then embarked on a second career as a deep-sea sailing explorer in a series of ancient Bristol pilot cutters, two of which he sank in unexpected encounters with the land. After a lifetime of inventive expeditions to high mountains and cold seas, he and his crew eventually disappeared on an Antarctic voyage in his 80th year, a mystery to the end.

Tilman was something of an enigma. Clearly traumatised by his experiences as a 17-year-old in the First World War, he appeared to grow a crust over his emotions which made him appear indifferent to his own or others' sufferings. He was gruff and taciturn, but not irritable. In appearance he was stocky, wore a moustache and smoked a pipe. He never married and appeared to prefer the company of men, but didn't show any interest in either sex. He seemed to exert an iron grip on his emotions, and one wonders what would have tumbled out had he ever let go. The key to Bill Tilman seems to be what happened to him during the most terrible conflict the world has ever seen. Coming out of it aged just twenty, he asked the question: 'Why was I spared when so many of the best of my companions were not?' Like Howard Somervell who asked just the same question, he seemed to suffer from that paradoxical complaint: survivor's guilt. In the end, Tilman seemed happiest on the open road: 'I felt uncommonly happy at trekking once more behind a string of mules with their bright headbands, gaudy red wool tassels, and jingling bells, over a road and country new to me with the promise of sixteen such days ahead. I felt I could go on like this for ever, that life had little better to offer than to march day after day in an unknown country to an unattainable goal.'*

Being Tilman, though, he immediately undermined the conceit by self-deprecation: 'The morning was well advanced and it was uncommonly hot, so that my thoughts underwent

* H. W. Tilman, *Two Mountains and a River* (Vertebrate Digital, 2016).

a gradual change. Far from wishing the march to go on for ever, I did not care how soon it would be over. I did not care if it was my last.'

His enduring achievement is his series of fourteen travel books, some of them classics of the genre. He is the master of a good travel tale, with a self-deprecating black humour which is sometimes misunderstood.

Turning to the subject of the yeti, or Abominable Snowman, firstly we have to concede that Tilman had an ambivalent attitude to science. As one of his biographers, J. R. L. Anderson, pointed out,[*] he held that travel and mountain climbing should be ends in themselves and science should not be allowed to compromise the adventure. He himself wrote: 'The idea of sending a scientific expedition to Everest is really deplorable; there could be no worse mixture of objectives.'[†] In this he was controversial, as some might say that the only reason Everest was eventually climbed (on the ninth attempt, in 1953) was by Griffith Pugh's application of science in the form of oxygen equipment, diet and clothing. Adventurers of the hardy variety would retort that Everest was only climbed properly in an ethical way in 1978 by Reinhold Messner and Peter Habler when they succeeded without using supplementary oxygen.

Despite this, Tilman was a careful observer, taking great trouble to check geographical locations and work out heights on his spying mission in Chitral: 'We used an aneroid barometer and at specially important points took boiling point thermometer readings. As there were no basic stations sufficiently near for the reduction of the barometer to sea level, the barometrical readings taken during three days before leaving Urumchi were used as a check. For this period a correct mean height of the barometer was ascertained by using the obser-

* J. R. L. Anderson: *High Mountains and Cold Seas* (Gollancz, 1980).

† H. W. Tilman, *Mount Everest, 1938* (Cambridge University Press, 1948).

vations made by Strowkowski over a period of three years in Urumchi.'*

A sailor would know just how proficient Tilman was at celestial navigation, finding himself around the oceans of the world armed only with paper charts, compass, sextant and a copy of Lecky's *Wrinkles In Practical Navigation:* 'The amateur sailor, or haphazard navigator, should ponder a remark of the editor of the new edition of Lecky's Wrinkles: "There is nothing more distressing than running ashore, unless it be a doubt as to which continent that shore belongs."'†

However, it cannot be denied that Tilman sometimes derided science and scientists in his books, and I suspect that, like his friend Eric Shipton, he had a sense of humour and may have played fast and loose with the truth when it came to the Abominable Snowman.

On Mount Everest in 1938, Tilman's team included Eric Shipton and Frank Smythe: the very two men accused by Ernst Schäfer of using yeti footprints to raise expedition funding. All three of these men had seen strange footprints in the Himalayas. One can imagine the campfire stories about the Abominable Snowman. Rongbuk is an eerie valley at the best of times; I have walked alone there at night with the ghosts of Mallory and Irvine at my back and can imagine that the shifting shadows beyond the firelight might have caused the odd shiver of fear.

These same three climbers had just had a minor spat in the newspapers before the expedition. Smythe had reported his find

---

* H. W. Tilman, *China to Chitral.*
† H. W. Tilman, *Mischief in Greenland.*

of what he insisted were bear tracks in *The Times* of 10 November 1937, perhaps with a view to some helpful pre-publicity for his next book; and Tilman, under the pseudonym of Balu (the bear), had put up a defence of the Abominable Snowman in the letters page on 13 November where he wrote: 'Mr Smythe's article, if it was an attempt to abolish that venerable institution, the "Yeti", was hardly worth the paper on which it was written.'

This was nicely calculated to wind up the irascible Smythe (note that this was one of the first public uses of the term 'yeti' instead of Abominable Snowman). Shipton, also writing pseudonymously (as The Foreign Sportsman, one of the Sherpa's nicknames), had given his own first-hand experience of footprints in the snow, and supported Balu. He wrote: 'Balu's contribution to the discussion was welcome. His spirited defence of the Abominable Snowman wilting under the combined attack of Mr Smythe and the Zoological Society reminded me of Kipling's lines: "Horrible, hairy, human, with paws like hands in prayer, making his supplication rose Adam-Zad the bear."'

In short, Tilman and Shipton were having a bit of fun taking the mickey out of the presumptuous Frank Smythe and a bunch of self-important scientists. This was altogether more amusing than the annual 'first cuckoo of spring' type of letters to *The Times*, and this controversy between Himalayan rivals, I suggest, may have provided the spark for what I think was the biggest yeti hoax of the century. (But that was to come much later, in 1951, after Smythe was dead.)

Tilman loved the Abominable Snowman story and had had first-hand experience of it. This is what he reported in his *Times* letter. He told the 1938 Everest party how in the previous year, during his great journey of exploration across the Karakoram with Eric Shipton, he and two Sherpas came across the footprints of a strange animal:

While contouring round the foot of the ridge between

these two feeder glaciers, we saw in the snow the tracks of an Abominable Snowman. They were eight inches in diameter, eighteen inches apart, almost circular, without signs of toe or heel. They were three of four days old, so melting must have altered the outline. The most remarkable thing was that they were in a straight line one behind the other, with no 'stagger' right or left, like a bird's spoor. A four-footed animal walking slowly puts its hindfoot in the track of its forefoot, but there are always some marks of overlapping, nor are the tracks immediately in front of each other. However many-legged it was, the bird or beast was heavy, the tracks being nearly a foot deep. We followed them for a mile, when they disappeared on some rock. The tracks came from a glacier pool where the animal had evidently drunk, and the next day we picked up the same spoor on the north side of Snow Lake.

The Sherpas judged them to belong to the smaller type of Snowman, or yeti, as they call them, of which there are apparently two varieties: the smaller, whose spoor we were following, which feeds on men, while his larger brother confines himself to a diet of yaks. My remark that no-one had been here for thirty years and that he must be devilish hungry did not amuse the Sherpas as much as expected! The jest was considered ill-timed, as it perhaps was, the three of us standing forlorn and alone in a great expanse of snow, looking at the strange tracks like so many Robinson Crusoes.*

Tilman attempted to take a photograph but claimed that he managed to make two exposures on the same negative and so nothing came out. This seems odd, as he seemed perfectly competent with his camera on other expeditions. One might begin to smell a horrible, hairy rat. Later, his team saw bear tracks and agreed that they were completely unlike what they

* E. Shipton, *Blank on the Map* (Hodder & Stoughton, 1938).

had seen earlier. The first set of prints he reported as circular, with no toes. Tilman speculates on the nature of the creature: 'A one-legged, carnivorous bird, weighing perhaps a ton, might make similar tracks, but it seems unnecessary to search for a new species when we have a perfectly satisfactory one at hand in the form of the Abominable Snowman – new perhaps to science but old in legend.'

They followed the footprints for a mile. His diary notes tersely: 'Sixteen inches apart and about 6–8 inches in diameter. Blokes say it is hairy like a monkey.'

On *The Times* letters page, Shipton chipped in with his own sighting. 'With two Sherpas I was crossing the Bireh Ganga glacier when we came upon tracks made in crisp snow which resembled nothing so much as those of an elephant. I have followed elephant spoor often and could have sworn we were following one then but for the comparative scarcity of these beasts in the Central Himalaya.'

If you are attuned to the Shipton–Tilman dynamic, you might begin to hear the gentle sound of the piss being taken. Then – and here's a point relevant to Ernst Schäfer's accusation – Tilman chimed into suggest a search expedition: 'I notice regretfully that the correspondence appears to be failing and that a zoologist (Huxley) has been afforded space to drive yet another nail into the coffin of our abominable friend having first poisoned him with another dose of Latin. Difficult though it is, the confounding of scientific sceptics is always desirable, and I commend the suggestion that a scientific expedition should be sent out. To further this an Abominable Snowman Committee, on the lines of the Mount Everest Committee, might be formed, drawn from the Alpine Club and the Natural History Museum.'

Were Tilman and Shipton hinting that more public money might be raised to pay for their expeditions, this time to pursue the Abominable Snowman?

Despite including seven strong climbers, Tilman's 1938 Everest expedition got no higher than the Norton and Somervell high point of 28,000 feet. Food became a point of contention among the team members; in the name of austerity Tilman had refused the gift of a crate of champagne from a well-wisher, and listed porridge and soup as luxuries. Noel Odell, in particular, objected to the ration of two pounds per day of flour and lentils after enjoying quails in aspic and chocolates on the 1924 Everest expedition. He blamed the parsimonious diet for the recurrent illness and weakness of the party. Bill Tilman gave a typically sarcastic response to this in Appendix A of his expedition book: 'I must confess I was surprised to hear any criticism of the food, except from Odell, who has not yet finished criticising the food we ate on Nanda Devi in 1936 and who, in spite of his half-starved condition, succeeded in getting to the top.'*

However, Odell did have a point: once again, the British had failed on Everest. Little did they know that their youngest Sherpa, 24-year-old Tenzing Norgay, would finally manage to climb the mountain in 1953 with Edmund Hillary. He was described by the leader as young, keen, strong and very like-able. Shipton had employed him on the 1935 Everest reconnaissance expedition, catching his flashing smile in the employment lines. Nor could they suspect that a British woman, Rebecca Stephens, would climb Everest in 1993; a 13-year-old boy, Jordan Romero, would climb it in 2010; or an 80-year-old Japanese man, Yuichiro Miura, in 2013. Surely, they wouldn't believe that 234 people would reach the top in a single day in 2012. One of the greatest mysteries about moun-

* Tilman, *Mount Everest, 1938,* op. cit.

tains is how they appear to lose their difficulty. As British mountaineer and author Albert Mummery said: 'It has frequently been noticed that all mountains appear doomed to pass through the three stages: An inaccessible peak – The most difficult ascent in the Alps – An easy day for a lady.'* This is not a topic for this book, but it has been addressed at length in at least one other.†

Once again, the weather was bad that year so they retreated to the Rongbuk monastery, where they had already noticed that someone had demolished the monument to those who died in 1924 (the carved stone panels on this had been executed by Howard Somervell, the polymath, in an Arts and Crafts style). Tilman and the other climbers questioned the lamas:

> Odell, who as a member of the 1924 expedition was particularly interested, then asked who had destroyed the big cairn erected at the Base Camp . . . The abbot disclaimed all responsibility on the part of the monastery and suggested that the culprits were the 'Abominable Snowmen'. This reply staggered me, for though I had an open mind on the matter I was not prepared to hear it treated so lightly in that of all places. I was shocked to think that this apparently jesting reply, accompanied as it was by a chuckle from the abbot and a loud laugh from the assembled monks, indicated a disbelief in the 'Abominable Snowman' . . . Further questioning showed clearly that no jest was intended, and we were told that at least five of these strange creatures lived up near the snout of the glacier and were often heard at night.‡

Another explanation could be that the monument, which might

* A. F. Mummery, *My Climbs in the Alps and Caucasus* (Nabu Press, 2014).

† Hoyland, op. cit.

‡ Tilman, op. cit.

have been considered to sacrilegiously resemble a Tibetan religious chorten, had indeed been demolished by the lamas.*

There was more to see in the Rongbuk monastery. In the innermost shrine, they were shown a piece of rock with 'the very clear impress of a large human foot'. Odell, a geologist of some standing, could not provide an explanation. Another mysterious footprint!

Tilman's book of the expedition, *Mount Everest 1938*, was not published until ten years later, after the war. In it he discusses the Abominable Snowman at length: 'Since no book on Mount Everest is complete without appendices, I have collected all the available evidence, old and new, and relegated it to the decent obscurity of Appendix B.' As well as being obscure, Appendix B† is now extremely hard to find (having been unaccountably left out of the otherwise excellent Diadem edition of his collected Mountain-Travel books). It is written in a suspiciously jocular manner – 'Nothing like a little judicious levity' – but Tilman manages to make the case for the Abominable Snowman whilst undermining him and at the same time hinting that he doesn't take the whole phenomenon entirely seriously. In fact, this is a masterpiece of sustained comic irony, a difficult rhetorical trick to pull off but one that Tilman manages, time and time again.

He firstly deals with the genesis of the Western yeti, thanks to Howard-Bury's missing exclamation marks, then suggests that the journalist Henry Newman may have had one explanation of the phenomenon:

---

* I witnessed the final bulldozing of this by a Chinese digger in 2011.

† Tilman, op. cit. App. B.

... in Tibet there is no capital punishment, and men found guilty of grave crimes are simply turned out of their villages and monastery. They live in caves like wild animals, and in order to obtain food become expert thieves and robbers. Also in parts of Tibet and the Himalaya many caves are inhabited by ascetics and others striving to obtain magical powers by cutting themselves off from mankind and refusing to wash.

In other words, was the yeti phenomenon merely wild Tibetans trying to make ends meet? Henry Newman had translated the porters' name for the wild men as '*metch* kangmi', *kangmi* meaning snowman and *metch* meaning disgusting, or abominable, but it appears that the word '*metch*' actually means someone wearing tattered or disgusting *clothes*. This fitted better with the idea of exiled wild men wearing the remnants of their original clothing, attacking travellers; or indeed, hermits wearing rotting rags. This seems a possible origin for the story.

Tilman points out that snow is an unsatisfactory medium for footprints. A foot changes shape as the body's weight comes onto it and the resulting print can look nothing like the foot that made it. And the effect of intense high-altitude sun is first to collapse the sides of the print by melting, then to enlarge the whole thing, ending with a vague circular shape. An explanation for bare footprints in snow was provided by one of Tilman's correspondents:

In 1930 on the summit of a 17,000 ft pass in Ladakh, Capt. Henniker met a man completely naked except for a loincloth. It was bitterly cold and snowing gently. When he expressed some natural astonishment, he was met with the reply in perfect English: 'Good morning, Sir, and a Happy Christmas to you' (it was actually July). The hardy traveller was an MA of an English university (Cambridge, one suspects) and was on a pilgrimage for the good of his soul. He explained that one soon got used to the cold and that many Hindus did the same thing.*

Tilman then records the series of letters to *The Times* which had produced more eyewitnesses. One of them was from Ronald Kaulback, who on a journey to the Upper Salween in 1936 reported seeing at 16,000 feet five sets of tracks which looked exactly as though made by a bare-footed man. Two of his porters thought they had been made by snow leopards, but two claimed they were made by mountain men, which they described as like a man, white-skinned, with long hair on head, arms and shoulders. There were no bears recorded in that area. This letter produced another witness, Wing-Commander Beaumont, who had seen similar tracks near the source of the Ganges (however, bare-footed pilgrims are known to visit this sacred site). These letters in turn produced a volley from the zoologists, who suggested langurs might produce such footprints. Or giant pandas. Kaulback responded drily that he had seen and heard of no monkeys despite exploring the area for five months, and as for giant pandas there were no bamboo shoots, 'a *sine qua non* for pandas without which they languish and die'.

At this point, Tilman summarises the evidence: 'So far then we have as candidates for the authorship of queer tracks seen on three several occasions, snow leopards, outlaws, bears, pandas, ascetics, langurs, or X the unknown quantity (which we may as well call the 'Abominable Snowman') roughly in that order of probability.'

But Tilman is equivocal about the actual existence of the Abominable Snowman: '. . . everything turns upon the interpretation of footprints. And if fingerprints can hang a man, as they frequently do, surely footprints may be allowed to establish the existence of one.' However, despite his taciturnity, Tilman did have a tongue and at times it was in his cheek. His

* Ibid.

dark humour was sometimes misunderstood. Earlier in the same book, *Mount Everest, 1938*, he discusses the idea of dropping expedition stores onto the slopes of Everest: 'There is a good case for dropping bombs on civilians because so few of them can be described as inoffensive, but mountains can claim the rights of "open towns" and our self-respect should restrain us from dropping on them tents, tins, or possibly men.' One American reviewer complained of Tilman's complete lack of humour.

Tilman the satirist (and admirer of Jonathan Swift) reserves his ammunition for the irascible and scientific Frank Smythe, who had clearly irritated him on and off the slopes. He details his careful measuring of the prints 'with the calm scientific diligence of a Sherlock Holmes' and the way his photographs were carefully submitted to the 'Zoological pundits', who pronounced them to be made by a bear. 'Whereupon, Mr Smythe, triumphantly flourishing his Sherpa's affidavit, announced to his expectant audience that "a superstition of the Himalaya is now explained, at all events to Europeans". In short, *delenda est homo niveus disgustans;** moreover, any tracks seen in the snow in the past, the present, or the future, may safely be ascribed to bears. As a *non sequitur* this bears comparison with the classic example: "No wonder they call this Stony Stratford, I was never so bitten by fleas in my life."†

He makes a good point: Smythe's tracks were almost certainly those of the bear, but mystery footprints come in all shapes and sizes. Because his Sherpas had identified undisputed bear tracks as those of a wild man, Smythe had leaped to the conclusion that *all* mysterious tracks were made by bears. It was not his facts that were suspect but his inferences.

Tilman then produces his one-legged, carnivorous, hopping bird, weighing perhaps a ton, which he thought might explain

* Translation: 'The Abominable Snowman is destroyed.'

† Tilman, op. cit.

the circular footprints he had seen. Perhaps pulling another leg, he suggests that a more likely explanation was that Abominable Snowmen had developed a primitive kind of snowshoe, despite these being unknown to the natives of the Himalayas.

Why was Tilman so anti-science? This is something that comes up again and again, and you can see the same tendency in the Bigfoot believers. Perhaps he wanted a space left for mystery in the Himalayas. In all of his writings about the yeti, Tilman adopted an anti-science 'unbecoming levity'; as one interviewer found, '. . .it was obvious that he also belongs to the school which considers that the mystery of the yeti should be left uninvestigated; that once the unknown becomes known and the glamour dispelled, the interest evaporated.'*

This is an odd position. Tilman spent his exploring lifetime attempting to know the unknown among high mountains and cold seas. Was the glamour dispelled once the blanks on the maps and charts were filled in? In line with his generation, Tilman attended church and was a believer. However, he doesn't seem to have ever been a lover. Unknowns that become knowns in these circumstances might be too disillusioning. Maybe he just preferred the yeti to be left as a mystery.

Towards the end of Appendix B, Tilman describes how on his return march from Everest in 1938 he took a side trip and bumped into Ernst Schäfer's SS Tibet expedition. Over a few glasses of kümmel† he begged the Auschwitz anthropologist Bruno Beger to look into the mystery of *Homo odious* and quite possibly asked him not to upset the applecart. This may have prompted Schäfer's curt dismissal in his letter to Messner. I also suspect that Schäfer may have mixed him up with Smythe.

Tilman ends Appendix B with an account of what happened next. He and two Sherpas set out to make the first crossing of

* R. Izzard, *Abominable Snowman Adventure* (Hodder & Stoughton, 1955).

† A drink enjoyed by the flatulent golfers of 1930s Surrey.

the Zemu Gap, a 19,000-foot col near Kangchenjunga. They noticed a single track of booted footprints ahead of them that Tilman disappointedly noted went *over* the col (thus making it a pass). Enquiring in Darjeeling, they could find no climbers boasting of the ascent: 'men who climb in the Himalaya, though they may be strong, are not often silent.' Further enquires elicited a response from John Hunt, the future leader of the successful 1953 Everest expedition, who said he had also seen tracks the previous year, and not only were there tracks, but actual *steps* had been cut in the far side of the pass.*

Tilman suggests that the maker of the tracks had picked up a pair of discarded climbing boots from the old German base camp near Kangchenjunga, and used them to cross the Zemu Gap. 'I have hinted that the subject of our inquiry may not be as "dumb" as we think, and we are not to assume that a Snowman has not wit enough to keep his feet dry if they happen to be the shape that fits into boots.'

Tilman's conclusion is that *something* has made the strange footprints he enumerates, including the strange Rongbuk stone footprint, and that something might as well be the Abominable Snowman. There is a dubious logic about this. He concludes with a veiled threat, which we may quail at: 'I think he would be a bold and in some ways an impious sceptic who after balancing the evidence does not decide to give him the benefit of the doubt.'

So, covered with footprints, we end Appendix B perhaps more confused than when we began it, but with a vague feeling that we've been hoodwinked.

---

* I met Lord Hunt in the 1990s and he corroborated this account.

My next bookish proposition has been virtually unknown to the reading public since it first appeared in 1956. 'For most people, it appears . . . the funniest book they have never heard of,' wrote Bill Bryson, in a lavish preface that puts it on a par with *The Diary of a Nobody* (which Evelyn Waugh, in his turn, described as 'the funniest book in the world'). This cult book is so loved by the mountaineering tendency that it has been taken around the world by climbers and Antarctic scientists, and inspired the names of a mountain in the Masson range in Antarctica, the northeast ridge of Pikes Peak, Colorado, and (perhaps more usefully) the famous bar and restaurant in Kathmandu, Nepal. It also presents solid evidence of the 'Atrocious Snowman'.

The Ascent of Rum Doodle is a lethal parody of the stiff-upper-lipped, tight-arsed English school of expedition literature in which the sadder of us are steeped. It is the story of a group of utter incompetents who set out to climb the world's highest mountain, the 40,500-foot Rum Doodle, a mountain 'celebrated but rarely seen' (a 'rum do' means a strange event). It is claimed by Bryson and others that *The Ascent of Rum Doodle* is based on Bill Tilman's *The Ascent of Nanda Devi*, but I don't think that is entirely correct. There is already quite enough self-parody in that book: when they reach the summit, Tilman writes, 'we so far forgot ourselves as to shake hands on it'. No, I suggest that more likely texts to be satirised are Noel Odell's *Everest, 1925*, Ralph Barker's *The Last Blue Mountain*, and John Hunt's *The Ascent of Everest*; robust, militaristic accounts redounding to the credit of the writers. However, I could be wrong; you might also detect something in *Rum Doodle* of the underlying squabbles of Tilman's book *Mount Everest 1938* ('we were forced to breakfast on lentils and pemmican.')

The writer was W. E. Bowman, who seemed to have so much knowledge of high-altitude climbing that many readers assumed the name was a pseudonym for Tilman. Bowman was in fact a civil engineer who spent his time hill-walking, painting, reading rather too many expedition books and writing (unpublished) books on the Theory of Relativity. He only saw high mountains once, on a trip to Switzerland. As Bill Bryson recounts, the book did not fare well at first. One reviewer from *Good Housekeeping* admitted that she had got quite far in, before realising it wasn't entirely serious. Thirty years after its publication in hardback, Arrow Books issued a paperback edition, which has to be some kind of a record. Bowman's characters are all immediately recognisable to anyone who has been on a Himalayan expedition. They are:

Burley, the expedition leader, the strong thrusting and unsympathetic climber type.

Binder, the narrator (a Bounder, perhaps?)

Prone, the doctor, who spends the whole time lying down suffering from various appalling diseases.

Shute, the photographer, who accidentally exposes all his film stock to daylight.

Wish, the scientist, who wants to take a three-ton pneumatic geologist's hammer, and who while testing his altitude measuring equipment during the voyage to Yogistan discovers that the ship is 153 feet above sea level.

Then there is the language expert **Constant** (consonant?), who manages to infuriate the leader of the 30,000 Yogistani porters by informing him that he lusted after his wife.

However, my favourite is **Jungle**, the navigator, who gets lost on the way to the initial expedition meeting and sends telegrams from London requesting more money when the team are on the way to the mountain. (If you think this is far-fetched, I was on one expedition to Sikkim when my leader failed to apply for the correct Indian visa and was leading the party from London while we were herding yaks up the slopes of Kangchenjunga. We also ended up climbing the wrong mountain, but that is a shameful memory I try to repress.)

There are various bungling adventures which parody events in the source books. The members wander in the fog, coming across their own footprints and re-encountering each other until they realise that Jungle's compass is locked on north and they are walking in circles. They have the obligatory fall into a crevasse, a mainstay of expedition books, except that the rescue team remain at the bottom demanding further supplies of 'medicinal' champagne. There is even a curious homo-erotic passage which I think may refer to Gerald and Rupert's naked wrestling match in D. H. Lawrence's *Women in Love*. The narrator Binder and Constant are lying close together in a high-altitude tent:

> I awoke suddenly under the impression that a prehistoric monster had crept into the tent and was about to do me an injury. I seized the nearest solid object – which happened to be a climbing boot – and hit the monster as hard as I could. It was Constant, of course. I asked if I had woken him; and if he said what I thought he said he is not the man I thought he is . . . Constant flung himself on me. Still dazed by sleep and terror I fought back madly, and we were wrestling all over the tent . . . we were locked in a complicated embrace, half in and half out of our sleeping bags, with ropes and clothing wrapped around us . . . 'This can't go on,' said Constant.*

In an attempt to escape the dreadful cooking of the cook, Pong, the team ascend the mountain:

We were naturally all agog to catch sight of the Atrocious

---

* W. E. Bowman, *The Ascent of Rum Doodle* (Arrow, 1956).

Snowman, about whom so much has been written. This creature was first seen by Thudd in 1928 near the summit of Raw Deedle. He describes it as a man-like creature about seven feet [tall] covered with blue fur and having three ears. It emitted a thin whistle and ran off with incredible rapidity. The next reported encounter took place during the 1931 Bavarian reconnaissance expedition to Hi Hurdle. On this occasion it was seen by three members at a height of 25,000 feet. Their impressions are largely contradictory, but all agree that the thing wore trousers. In 1933 Orgrind and Stretcher found footprints on a snow slope above the Trundling La, and the following year Moodles heard grunts at 30,000 feet. Nothing further was reported until 1946, when Brewbody was fortunate enough to see the creature at close quarters. It was, he said, completely bare of either fur or hair, and resembled a human being of normal stature. It wore a loincloth and was talking to itself in Rudistani with a strong Birmingham accent. When it caught sight of Brewbody it sprang to the top of a crag and disappeared.

The *Rum Doodle* team continue upwards, and the most desirous to see the Atrocious Snowman is the scientist Wish:

. . . who may have nourished secret dreams of adding *Eoanthropus wishi* to mankind's family tree. Wish spent much time examining any mark which might prove to be a footprint; but although he heard grunts, whistles, sighs and gurgles, and even, on one occasion, muttering, he found no direct evidence. His enthusiasm weakened appreciably after he had spent a whole rest day tracking footprints for miles across a treacherous mountain-side, only to find that he was following a trail laid for him by a porter at Burley's instigation.

This was a fairly accurate assessment of the evidence gathered so far for the Abominable Snowman/yeti.

In the end, surmounting a South Col (in Hunt's book, not *Mount Everest, 1938*), our narrator finds that the members have climbed the wrong mountain, North Rum Doodle, only 35,000 feet, and the author Bowman finally parodies all those over-blown descriptions of Mount Everest. 'I looked up at the summit of Rum Doodle, so serene in its inviolate purity, and I had a fancy that the goddess of the mountain was looking down with scorn upon her slopes, daring them to do their utmost, daring the whole world . . .'

However, they soon see that their porters have climbed the correct mountain by mistake.

There is a last, serious, point to make about the prevailing English tight-lipped manner, so brilliantly captured later by the actor, John Cleese. It seems to contain a deeply suppressed rage at the universe which may have come partly from Victorian repression, partly from the horror of seeing your friends blown into bits in front of you during the war. Ways to feel better might be to conquer virgin mountains or capture mystery beasts; or, in Bowman's case, just to rip the piss out of it all.

CHAPTER FOUR

*Yeti prints on Everest. . .an English Ulysses. . .RAF Mosquito
over Everest. . .climbing in women's clothing. . .a sex
diary. . .the Daily Mail Snowman Expedition. . .Casino
Royale. . .a yeti scalp. . .a giant panda cub.*

More yeti footprints appeared near Mount Everest in 1951,
and this time they were properly photographed and created
a sensation in the popular press. These ones were monstrous,
with hideously misshapen toes. They were the Ur prints, the
image which finally confirmed the Abominable Snowman in
the public mind as a real, living monster. They shook the
scientific establishment and kicked off a literary war between
biographers. And they were presented to the public by Eric
Shipton, whose name will therefore be associated forever with
the yeti.

Of all our explorers, Shipton most closely approximates to
the protagonist of Tennyson's dramatic monologue 'Ulysses',
from which poem he took an epigram for his *Blank on the
Map*, and for the title of his second autobiography, *That
Untravelled World*. The poem obviously meant something to
him as an epic traveller. But Homer's Ulysses was also a smooth
talker and a trickster with an eye for the ladies.

As his biographer Jim Perrin explained,* Shipton was an explorer-mystic who never really fitted into the Establishment way of thinking. In 1930, as a young planter in Kenya, he received a letter out of the blue from the fellow-colonialist Bill Tilman suggesting that they might try some climbing together. That letter sparked one of the most successful climbing and exploring partnerships in history. Later that year, they made the first ascent of the West Ridge of Mount Kenya, and for the rest of that decade they completed an unmatched series of climbs and explorations, from the penetration of the unvisited Nanda Devi Sanctuary and expeditions to Mount Everest in 1935 and 1938, to the first crossings of huge expanses of unexplored Himalayas. The whole decade was spent in their trademark lightweight unsupported Himalayan exploration, the full extent of which is still unacknowledged.

A strange connection between yetis and spying begins to emerge. During and after the Second World War, Shipton served as the British Consul-General in Kashgar, fighting a rearguard action against the foreign players in the last rounds of the Great Game. Every month he would write letters headed 'Secret' in which he detailed the latest activities of the main Russian and Chinese players of the game. In Persia during the war, he acted as a 'double hatter', ostensibly acting as an agricultural advisor but also reporting on political matters on the border between Persia and Iraq. Then in 1951, on a reconnaissance expedition to Mount Everest in just-opened Nepal, he and Ed Hillary spotted the eventual route to the top on the southern slopes of the mountain. It was on this trip that he discovered his evidence for the yeti.

Then disaster struck: not a climbing accident, which might have been expected, but something far more treacherous. He had been asked to lead the 1953 British Mount Everest expedition,

* J. Perrin, *Shipton and Tilman: The Great Decade of Himalayan Exploration* (Arrow Books, 2013).

and, having accepted, was then dumped by the Mount Everest committee, some of whom felt that he lacked the killer instinct and Establishment ties to fulfil the role. The less experienced Colonel John Hunt was appointed and the rest is history. Success and fame all round: except for Eric Shipton. 'I leave London absolutely shattered,' he wrote. Anyone who has been shafted by bureaucrats will sympathise. But there might have been another reason why the committee didn't trust Shipton.

After this shameful episode, Eric Shipton's marriage broke up, he lost his job as warden of an Outward Bound school and he then worked for a while as a forestry labourer. He became a sort of international tramp, but he did have a final decade of enjoyable and fruitful exploration in Patagonia. He ended his days leading easy treks in the Himalayas and lecturing on cruises. However, he will always be remembered as a kindly, wise and amused man who imbued confidence in his fellow climbers. Frank Smythe described a particularly trying day on Kamet: 'We sank in knee deep, and I reflected grimly that we should have to retrace our steps up that slope towards the end of the day. But no one who climbs with Shipton can remain pessimistic, for he imparts an imperturbability into a day's work which are themselves a guarantee of success.'*

There we have it, our thumbnail sketch of the man. But what did he discover about the yeti? When Nepal's borders had finally opened after the Second World War, it was at last possible to explore the southern approaches of Mount Everest. In 1950, Bill Tilman had penetrated to the foot of the icefall in the Khumbu valley that was to prove the key to the summit. He thought the route would work but he felt that the risks were unacceptable. The route has since proved to be the main highway in the many successful climbs of the mountain, but the icefall has also seen the deaths of dozens of Sherpas and

* F. Smythe, *Kamet Conquered* (Gollancz, 1932).

somewhat fewer Westerners. (I myself narrowly escaped disaster in the icefall on two occasions: once by avalanche and once by a collapse of ice seracs.) In the following year Eric Shipton, the second half of the Tilman–Shipton exploring partnership, lead the impressively titled Mount Everest Reconnaissance Expedition of 1951 to the same valley. Included in the party was Edmund Hillary, who was going to get to the summit two years later. They managed to climb the 2,000-foot icefall despite deep snow and saw a clear route to the top. Shipton saw that the mountain was climbable, given enough resources.

Some might have staged a shot at the summit from there (and changed history), but Shipton always seemed more inter-ested in exploration than peak-bagging. He turned away from Everest, and in so doing probably gave ammunition to those who so humiliatingly sacked him from the leadership of the successful British expedition of 1953. This was unfair, as his expedition was far too late in the season to go high; it was 28 October and the winter cold had set in. (I was on the summit on 6 October and was lucky to get away with just frost-bitten fingers.) The reconnaissance expedition split into three parties, with Edmund Hillary exploring other possibilities behind the Shipton party. Then Shipton, Michael Ward and Shipton's long-term Sherpa companion Sen Tensing found something else entirely:

It was on one of the glaciers of the Menlung basin, at a height of about 19,000 feet, that, late one afternoon, we came across those curious footprints in the snow, the report of which has caused a certain amount of public interest in Britain. We did not follow them further than was convenient, a mile or so, for we were carrying heavy loads at the time, and besides we had reached a particu-larly interesting stage in the exploration of the basin. I have in the past found many sets of these curious footprints and have tried to follow them, but have always lost them on the moraine or rocks at the side of the glacier. These particular ones seemed to be very fresh, probably not more than 24 hours old. When Murray and Bourdillon followed us a few days later the tracks had been almost obliterated by melting. Sen Tensing, who had no doubt whatever that the creatures (for there had been at least two) that had made the tracks were 'Yetis', or wild men, told me that two years before, he and a number of other Sherpas had seen one of them at a distance of about 25 yards at Thyangboche. He described it as half man and half beast, standing about five feet six inches, with a tall pointed head, its body covered with reddish brown hair, but with a hairless face . . . He left no doubt as to his sincerity.*

And then, writing in *The Times*:

The tracks were mostly distorted by melting into oval impressions, slightly longer and a good deal broader than those made by our mountain boots. But here and there, where the snow covering the ice was thin, we came upon a well-preserved impression of the creature's foot. It showed three 'toes' and a broad 'thumb' to the side. What was particularly interesting was that where the tracks crossed a crevasse one could see quite clearly where the creature had jumped and used its toes to secure purchase on the snow on the other side. We followed the tracks for more than a mile down the glacier before we got on to moraine-covered ice.†

* E. Shipton, *The Mount Everest Reconnaissance Expedition 1951* (Hodder & Stoughton, 1953).

† See *The Times*, 6 December 1951.

This little detail of the dug-in toes reminded me of the way I felt when I saw the way my yeti's toes had dug into the snow.

Shipton's ice axe and the footprint: true and false?

The photographs caused a sensation. Shipton's extraordinary footprint led all who saw it to conclude that the creature that made it was an enormous snow-dwelling ape. On his return flight, Shipton was told by an air hostess at Karachi that journalists were waiting for him when they landed at London. He was mobbed at the airport on arrival and photographs of the footprint with an ice axe for scale, the footprint with a boot and another one featuring a trail of footprints made up the whole front page of *The Times*.

Scientists took the photographs seriously. John Napier was a British primatologist and paleoanthropologist who was widely considered as the leading authority on primate taxonomy. He was also the author of the first authoritative study of our subject: *Bigfoot: The Yeti and Sasquatch in Myth and Reality.*[*] He explains in his book that it was Shipton's photograph which really kicked off his own interest in the yeti. He thought that the previous eyewitness stories were merely travellers' tales. 'But with the publication of Shipton's picture – sharp, undistorted and precisely exposed – the legend of the yeti took a giant step forward and entered the public domain.'

Scientific publications took it seriously, too. In the *New Scientist*, an editorial gasped: 'The discovery would have profound scientific importance, as well as being a certain winner at the Zoo.'[†] The Zoo?! Well, yes. Not to mention TV chat shows and a royal presentation. And, just by the way, overturning most theories of human evolution.

Shipton's story was later corroborated by his companion Dr Michael Ward, who wrote: 'This was no hoax and the events occurred exactly and precisely as described in Shipton's book on the Everest reconnaissance and by myself in this article. There must, therefore, be some rational explanation.'

Dr Ward was one of the uncelebrated men behind the success of 1953. During his national service with the Royal Army Medical Corps, he had come across a roll of 35mm film shot by an RAF Mosquito fighter-bomber during an 'accidental' flight over Everest.[‡] He saw at once that there was a climbable route from the Western Cwm. He helped to persuade the Joint Himalayan Committee of the Alpine Club and the Royal Geographical Society to approve the Everest reconnaissance of 1951, and joined the successful British expedition of 1953 as

[*] Napier, op. cit.

[†] 'It Seems To Me,' *New Scientist*, 12 May 1960, p. 1218.

[‡] It was 400 feet of 35mm film. The aircraft belonged to RAF 684 Squadron, based at Alipore airfield, Calcutta. Quoted service altitude was 37,000 feet. See http://www.colonialfilm.org.uk/node/5133.

doctor. James Morris gave us a thumbnail sketch of Ward at the top of the icefall: 'He was a slender, lithesome man, and it always gave me great pleasure, even in those disagreeable circumstances, to watch him in action. His balance was so sure, and his movements so subtle, that when he turned his grinning and swarthy face upon you it was as if someone had drawn in a moustache upon a masterpiece by Praxiteles.'

Meanwhile, John Napier was making an exhaustive study of the yeti/Bigfoot phenomenon for his 1973 book on the subject, concentrating on the Shipton photograph, in particular. Napier was well qualified to pronounce on primate footprints, as before his career as a primatologist and paleoanthropologist he had worked as an orthopaedic surgeon and later became an expert on human and primate hands and feet. He was the founder of the Primate Society of Great Britain (they must have had great tea parties), and helped to name *Homo habilis* ('handy man') in the 1960s. Later, he became the Director of the Primate Biology Program at the Smithsonian Institution, where he examined the footage of an actual walking Bigfoot (the Patterson film, see Chapter Eight), and he also investigated the frozen Bigfoot specimen, the Minnesota Iceman.

Napier first of all takes us through the previous evidence for what we are calling the Western yeti and finds it unconvincing. Sherpas and mountaineers, he says, are seeing *something*, but what? 'The behaviour and ecology of wild animals are only determined by long and arduous field studies followed by months of careful statistical analysis, and not by isolated encounters by untrained observers.' By untrained observers I think he means us: the layman trekkers and climbers.

However, he allowed that mountaineers might add something to science. Napier notes that there are repeated accounts of yetis falling over while running down mountainsides because of the long hair over their eyes. This story comes up again and again, and the plant hunter Hooker first mentioned it in connection with his Sikkimese Lepcha porters. When traversing snowfields in bright sunlight, they combed their long black hair over their eyes to avoid snow blindness, not possessing glacier goggles. I have seen this myself in Tibet, and I suspect some of the stories of unexpected encounters with man-like beasts at night with long hair over their faces might just stem from unexpected meetings with other men with this particular hairstyle.

Napier examined Shipton's photographs with great care and in the light of his particular expertise, human feet, which he states are the most specialised part of the body after the brain. He explains that modern humans walk in a unique way that distinguishes us from other primates. We walk with a stride, which begins with the desire to move forwards. The body sways forwards from the ankles until its centre of gravity moves in front of the feet and the body begins to fall forwards. At this point, we are about to fall flat on our faces. The reason that we don't is because of a reflex action by the leg: it is swung forwards to intercept the fall and prop up the body. This continues in a succession of near-falls (rather like the progress of a bicycle, which is constantly steered to keep its centre of mass over the wheels). Disaster is never far away, as the observation of toddlers and drunks will confirm.

When a human foot hits the ground, it strikes heel first. For most individuals, the outside of the back of the heel touches first (as a quick look at your shoes will confirm), then as the stride progresses and the body catches up, the point of contact of the foot with the ground rolls along the shank to the ball of the foot behind the big toe, then the heel is lifted off the ground. The final push-off is performed by the big toe alone, which is why it is so much larger than the other toes. The foot is flexible, of course, which is one reason why, in soft sand and snow, you will see a narrow ridge of sand formed as the smaller toes curl up and depart.

In this context, then, a number of characteristics of the

Shipton footprint seemed to bother Napier. He noted that the foot was not excessively long (13 inches), but extremely wide (8 inches across the forefoot). This was well outside the range of most known primate footprints. Then there appeared to be a presumptive or conjectured big toe in addition to what looked like a 'normal' big toe. This huge extra big toe was almost circular and had an odd V-shaped indentation behind it marked in the snow, which didn't accord with any other known footprint. There were five toes in all. All known apes have the big toe much further back to allow for grasping, so whatever made the print was more human than *gigantopithecus*. Strangely, the imprint of the foot was convex in the region of the ball precisely where one would expect it to be concave, where the weight of the animal would have borne down in the snow. If this creature was walking like a human, it wasn't leaving a print consistent with our style of locomotion.

Napier, seeking answers, then stresses that there was no certainty that the footprint as photographed was the same as the footprint when it was made. Melting or sublimation of the snow had probably enlarged the print in some unpredictable way. But still, two big toes seemed excessive. Also, what part of the foot had made the V-shaped indentation, and how could the snow be convex under the ball of the foot where it should be concave? Could it have been made by a human wearing some kind of moccasin with a V-shaped ruck in the leather of the sole?

He was deeply puzzled and was clearly flailing for an answer when he suggested that it might be double: two tracks superimposed. But a double what? He didn't know.

Something must have made the Shipton footprint. Like Mount Everest, it is there and needs explaining. I only wish I could solve the puzzle; it would help me sleep better at night. Of course, it would settle a lot of problems if one could simply assume that the yeti is alive and walking about the Himalayas on gigantic feet with two big toes on each foot, and leave it at that. The trouble is that such an assumption conflicts totally with the principles of biology as we know them.*

It is painful watching this serious scientist floundering around for an answer when it should have been staring him in the face. Even when he gained access to the uncropped version of Shipton's footprint and saw a second, different, part-footprint, the truth did not dawn on him. He concludes: 'At first sight the Shipton print seems to offer unequivocal evidence for the reality of the Yeti; but perhaps it is too much to expect that the Himalayas would surrender one of its outstanding mysteries as easily as that . . . The Shipton print, at the moment of writing, is the one item in the whole improbable saga that sticks in my throat; without it I would have no hesitation in dismissing the Yeti as a red herring, or at least, as a red bear.'

After *The Times* headlines of 1951, some doubts were quietly raised among more sceptical yeti-hunters. A monstrous footprint, yes, but where was the foot? Careful readers noticed that Shipton's account moved seamlessly from a first-person eyewitness statement to hearsay from a third party, Sen Tensing. Some remembered the teasing *Times* letters of the 1930s. Others were aware that there was a tradition of Everest expedition parties leaving practical jokes for the party following behind. For example, in Somervell's diary for 1924: 'March 31ˢᵗ . . . Down to a quaint and primitive Tibetan bungalow, where we left a whisky bottle filled with cold tea, with a note saying we had too much and this was left over. The second party completely fell, having not realised what it was April 1ˢᵗ . . . They dished it out all around before they discovered its true nature!'†

Shipton's four photographs came up for sale at Christie's

* Napier, op. cit.

† T. H. Somervell, *After Everest* (Hodder & Stoughton, 1936).

auction house and so the public was able to study them more closely. Two of them featured the monstrous footprint, one with an ice axe for scale, and one with Michael Ward's size eight-and-a-half climbing boot. Then there were two showing the line of tracks, one including Ward for scale, and one with a rucksack.

Snowy Prints

One problem is that the footprints in the wide-angle shots of lines of tracks do not match the single footprint in either size or shape. This is particularly evident in the 'rucksack' shot. This had also bothered John Napier, who had also seen the uncropped photographs.

When Napier quizzed him about the tracks eighteen years later, Ward then said that there were two sets of tracks, one from the yeti and one from maybe a goat. He said that the photograph including the rucksack was taken at a different time and wrongly put in a file with the 'yeti footprint' photos. Shipton corroborated this account, blaming a sub-editor at *The Times* for putting the 'goat' tracks in the same folder as the 'yeti footprints', or maybe they were filed together in the archives of the Mount Everest Foundation. Napier seized upon this explanation gratefully, even putting his conclusion in italics: 'The truth of the matter, according to Michael Ward, and later confirmed by Eric Shipton, is that *the trail has nothing whatever to do with the footprint.*'

Unaccountably, though, Napier puts this particular photograph, which he now says has nothing to do with the yeti prints, on the cover of the Readers' Union edition of his book.

What about the second photograph, featuring Michael Ward and another line of tracks? They don't match the single footprint either. Napier doesn't address this issue. There is a further problem: in the uncropped ice axe shot there is part of a second footprint but it doesn't resemble the full footprint, as there is no sign of the second big toe. Did yetis have differently shaped feet? This second footprint appears to be another left foot. Did yetis therefore have two left feet, or was it hopping?

Now let us look at what Ward himself originally said:

In 1951 Sen Tensing, Shipton, and I descended from the Menlung La . . . at about 16,000–17,000 feet (Shipton said 19,000 feet) we came across a whole series of footprints in the snow, on the lower part of the glacier. There seemed to be two groups, one rather indistinct in outline leading on to the surrounding snowfields. The others were much more distinct with, in places, a markedly individual imprint etched in the 2 to 4-inch covering of snow. We had no means of measuring so after examining them Shipton took four photographs: two of the indistinct prints with myself, my footprints, and rucksack beside them for comparison; the other two photographs were of one of the most detailed and distinct group of prints, with my ice axe for scale, and a second one with my booted foot. The footprint was about the same length as my boot, and I take a size 42 continental, or 8½ British, which is about 12 to 13 inches long. The print was nearly twice as broad as my boot (3 to 4 inches) and had clear-cut edges in the crystalline snow on a base of firm snow ice. There was the definite imprint of a big toe that was broader and shorter than the other rather indistinct toes, of which there seemed to be four or five. We followed these tracks for some way down the easy glacier and noticed that whenever a narrow 6-inch-wide crevasse was crossed there seemed to be claw marks in the snow at the end of the toe imprints . . . Two days later we were joined by Murray and Bourdillon, who, after visiting the Nangpa La . . . had followed our route into the Menlung Basin. All tracks had been deformed by the sun and wind.*

So was there one set of tracks, or two? Edmund Hillary stated later that he was not aware of a second set of tracks. Bourdillon only mentioned one set of tracks when he followed a couple of days later. And claw-marks, made repeatedly? Why didn't Shipton mention claws, and why were there no claw-marks in the monstrous single footprint photographs? Napier, clearly puzzled, wrote 'there is only one footprint which disturbs me, and that is Shipton's . . . this is my chief hang-up over the Yeti problem. It could be the one single piece of evidence that underwrites the existence of the Yeti, but I don't think it is.'

Questions began to mount up. One possible answer, of course, was that Shipton's footprint was . . . Shipton's.

* M. Ward, 'Everest 1951: the footprints attributed to the Yeti – myth and reality,' *Wilderness & Environmental Medicine*, vol. 8, 1997, pp. 29–32.

In 1989, the mountaineering journalist Peter Gillman published an article in the *Sunday Times* magazine about Eric Shipton's footprint: 'A Most Abominable Hoaxer'. It at last said what everyone had been thinking. In the *Alpine Journal* of 2001, he described how he and his collaborator Audrey Salkeld, the indefatigable mountain researcher and writer, pored over the photographs. They discussed the issue of the contradictory stories about the sets of tracks, and then:

> We obtained the full version of the 'ice-axe' photograph – the version that is usually published has been cropped – and found that it contained the top half of a second footprint. Unlike the full footprint above it, it had only vague impressions of the smaller toes; and where you would expect a big toe to match the one in the main footprint, there was nothing at all. It was after pondering all the evasions and inconsistencies that we concluded that the most obvious explanation for the unique and anomalous single footprint was that it had been fabricated by Shipton. It would have been the work of moments to enhance one of the oval footprints by adding the 'toe-prints' by hand, particularly a hand wearing a woollen glove. The crisp indentations delineating the inner side of the print could have been made by Shipton's ice axe. Hillary agreed with us, saying that he could quite imagine Shipton 'tidying up' the footprint in such a way.

In short, Gillman suggested that Shipton fabricated the footprint, which he photographed together with the ice axe and Ward's boot; but unfortunately, the joke got out of hand. So, Gillman maintained, Shipton had to keep up the story, partly in retribution to the Everest Establishment that had so shamefully dumped him as leader of the 1953 expedition. In the article, he described Shipton as 'mercurial and disrespectful of authority' and 'defiant, non-conformist, restless and embittered' (compliments, I would have thought, apart from the last epithet). Gillman seems mildly shocked that Shipton should get up to such a prank, but perhaps he forgot the peculiar dynamic between his subject and his companions, Tilman and Sen Tenzing. These three men had kept this particular canard flying for decades.

Gillman's article provoked fury in Peter Steele, who published a biography of Eric Shipton in 1998. In it, he wrote about the Gillman article: 'It is difficult to take seriously, being full of scurrilous invective . . .' and he objected to Gillman's 'churlish appraisal' of Shipton's character. This was unnecessarily personal but fairly typical of Shipton's supporters, who always considered that he had a raw deal. Gillman put up a stout defence in an article in the *Alpine Journal* in which he also responded to Ward's 'The Yeti footprints – myth and reality' in the *AJ* of 1999, in which he was again taken to task. In it, Gillman revealed that Ed Hillary was an early sceptic who quizzed Shipton about the photographs: 'Eric,' said Hillary, 'tended to rather dodge giving too much of a reply.'

John Napier had clearly been bothered by the discrepancy between the big footprint and the two photographs of tracks, but throughout his book he had carefully dodged the first question that a scientist would be expected to ask: are these real?

All the witnesses had originally only spoken of one set of tracks; Shipton and Ward, and then Bourdillon and Murray, who had followed a couple of days later. When pressed, Ward then suggested that one set of tracks could have melted away by the time Bourdillon and Murray saw them. One set of tracks melting away preferentially? This seems odd. Gillman suggests that Ward was by now flailing around in the attempt to reconcile all the versions of the tale. The truth was simple, says Gillman: Shipton faked the footprint, and the loyal Ward did his best to cover up his tracks. Then Ward came up with another theory, in an article in the *Alpine Journal* of 1999,* where he speculates that the prints were actually made by a human with deformed feet.†

Ward, a doctor used to describing physical abnormalities, pointed out that porters routinely travelled across snow barefoot. It would take only one such individual with a deformed foot and one such event to start an enduring myth amongst the Sherpas. But would he really have two identically deformed feet? And why would he be trekking in bare feet at 19,000 feet along the Nepal-Tibet border well away from any kind of trading route?

In his conclusion, which is relevant to our study of cryptids, Gillman writes that as an investigative journalist he has learned one lesson: 'No matter how implausible a set of alternative theories may appear, there has to be one which is true. The best rule of thumb is to select the explanation which is both the simplest and least implausible – which in this case brings us back to the hoax.' In this, he conflates Sherlock Holmes and William of Ockham.

Jim Perrin, the celebrated mountaineering writer, is in no doubt. In his biography of Shipton and Tilman, he reports an interview with Edmund Hillary who was on the same expedition in 1951:

What you've got to understand is that Eric was a joker. He was forever pulling practical jokes, fooling around in his quiet way. This footprint, see, he's gone round it with his knuckles, shaped the toe, pressed in the middle. There's no animal could walk with a foot like that! He made it up, and of course he was with Sen Tenzing who was as

---

* M. Ward, 'The Yeti Footprints: Myth and Reality,' *Alpine Journal* (1999). See https://www.alpinejournal.org.uk/Contents/Contents_1999_files/ AJ%201999%2081-87%20Ward%20Footprints.pdf.

† See https://uk.pinterest.com/pin/325525879292759740/.

big a joker as he was. They pulled the trick, and Michael Ward just had to keep quiet and go along with it. We all knew, except Bill Murray maybe, but none of us could say, and Eric let it run and run. He just loved to wind people up that way.*

Jim Perrin then tells a tale of leading Ward on a tight rope on a tricky rock climb, years after the Hillary interview. He gave him some worrying slack, then quizzed him about the yeti photograph. His smile, he said, told him everything.

This all leaves some rather interesting questions. What was Edmund Hillary doing in accepting money for a search expedition for the yeti in 1960, if he knew Shipton's photo was a hoax? And why did Ward publish his article in the 1999 *Alpine Journal* if, as Gillman and Perrin claim, he knew the Shipton print was a fake? Was he suffering from some kind of double-think, torn by loyalty to Shipton? And why was Napier so unwilling to accommodate the idea of a simple hoax?

Eric Shipton was indeed prone to playing practical jokes. Audrey Salkeld managed to detect two more hoaxes perpetuated by Shipton. One was connected to the 1938 Everest expedition, after which Shipton claimed that the party's geologist Noel Odell was so affected by oxygen deprivation that he tried to eat some rocks, thinking they were sandwiches. Odell told Salkeld it was 'complete nonsense'.

The second joke Salkeld discovered was in rather questionable taste. On their 1935 Mount Everest Reconnaissance

---

* J. Perrin, *Shipton and Tilman, The Great Decade of Himalayan Exploration* (Hutchinson, 2013).

expedition, Eric Shipton and Charles Warren had found the body of the Englishman Maurice Wilson lying near a tattered tent at the foot of the North Col.

Wilson had announced to the world in 1933 that he would fly an aeroplane to Mount Everest, crash-land it and make the first ascent of the mountain, completely alone. This he would do by the power of a new religious system he had developed based on fasting, despite the fact that he had never climbed a mountain and could not fly a plane.

Wilson was another of those lost souls who had been through the First World War and couldn't settle down. He had won the Military Cross by an act of huge bravery, then been badly injured by machine-gun fire at Ypres, and on his return home to Bradford found life too dull. The pain in his chest and left arm plagued him all his life. He emigrated first to the United States and then to New Zealand, where he became successful running a women's clothing business. However, he was clearly approaching a nervous breakdown and returned to England. On the voyage home, he claimed to have had an encounter with a mysterious Eastern mystic who healed him with a 35-day regime of fasting and prayer. He emerged from the cure a new man with a new purpose in life: to spread the word of his new faith. 'He believed that if he could get divine help he'd be able to prove that he could do something marvellous,' said Audrey Salkeld.

So, inspired by the 1924 Mallory and Irvine climb and the previous year's Houston flight over Everest, Wilson settled on the idea of climbing the mountain solo. He bought a Gipsy Moth biplane that he named *Ever Wrest* and learned to fly. Publicly defying the British authorities, he gained a great deal of press coverage. On the day of departure from England and distracted by the watching journalists and photographers, he took off downwind instead of facing the wind, but somehow made it into the air. He flew out to India, covering 4,350 miles in 17 days, and arrived at the same airfield used by the Duke of Hamilton on his flights the previous year. Here the British Raj caught up with him and his plane was impounded. Undaunted, he made it to Darjeeling, hired three Sherpas who had worked on the 1933 expedition, and all four of them slipped into Tibet disguised as Buddhist monks. Somehow they made it to Rongbuk monastery and Wilson made repeated attempts to climb the mountain. Beaten by a 40-foot icewall on the North Col, he lay down and died. His last diary entry recording his third attempt read: 'Off again, gorgeous day.'

Shipton claimed that Wilson was found wearing women's clothing and that a second diary of a sexual nature was discovered in the tent. Oddly enough, the story was given credence by the find of a woman's shoe at 21,000 feet by the 1960 Chinese expedition. Audrey Salkeld said: 'We can't pin the woman's shoe find on Wilson, but knowing that he worked in a ladies' dress shop in New Zealand, all these things have come together to build a picture of Maurice Wilson as a transvestite or shoe fetishist.' But no evidence has been put forward to support Shipton's story.

Perhaps the professional climber Shipton was amused by the deluded amateur; whatever the reason, the mud stuck, and, despite his heroic war record, impressive flight and solo attempt on the mountain, Wilson is still regarded as something of a failed oddity.

Whether or not Shipton was a hoaxer and practical joker, I would like to suggest what might have happened. He had just spotted a clear route to the summit of the world's highest mountain, and he knew that the Swiss were snapping at his heels: they would go on to nearly climb the mountain the very next year. Britain was on her knees financially after the Second World War, and the British public was probably reluctant to cough up again for yet another expensive failed expedition. What better way to enthuse possible sponsors than to tantalise them with the discovery of a monster? And what could be more fun than to wind journalists up in this way?

Ernst Schäfer was probably right all along. Shipton et al. saw faint footprints, perhaps made by a bear. These were probably kneaded by him into a monstrous shape using his gloved hands and then photographed by him with the collusion of Sen Tenzing, possibly to fool the party following behind, possibly with a larger audience in mind. Ward loyally supported his story.

The doubts in other people's minds may just have contributed to Shipton's downfall at the hands of the Mount Everest committee two years later. Peter Gillman's assessment and Jim Perrin's and Audrey Salkeld's evidence clearly point to Eric Shipton and Sen Tenzing engaged in a practical joke, despite Michael Ward's collusion with him providing a sober and convincing explanation. John Napier, a serious scientist, seemed deeply conflicted: he just couldn't accept the possibility that Shipton and Ward were lying to him. Fake or deformed foot, either way it wasn't a horrible, hairy beast.

In the end, the money for yet another Everest expedition was raised, and after a heart-stopping near-miss by the two Swiss expeditions of 1952, the world's highest mountain finally fell to the British expedition of 1953. The greatest prize in mountaineering was theirs. After the successful conquest, the climbers were besieged by journalists, but some of them weren't as interested in the summit so much as what might live there. They wanted to know if yeti tracks had been found on the mountain as they had the previous year by the Swiss team. Ed Hillary and Sen Tenzing had also been reported as seeing large footprints, but the leader John Hunt was less encouraging. 'I am sorry to disappoint you,' he said, 'but we saw no trace of him at all. I think we were too big a party for any Abominable Snowman. They like seclusion and solitude.' However, in his book of the expedition, he described an interesting encounter just after reaching base camp at Thyangboche monastery:

That afternoon we paid our first official visit to the Monastery at the invitation of the monks. There was a simple ceremony to perform on arrival, the laying of scarves on the thrones of the present Abbot as he, a young boy, was away in Tibet . . . Coached in this formality by Tenzing, I also presented to the acting Abbot our expedition flag. We were briefly shown round the sanctuary, after which a meal was served in an upper room. Seated with Charles Wylie and Tenzing beside our host, a rotund figure robed in faded red, I questioned him about the Yeti, better known to us as the 'Abominable Snowman'. The old dignitary at once warmed to this subject. Peering out of the window on to the meadow where our tents were pitched, he gave a most graphic description of how a Yeti had appeared from the surrounding thickets a few years back in winter, when the snow lay on the ground. This beast, loping along sometimes on his hind legs and sometimes on all fours, stood about five feet high and was covered with grey hair, a description which we have heard from other eyewitnesses. Oblivious of his guests, the Abbot was reliving a sight imprinted on his memory as he stared across at the scene of this event. The Yeti had stopped to scratch, the old monk gave a good imitation, but went on longer than he need have done to make his point. It had picked up snow, played with it and made a few grunts; again he gave us a convincing rendering. The inhabitants of the Monastery had meanwhile worked themselves into a great state of excitement, and instructions were given to drive off the unwelcome visitor. Conch shells were blown and the long traditional horns sounded. The Yeti had ambled away into the bush.*

* Hunt, op. cit.

Here was an *ex cathedra* statement from a trustworthy source, a religious leader. But this sounds very much like a description of the *dzu-teh*, or bear. It also reinforces the theory that, for the Nepalese, the yeti has no particular religious significance: the monks drove the creature away. Hunt called for another expedition to look for the yeti, and Sen Tenzing said that he believed in the creature because his father had seen one. In his second autobiography, however, he said he had become more sceptical about it.

The 1950s were the Golden Age of Himalayan climbing, with all of the fourteen 8,000-metre peaks 'knocked off' within ten years of each other. It was also the Golden Age of yeti-hunting expeditions. In 1954, enthused by the successful Everest expedition of the previous year, the *Daily Mail* newspaper sent a hugely expensive Snowman expedition to find the yeti. The mountaineering leader was John Angelo Jackson, who was ex-RAF and had flown supplies into Burma during the war. He was a fine climber and had been on the back-up climbing team for the previous year's Everest expedition. Accompanying them was 1953 Everest cameraman Tom Stobart. Significantly, the team also included the poker-playing journalist Ralph Izzard. He was another who contributed to the character of James Bond, for like many journalists (and yeti-hunters) he had a second life as a spy, and I suspect he may have known Ivan Sanderson.

After graduating from Cambridge in 1931, Izzard worked for the *Daily Mail* and remained there as foreign correspondent for the next 31 years. He was the newspaper's Berlin bureau chief during part of the Cold War, but it was during the Second World War that he worked in military intelligence. Fluent in German, he interrogated captured agents, and it was during this time that he came up with Operation Ruthless. The idea was to capture one of the German Navy's Enigma encryption machines. His plan was for an RAF crew dressed in Luftwaffe uniforms to crash a captured German bomber into the sea near a German Navy vessel. After rescue, the RAF crew would then kill the German crew and hijack the vessel, thus acquiring one of the Enigma machines.

Any one of us could see some slight flaws in this cunning plan, but two factors intervened. Firstly, the RAF pointed out that the Heinkel bomber would sink too quickly to allow the crew to escape. Then, before the plan could be changed, a British destroyer, HMS *Bulldog*, beat them all to it in May 1941, capturing an Enigma machine from a German submarine. After being forced to the surface by depth-charge attack, U-boat U-110 was boarded by personnel from *Bulldog* who stripped it of everything portable, including her Kurzsignale code book and Enigma machine.

Before the US entry into the war, American intelligence operatives were sent to Britain to observe the interrogation of enemy prisoners. Izzard was their liaison officer. He was then sent to New York to assist the British Security Co-ordination, headed by Canadian William Stephenson, where he almost certainly met his colleagues Ivan Sanderson and the future children's writer Roald Dahl. Could they have discussed the wild man of Tibet? We will never know. However, there seems to be a strange connection between spies, black propaganda and the yeti.

Izzard achieved a certain kind of spying immortality. While serving with Naval Intelligence, his commander was Ian Fleming. During the operation against German interests in Brazil, he found himself playing poker against his opposite number in German Navy Intelligence at a casino in Pernambuco. Fleming drew on this episode as the inspiration for the first lines of his first Bond novel, *Casino Royale,* in which Commander Bond plays baccarat with the SMERSH villain Le Chiffre:

The scent and smoke and sweat of a casino are nauseating at three in the morning. Then the soul erosion produced by high gambling – a compost of greed and fear and nervous tension – becomes unbearable and the senses awake and revolt from it.*

Casino Royale went on sale in April 1953, mere weeks before the first climb of Mount Everest. On that very day, Ralph Izzard had found his way to base camp, wearing a silk cravat, a golfing jacket and a pair of plimsolls. The team were impressed that a journalist had not only climbed to base camp unsupported but had also managed to shave and brush his hair. Izzard, like Bond, was always immaculately presented. However, he was eventually scooped by James Morris (later Jan Morris), the *Times* correspondent who, terrified that the *Daily Mail* would scoop *him*, raced down to Kathmandu a few weeks later with the news that the mountain had been climbed.

So it was that Izzard arrived the next year highly motivated to find a story even bigger than Everest. 'The *Daily Mail* Snowman Expedition' provided adventure for a large team of climbers, scientists and 370 porters who were employed for fifteen weeks to carry tons of supplies and bring back specimens. There was an ornithologist, an Indian zoologist and a specialist in the capture of wild animals. If a live Abominable Snowman was caught, it was to be shipped in a cage back to London to be examined. The whole bandobust must have cost around a million pounds in today's money.

The mountaineering leader John Jackson found and photographed many footprints in snow, some of which the expedition naturalists could not identify but admitted that they could have melted out from common animal tracks. Jackson also photographed hand-painted pictures of the yeti in Thyangboche monastery:

One of these frescoes created much interest because it depicted a symbolic *meh-teh* being chased by men on

* I. Fleming, *Casino Royale* (Jonathan Cape, 1953).

horseback. The creature's body was painted blue and had a repulsive green face topped by long green hair. A blue and red tongue protruded from its gaping mouth and snakes writhed about its neck and shoulders. None of us had heard of such a painting before, but a few days later Kapa Kalden, the lama from Kumjung who had painted the fresco, gave us a less symbolic painting of the *meh-teh*, as well as the *chu-teh* and the *dzu-teh*. From the paintings and by interrogation of the Sherpas, we got a clear impression that the *dzu-teh* is a bear, probably the Himalayan red bear (*Ursus arctos isabellinus*), which can kill the Sherpa yak. The *meh-teh* was depicted as a smaller animal. The *chu-teh* was the smallest – seemingly a gibbon-like creature said to live in Tibet. Or is it a langur monkey? We all hoped we might see a *meh-teh*, but not for long if it was anything like the painting on the gompa wall.*

Was there any significance in the body of the *meh-teh* being painted blue? Jackson goes on to speculate cautiously that the creature was actually the Tibetan blue bear *Ursus arctos pruinosus*,† a subspecies of the Tibetan brown bear. This is one of the rarest subspecies of bear in the world and is hardly ever sighted in the wild. It was first classified in 1854 by examination of pelts and bone samples. As a result, its conservation status is unclear, but this is bound to be threatened by the trade in bear bile in Chinese traditional medicine and the loss of habitat.

Jackson is cautious about his theory, because other zoologists do not mention the creature. But this could be because they hadn't encountered it. It is, however, mentioned by other writers, and in *The Himalaya*, edited by John Lall, the writer Ramjit Singh has this to say: 'The bear family is represented in the

* J. Jackson, 'The Elusive Snowman', *Alpine Journal*, 1999.
† P. Z. S. Lydekker, 'The Blue Bear of Tibet,' *Journal of the Asiatic Society Bengal, vol. XXII, 1897, p. 426.*

The Tibetan blue bear Ursus arctos pruinosus.

Himalaya by the brown and the Himalayan black bear. A third member, the Tibetan blue bear, is so rare that practically nothing is known about it.' He goes on to say that one was reported across the border in Tibet when he was camping on the Bhutan–Tibetan border: in 1965. 'Though pelts of this animal have been known for 150 years there has never been a Tibetan blue bear in captivity. Pelts were first brought out of Sichuan in northern China early in the last century, and since that time a number of hunters have brought back pelts from the Himalaya, but not the animal.'

We will meet another adherent to this theory later. Jackson's book of the expedition, *More Than Mountains,* is a classic of the genre but is little read nowadays. All the freshness and excitement of Himalayan mountaineering in the 1940s and 1950s is there, together with descriptions of the culture of the mountain people:

Butter is made from the milk of the yak or the *dzo* . . . this butter has many uses; it greases the hair, supplies fuel for butter-lamps, is carved into statues of Buddha for religious processions, floats on the surface of butter-tea, and often for the poorer people is the only storable source of wealth. In the Kargil and Paskyam area the peasants take the butter above the snowline and bury it beneath the ice. Before he dies a father gives instructions that his store of butter shall be passed on to his eldest son. Thus it accumulates. With Daniel Berger, the Swiss missionary, I once bought some of this butter of great age – over sixty years old, we were told, and it was still edible, though a little rancid and discoloured.[*]

Something even more exciting, though, was found at a monastery in the Pangboche village further up the valley. On 19 March 1954, the *Daily Mail* ran the story claiming that a scalp had been discovered, said to be taken from a dead specimen of the elusive yeti.

The team zoologist, Charles Stoner, considered that the specimen had quite clearly come from the head of a previously unknown animal, but that he was utterly unable to identify it. The hairs, which were black and foxy red in colour, were immediately sent to Professor Frederick Wood Jones, one-time president of the Anatomical Society, who believed that humans had evolved from an earlier, non-anthropoid strain of creature. He bleached the hairs, cut them into sections and examined them through a microscope, comparing them to hairs from orang-utans and bears. He concluded that the hairs were not actually from a scalp, as no known creature has a ridge of hair extending from the nape across the pate all the way to the forehead. He couldn't identify them, but was certain that the skin and hairs were not from an ape or a bear but had been taken from the shoulder of a coarse-haired animal such as a goat. The skin had then been worked and kneaded

[*] J. Jackson, *More Than Mountains* (Harrap, 1955).

into the shape of a cranium while the skin was still fresh, presumably by Nepalese lamas. Wood was a sceptic:'If the primate forms immediately ancestral to the human stock are ever to be revealed, they will be utterly unlike the slouching "ape men" of which some have dreamed and of which they have made casts and pictures during their waking hours.' He was to die later that year, still unconvinced that the *Daily Mail* had found the scalp of the yeti.

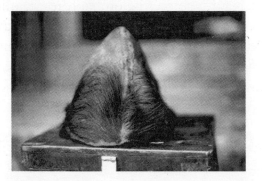

Scotland Yard: 'Sorry, we do not know this man.'

The hairs were also sent to Scotland Yard, the home of the metropolitan London police, together with a list of questions. After a delay of several days they replied with: 'Sorry, we do not know this man.'

After the expedition, Ralph Izzard published a long account of the trip in which he claimed to have followed footprints of two yetis for eight miles over two days. They were around 9 inches long and 5 inches wide, he said, with a stride of 2 feet 3 inches (rather like a pair of local Nepalese humans). These prints carefully avoided human pathways and villages. Izzard admitted that the footprints were not fresh and may have melted out in the sun.

Izzard was accompanied during those two days by the somewhat shadowy naturalist Gerald Russell, who was also on the *Daily Mail* team. When I spotted his name in the expedition members' list, my eyebrows rose. In 1936, Russell had acquired brief fame as one of the people who had been the first to capture a giant panda. In 1934, the husband of the American socialite and fashion designer Ruth Elizabeth Harkness had travelled to China to search for the mythical creature. However, he died of throat cancer in Shanghai in early 1936 and his wife decided to complete his quest.* She took with her a Chinese–American explorer, Quentin Young, and the naturalist Russell. They travelled through Chengdu, climbed into the foothills and had the good fortune to stumble across a nine-week-old panda cub on 9 November 1936. They immediately captured it (one wonders how its distraught mother felt). Harkness took it back to America in her arms rather than in a cage. They named it Su Lin, after Young's sister-in-law, unaware that it was in fact male. The panda died two years later in a zoo in Chicago.

Ruth Harkness and Su Lin.

Although born in the USA, Gerald Russell had attended Cambridge University where he had become a lifelong friend of . . . Ivan Sanderson! The plot thins: the same character keeps appearing. In 1932, Russell had accompanied Sanderson on an

---

* R. Harkness, *The Lady and the Panda: An Adventure* (Carrick & Evans, 1938).

expedition to Africa. It was on this trip, while in the British Cameroons, that the two young men claimed to have encountered the fabled Mokèlé-mbèmbé, a huge creature somewhat like the Loch Ness monster or a sauropod, the 'lizard-hipped' dinosaur. Two months later while in the Assumbo area, on the same expedition, they reportedly saw the giant bat-like-lizard, the kongamato. These two students clearly had remarkably good luck to spot not one but two Jurassic-era living dinosaurs.

After the success of the giant panda expedition, Russell served during the war as an American volunteer in the British Royal Navy. Again, we notice the curious military intelligence connection between Eric Shipton, Ian Fleming, Ivan Sanderson, Roald Dahl, Ralph Izzard and now Gerald Russell: tall-story tellers all. After the conflict, Russell travelled to China in search of the elusive golden takin, a goat-antelope whose coat is said to have inspired the legend of the Golden Fleece. Russell had to abandon this expedition on account of the civil war between Communist and Nationalist Chinese forces. However, he was employed by the *Daily Mail* in 1954 as one of its naturalists, clearly having had success in finding mythical beasts in the past. His team claimed sightings and collected droppings from the smallest type of yeti during the *Daily Mail* trip, but examination of the dung proved inconclusive. Russell's method of finding the yeti involved the use of a pendulum dangled over the map, which Jackson found unconvincing:

This pendulum was used by him much as a water-diviner uses a rod, although its 'extraordinary' powers were even greater, for by merely placing the pendulum over a map it would swing and indicate the position of our quarry . . . Once the pendulum stopped above the fantastic, impossible summit of Cholatse, and I felt like taking my hat off to the redoubtable *Meh-Teh*.*

---

* Jackson, op. cit.

If the *Daily Mail* expedition had produced little more than a few footprints and a faked scalp, at least it helped to popularise the idea of the yeti, and a second, more serious, book emerged after the trip. The naturalist Charles Stoner's book* described much new animal and bird life of the Nepal Himalayas, including this description of the yeti by Pasang Nima, one of the Sherpas who said he had seen one:

> He described it as the size and build of a small man. Its head was covered with long hair, as was the middle part of the body and thighs. The face and chest did not look to be so hairy, and the hair on its legs below the knees was short. The colour he described as both dark and light and the chest looked to be reddish. The Yeti was walking on two legs, nearly as upright as a man, but kept bending down to grub in the ground, he thought for roots. After a time it saw the watchers, and ran into the undergrowth, still on two legs, but with a sidling gait (which he imitated), giving a loud high-pitched cry.

Stoner concluded that no positive identification of a yeti could be made on the evidence his expedition found. However, the Tibetan stories he heard about the *dzu-teh* were undoubtedly sightings of the Himalayan red bear. Oddly enough, though, he concludes with these words: 'Some unknown and highly intelligent form of ape does in fact maintain a precarious foothold in the Alpine zone of the Himalayas.'

* C. Stoner, *The Sherpa and the Snowman* (Hollis and Carter, 1955).

CHAPTER FIVE

Yeti-mania. . .the CIA connection. . .the escape of the Dalai Lama. . .spies and damned spies. . .the Abominable Sanderson. . .Roald Dahl. . .sleeping with everyone worth over $50,000. . .the atomic bug. . .nuclear testing. . .death of a woman mountaineer. . .Nanda Devi.

The 1950s saw an increase in the number of yeti-hunts, and soon newspapers all over the world were carrying stories about the beast. The Nepalese authorities began charging for permits to hunt for the animal: £400 per yeti. Then, in 1956, along came a Texan oilman roaming through the Himalayas with the glorious name of Tom Slick. What is more, there is a curious connection between Slick, the CIA and the escape of the Dalai Lama after the Chinese invasion of Tibet.

Far from the popular image of a Texan oil millionaire, Tom Slick was a thoughtful man who wrote a book about the best way to achieve world peace. Slick's father, 'the King of the Wildcatters', had become immensely rich after discovering Oklahoma's largest oil field, and Tom Jnr spent the money on his interests in peace politics, art, aircraft, adventure and cryptozoology, a pseudoscience that attempts to prove the existence of mythical creatures. He mounted expeditions to look for the Loch Ness monster, the Trinity Alps giant sala-mander and Bigfoot. He also financed three expeditions to look for the yeti after a trip to Central Asia in 1956. In that year, he met the Irishman Peter Byrne, an explorer and big-game hunter, who later became instrumental in Bigfoot hunts. In his biography of Slick,* Loren Coleman discovered that both Byrne and Slick were by then working for the CIA, which was concerned about newly formed Communist China's intentions towards Tibet.

Slick was a valuable asset to the Agency, as there were few Americans in the post-war era with money, connections and an interest in the politics of Central Asia. In 1957, he spent at least a month roaming the mountains in the north of Nepal. Little came of this trip apart from some more footprints; however, the next year he employed Gerald Russell of the *Daily Mail* expedition and claimed that this time he would be successful and that the yeti would be found by the end of the year. The expedition numbered 100 in all, and this time they took dogs: three bluetick coonhounds known for their hunting ability. They also carried tranquilliser guns and Russell insisted that 'all white hunters will be disguised as natives. We will wear rough woollen Sherpa vests, woollen hats, and felt Tibetan hats. Our faces will be stained brown.' (Howard-Bury would have fitted right in.) They roamed the Himalayas for months, heavily stained, sending back reports that the newspapers found irresistible. One memorable head-line in the *Washington Post* on 17 June 1958 screamed 'Snowman Reported Eating Himalayan Frogs', while the *Boston Globe* of 30 April had 'Americans Find Cave of Abominable Snowman'. Tom Slick trumpeted 'Expedition a Success, Proves Yeti Exists' in his summary in the *Boston Globe* of 26 July. In reality, there was still no Snowman. Or foot. But at least this time there was a hand.

* L. Coleman, *Tom Slick and the Search for the Yeti* (Faber & Faber, 1989).

In a BBC interview in December 2011, Peter Byrne described what happened:

> We found ourselves one day camped at a temple called Pangboche [the same monastery that had preserved the yeti scalp]. The temple had a number of Sherpa custodians. I heard one of them speaking Nepalese, which I speak. He told me that they had in the temple the hand of a yeti which had been there for many years. It looked like a large human hand. It was covered with crusted black, broken skin. It was very oily from the candles and the oil lamps in the temple. The fingers were hooked and curled.*

On his return to London during a meal at a restaurant at Regent's Park Zoo, Byrne repeated his story to Professor William Osmond Hill, a primatologist. This meeting had been set up by the well-connected Slick. Osmond Hill said: 'You've got to get this hand. We've got to see it. We want to examine it.' But Byrne said he had already asked the lamas if he could have the hand and they said no, it would bring bad luck, disaster to the temple if it was taken away.

Professor Hill and Slick persuaded Byrne to return the following year and try to remove one finger from the temple. Their plan was to substitute the missing finger with a human finger. Subterfuge was being proposed by not telling the lamas about the substitution. Professor Hill then produced a brown paper bag and shook out a human hand on to the restaurant table: 'It was several months old and dried. I never asked him where he got it from.'

So, armed with a hand, as it were, Byrne returned to the temple in Nepal in 1959. He later said that he gave a donation in exchange for the finger, and then wired a dried human

---

* See http://www.bbc.co.uk/news/science-environment-16264752.

finger from the dried hand onto the holy relic. Slick wanted to make sure that the yeti finger would reach London safely, so he asked his friends, the Hollywood actors James Stewart and his wife Gloria Stewart, to help. They were touring India and Byrne met them at the Grand Hotel in Calcutta with the stolen digit. 'They were a little bit worried about customs, so Gloria hid it in her lingerie case and they got out of India, no trouble. They arrived at Heathrow, but the lingerie case was missing.'

A few days later, a customs official returned the case personally to Gloria Stewart, assuring her that no British customs official would ever open a lady's lingerie case. (This was a rash statement to make. Surely it would depend on the lady?) The finger duly made its way to Professor Hill, and Byrne lost touch.

Years passed, but eventually Professor Hill's collection turned up in the vaults of the Royal College of Surgeons' Hunterian Museum in London, where there are thousands of anatomical specimens from both human and animal species. Somewhat like Indiana Jones's Lost Ark, it had been forgotten in a huge collection. In 2008, a box was found containing plaster casts of a footprint, hair, scat (droppings) – and an object recorded as a yeti's finger. The specimen was 3.5 inches long and 0.8 inches wide at the widest part, curled and black at the end with a long nail. DNA tests were made and the finger was found to be of human origin, according to Dr Rob Jones, senior scientist at the Zoological Society of Scotland. 'We have got a very, very strong match to a number of existing reference sequences on human DNA databases. It's very similar to existing human sequences from China and that region of Asia but we don't have enough resolution to be confident of a racial identification.'

This 'yeti's finger' is now all that remains of the original yeti's hand, which was stolen from Pangboche monastery in the 1990s. There are suggestions that it should be handed back.

Yeti-mania reached boiling point in 1959 and 1960, when no fewer than eleven expeditions from Japan, France, Great Britain and China scoured the Himalayas. The Chinese, who were consolidating their grip on their sovereign neighbour Tibet, began to be suspicious about the real motives behind these incursions. In 27 April 1957, the *New York Times* had published an item entitled: 'Soviet Sees Espionage in US Snowman Hunt'. The piece claimed that Tom Slick was behind an attempt to subvert the Chinese and free Tibet. What was more, the Russians complained that relations were being deliberately strained between Nepal and Communist China 'by the missing link in the story of the mysterious scientific expeditions sent to the Himalayas in quest for the "snowman".'

The Americans were taking the reality of the yeti very seriously. I have seen a declassified document originating from the US embassy in Kathmandu entitled: 'Regulations Covering Mountain Climbing Expeditions in Nepal Relating to Yeti'. It lays out the need for the correct permit to search for the animal from the Nepalese government, and furthermore stipulates that, although it was acceptable to photograph or capture a living specimen, 'it must not be killed or shot at except in an emergency arising out of self defense'. Curiously, a copy of this document is lodged in the archives of the CIA.

Then, right at the height of yeti-mania, the young God-King, the 14th Dalai Lama, fled the country. On the night of 17 March 1959, aged just 23, he slipped out of Norbulingka, his summer residence in Lhasa, and began his flight to India. He was so well disguised that his faithful subjects mistakenly prostrated themselves before a monk in his party. He crossed the most rugged terrain in the Himalayas, ending up in the safety of India.

Leroy Fletcher Prouty, a US Air Force colonel who supervised secret air missions for the Office of Special Operations, wrote a book which claimed the Dalai Lama's flight was masterminded by the CIA. 'This fantastic escape and its major significance have been buried in the lore of the CIA as one of those successes that are not talked about. The Dalai Lama would have never been saved without the CIA.'* The book can hardly have pleased the Agency, as it also claimed that President Kennedy was assassinated to keep the USA and its defence budget in Vietnam, and that the U-2 Crisis of 1960 was staged to sabotage the Eisenhower–Khrushchev talks.

However, there were persistent rumours that Tom Slick and Peter Byrne were somehow complicit in the Dalai Lama's escape. In his 1986 book, *Presidents' Secret Wars*, John Prados stated that 'the best information [about the fleeing Dalai Lama] came from the CIA . . . The CIA was so well informed because it had furnished an American radio operator, who travelled with the Dalai Lama's party . . . There may have been other CIA agents with the party as well.' And who got them into Tibet? According to Slick's biographer Loren Coleman, it was none other than Peter Byrne, Slick's man in Nepal.†

Conspiracy theory or historical fact? It is fairly well known now that the Americans ran a 2,000-strong Tibetan Khampa rebel camp in Mustang, Nepal, during the 1950s and 60s, and trained Tibetan guerrilla fighters at Camp Hale, Colorado. I know one elderly CIA operative who ended up staying in Kathmandu. The yeti expeditions were a perfect cover for reconnaissance trips and for passing people across the Tibetan border.

Whatever happened to Tom Slick? On 6 October 1962, he was flying his Beechcraft Bonanza back from a Canadian

---

* L. Fletcher Prouty, *The Secret Team: The CIA and its Allies in Control of the United States and the World* (Ballantine Books, 1974).

† See http://www.umsl.edu/~thomaskp/dalai.htm.

hunting trip when it exploded in mid-air over Montana. He was killed immediately, taking all his secrets with him.

A significant book (first mentioned back in Chapter Two) was published at this time – the apogee of yeti-mania, which exaggerated and distorted the original Howard-Bury and Waddell reports and claimed that there were 'sub-humans' on five of the continents. I am referring to *Abominable Snowmen*, written by our old acquaintance, Ivan T. Sanderson, and published in 1961. This tome features a lurid cartoon of a threatening yeti striding towards us, pushing aside the subtitle: *Legend Come to Life*. The one Amazon reviewer writes 'Great research. Full of undeniable evidence', and awards five stars. Ivan Sanderson was the author of other undeniable works such as *Invisible Residents: The Reality of Underwater UFOs,* the amazing *Pursuing the Unexplained: Puzzling Mysteries of the Natural World,* and (my personal favourite) *'Things' and More 'Things'.*

Sanderson claimed to have coined the word 'cryptozoology' when he was a student, and if so it seems particularly appropriate. His book is full of the same assertions, half-truths and downright fabrications that you might find today on any cryptozoological website. *Abominable Snowmen: Legend Come to Life* is further subtitled *The Story of Sub Humans on Five Continents from the Early Ice Age until Today*. At the beginning of his *Abominable Snowmen*, Sanderson adopts a breezy tone, describing Laurence Waddell as a blimpish colonel, attributing 'whoops of admiration even from the Major's mountain-born porters', something Waddell certainly does not describe, and dismissing his *Among the Himalayas* as 'a somewhat uninspired and uninspiring book'. This seems a strange conclusion, as from the very beginning Waddell's descriptions of travel up from Calcutta on the toy train to Darjeeling are exciting, fresh and colourful. Sanderson adds details about Waddell's tracks being made by bare feet and ignores his conclusion that they had been made by a bear. This is lying by omission. I suspect Sanderson never read the book, only the much-reprinted wild man footprints section, especially as he complains later about the difficulties of finding source texts. In the rest of *Abominable Snowmen*, he claims that there are hominids living in Canada, northern California, Africa, Central and Southern America, the Caucasus and so on. Later on, describing the 1950s yeti-hunts, he is effusive about the credentials of his friends, Gerald Russell and Tom Slick, without revealing his relationship with them. This kind of book, however, is very convincing to readers who want to be convinced.

Ivan T. Sanderson was born in Edinburgh. His father, who was involved in the whisky industry, was killed by a rhinoceros in Kenya when Ivan was only 14 years old. Mysterious murderous beasts seem to have dominated Ivan's life from then on. He was sent to Britain's top school, Eton College, which has produced 19 of Britain's prime ministers.

In *The Importance of Being Eton*, the author Nick Fraser explains that Etonians compete for office within the school; and (relevant to our discussion) their Eton Scientific Society admits members by election, rather than mere intellectual ability. According to Jonathan Aitken, the Old Etonian MP who was jailed for perjury, this 'breeds a certain speciality of behaviour. You know how to get elected. You know how to please. You have to learn to oil. And at Eton you do learn.'*

I worked with Aitken during the making of a TV documentary and I can confirm that he exhibited supreme charm: 'Eton Oil' combined with inventiveness is a powerful combination. This is what Sanderson had in buckets.

Sanderson gained an MA at Cambridge in botany, travelled widely in Asia and Africa and then became famous after

---

* N. Fraser, *The Importance of Being Eton* (Short Books, 2006).

claiming that he had spotted a giant kongamato in the Jiundu swamps of Western Zambia. He described it as 'the Granddaddy of all bats'. There were suggestions that this could be a surviving *rhamphorhynchus*, a devilish-looking Jurassic winged lizard. There were no photographs or specimens provided to prove the existence of this creature.

Sanderson's life then became even more extraordinary. During the Second World War, he was recruited by British Intelligence in charge of counter-espionage against the Germans in the Caribbean. German U-boats, operating at the extremes of their range, had become a problem in the Caribbean, where they hid among the islands and struck at strategically important oil refineries and tankers. The British Isles required four oil tankers a day during the early part of the war and most of that petroleum came from Venezuela, through the Royal Dutch Shell refinery on Curaçao. There was significant support for the Axis powers in South America, with pro-German paramilitary training undertaken in southern Chile, and Nazi supporters elsewhere routinely sending information to Germany about the routes of Allied merchant vessels. Sanderson's job was to spread disinformation and propaganda about German interests.

He worked for a shadowy outfit, the British Security Co-ordination, headed by Canadian William Stephenson.* This man was known by the code name Intrepid and was another model for James Bond. Ian Fleming himself stated: 'James Bond is a highly romanticised version of a true spy. The real thing is . . . William Stephenson.'† His much-decorated exploits in the Royal Flying Corps during the First World War in a Sopwith Camel may also have partly inspired the Biggles novels by W. E. Johns, and he has been credited with some responsibility

---

* W. Stephenson, *The Secret History of British Intelligence in the Americas, 1940–1945* (Fromm, 1999).

† H. Montgomery Hyde, *Room 3603* (The Lyons Press, 2001); see Preface.

for the birth of the CIA. He was, in short, a spook. And so was his colleague Sanderson.

The children's novelist Roald Dahl was one of Sanderson's fellow agents. He had a public relations role at the British embassy and, like James Bond, slept with countless high-society women while gathering intelligence against the Nazis in the United States. Antoinette Haskell, a wealthy friend of Dahl's, said the author had a whole stable of women. 'He was very arrogant with his women, but he got away with it. The uniform didn't hurt one bit, and he was an ace [fighter pilot],' she remembered. 'I think he slept with everybody on the east and west coasts that had more than $50,000 a year.'*

Roald Dahl, like Sanderson, was a charmer who also conjured up monsters, in his case for children. To date, over 200 million copies of his books have been sold. Among other monstrous events, his children are eaten by giants. Other children are changed into mice by hags. As child psychologist Bruno Bettelheim explained in his book *The Uses of Enchantment,*† the grotesque in children's literature serves a cathartic function. 'Without such fantasies, the child fails to get to know his monster better, nor is he given suggestions as to how he may gain mastery over it. As a result, the child remains helpless with his worst anxieties, much more so than if he had been told fairy tales which give these anxieties form and body and also show ways to overcome these monsters.' This might suggest an explanation for the childish desire to believe in large mythical beasts like yetis, Grendel and Bigfoot.

Dahl was not a particularly pleasant person. He was dubbed 'Roald the Rotten' by his actress wife Patricia Neal after she discovered that he had been cheating on her for years with her best friend. A friend of mine at the BBC had an unfortunate habit of interviewing elderly writers just before they died

---

* D. Sturrock, *Storyteller: The Life of Roald Dahl* (Harper Press, 2010).

† B. Bettelheim, *The Uses of Enchantment* (Thames & Hudson, 1977).

suddenly and unexpectedly (of natural causes, of course). She saw off William Golding in this way, and Roald Dahl as well. At least the waspish Dahl might have found this funny.

MI6 set up the British Security Co-ordination (BSC) operation in New York in 1940, under direct orders from Prime Minister Winston Churchill. It was at the nadir of British fortunes. The Blitz was at its height, the Nazis were triumphant everywhere and the only hope Britain had was to persuade a reluctant America into the war. In polling, it was revealed that 80 per cent of Americans were against the war and there was a strong anti-British sentiment. After the fall of France in June 1940, it was felt that Britain would be next, so why back a loser?

Under the command of William Stephenson, agents like Ivan Sanderson and Roald Dahl worked hard at making up monstrous stories to seduce the American public and scupper the Germans. The British Security Co-ordination operated under the cover identity of 'The British Passport Office'. It was run from three floors of the International Building at the Rockefeller Center. They worked hand in glove with the Office of Strategic Services, the predecessor of the CIA who came up with novel ideas such as introducing oestrogen into Hitler's food to deprive him of his trademark moustache and baritone voice. The BSC harassed German sympathisers with night-time phone calls, dead rats in their water tanks and punctured car tyres. They also forged the map of a purported future Nazi-run South America which was produced by President Roosevelt in a pro-war, anti-Nazi speech on 27 October 1941. 'This map makes clear the Nazi design,' Roosevelt declaimed, 'not only against South America but against the United States as well.' And, more importantly for our story, the BSC operated as a propaganda agency which influenced coverage in all the major US newspapers.

After the war, the *Washington Post* remarked: 'Like many intelligence operations, this one involved exquisite moral ambiguity. The British used ruthless methods to achieve their goals;

by today's peacetime standards, some of the activities may seem outrageous. Yet they were done in the cause of Britain's war against the Nazis, and by pushing America towards intervention, the British spies helped win the war.'

If any of this is sounding familiar, the 'psy-ops' operations of the data analytics firm that played a role in both the Donald Trump and Brexit campaigns used much the same methods of disinformation and untruths to sway an electorate, with the exception that today's data-mining of social media can identify the kinds of people who can be swayed. 'Finding "persuadable" voters is key for any campaign, and with its treasure trove of data Cambridge Analytica could target people high in neuroticism, for example, with images of immigrants "swamping" the country. The key is finding emotional triggers for each individual voter.'*

In the end, the events on the morning of Sunday, 7 December 1941 made the BSC's efforts unnecessary. The Japanese bombed Pearl Harbor and the USA was in the war.

After Pearl Harbor, Ivan Sanderson became a press agent, using the contacts and skills he had built up in the BSC. After the war was over, he became a naturalised US citizen, living at first in New York and later in New Jersey. He returned to his love of animals and opened 'Ivan Sanderson's Jungle Zoo' in New Jersey which rented exotic animals out to motion pictures and TV shows. He then became interested in the paranormal. In 1948, he published a *Saturday Evening Post* article, entitled 'There Could Be Dinosaurs', which inspired the so-called 'father of cryptozoology' Bernard Heuvelmans. Sanderson founded the Society for the Investigation of the Unexplained (SITU) in 1967. SITU was a non-profit organisation that investigated strange phenomena dismissed by mainstream science. And Sanderson admired Charles Hoy Fort, the researcher of anomalous phenomena (the *Fortean Times* was named after him).

* See https://www.theguardian.com/technology/2017/may/07/the-great-british-brexit-robbery-hijacked-democracy.

The retired magician and scientific sceptic, James Randi, knew Sanderson well: 'Ivan was a "character" in every way, a man who kept an odiferous cheetah named "Baby" in his New York apartment for weeks on end when he felt like it, and even slept with the beast. He had the claw marks to show for it. He was in the business of writing books about strange subjects, and he would never allow ugly facts to interfere with an otherwise attractive story. In person, he left no question about his doubts; in print he successfully resisted expressing any really serious reservations he had.'*

Ivan Sanderson is shown holding the monster cast print which appeared on the Suwannee riverbank in 1948. The well-publicised incident attracted Sanderson, and he summarised the case in his 1969 book More Things, *expressing his conviction that the case was authentic.*

* See http://archive.randi.org/site/jr/01-05-2000.html.

To be fair to Sanderson, he was also capable of scepticism. He established that the 1909 Jersey Devil sightings were a hoax: unscrupulous real estate speculators spread false stories of a winged devil to drive property prices down. Sanderson found the fake hooves used to make footprints in the snow.

In short, Ivan T. Sanderson was surely a gift to any psychologist interested in fabulism and tall stories. I would identify him as the man who did most to further the Western version of the yeti, and he did the same with the American Bigfoot.

If Sanderson's story sounds bizarre, what happened on Bill Tilman's Nanda Devi is almost unbelievable. In 1965, as the Vietnam War was escalating, the CIA and the Indian Intelligence Bureau tried to place a nuclear-powered listening device on the summit of the mountain, in an attempt to eavesdrop on the Chinese. The first Chinese nuclear bomb test, No. 596, had been conducted on 16 October 1964 at Lop Nor, not far from the site of the Tarim mummies which had so interested the Nazi Glacial Cosmogony enthusiasts. The Indians were concerned, as they had just fought a border war with the Chinese, and the Americans were also quite justifiably concerned, as the Chinese could be drawn into the Vietnam conflict more overtly and might then employ nuclear weapons. How effective were they? It was vital to know. Spy satellites were in their infancy, Pakistan had just banned American spy planes and the mountain chain of the Himalayas blocked out radio signals, so this was an attempt to peer over the Bamboo Curtain.

The whole extraordinary story is revealed in *Spies in the*

Himalayas,* a book by Mohan Kohli, the Indian Everest climber. Chinese missile test launches were being conducted in Xinjiang province a few hundred miles north of the Himalayas, and the plan was to intercept and relay their radio communications, which would reveal the progress of Chinese nuclear weapons technology. Mount Everest was at first proposed, as just two years earlier the first American team had climbed the mountain. General Curtis 'Bombs Away' LeMay, the US Air Force's most senior officer and a man who secured some funding for the 1963 expedition, wanted to know if the mountaineers would go back. However, the Everest option was soon rejected, as the Chinese border crossed the summit and so the bug could have been detected and retrieved by the opposite party.

On the Nanda Devi expedition, a 'Systems for Nuclear Auxiliary Power' or SNAP-19C device, using seven capsules of plutonium-238, was given to a porter, who reportedly suffered later from radiation burns to his back. This heat source and power generator was supposed to be connected to the actual listening device on arrival at the summit. However, due to poor weather the expedition failed to reach the top and retreated, leaving the bug anchored within a crevasse near the summit.

Then things got even worse. An Indian climbing party was despatched to retrieve the device but found nothing. So the task of retrieving the bug and replacing it with a fresh one went to another group of American Everest climbers. This aftermath is corroborated by the author Broughton Coburn in his book *The Vast Unknown: America's First Ascent of Everest*.† For months in 1966, the team flew in HH-43 Huskie helicopters converted for high-altitude operation, scanning the mountain with neutron detectors. 'There's some evidence that the whole hillside, the

* M. S. Kohli and K. Conboy, *Spies in the Himalayas* (University Press of Kansas, 2003).

† B. Coburn, *The Vast Unknown: America's First Ascent of Everest* (Crown, 2013).

whole area where it had been stashed had slid away in a land-slide and carried the device downhill,' Coburn says. 'There was no sign. The mission was abandoned. No readings, no leads where the device might have fallen . . . They believed they would have easily picked up a signal. And at least in the opinion of some of the climbers, they felt that Indian intelligence had secretly hiked up there before that spring mission and retrieved the device, and spirited it away, presumably in order to study it and possibly gather the plutonium.'

The whole area they were looking in had fallen down the mountain, landing somewhere below the watershed feeding the holy river Ganges. A plume of radioactive plutonium could therefore be spreading down through the rock and ice. As a result, the Nanda Devi sanctuary was closed to foreign expe-ditions through the rest of the 1960s.

However, the CIA did succeed in placing a SNAP unit and monitoring device onto another mountain, Coburn tells us. In 1967, a group of climbers placed one just below the summit of Nanda Kot, a 22,510-foot mountain just outside the Nanda Devi sanctuary. It stopped relaying messages after three months, although not before indicating that the Chinese, after all, did not yet possess a long-range nuclear missile. 'Ultimately, this wild operation was successful in gaining at least that much information,' Coburn writes, 'although the technique was obso-lete by the time spy satellites emerged. Still, it was close, and somewhere down the mountain a piece of Cold War plutonium might still be there.* At the Chinese Lop Nor Nuclear Weapons base, 45 atomic explosions were tested, which it has been calculated by the Japanese scientist Jun Takada could have caused the deaths of up to 190,000 people in China from nuclear-related illnesses.

I spoke to one of the climbers involved who confirmed the whole Nanda Devi bug story, somewhat shamefaced. Which

---

* Ibid.

only goes to show that mountaineers will do almost anything (or make up anything) to fund a climbing trip.

As a postscript, three American climbers, John Roskelley, Jim States and Lou Reichardt, went to climb Nanda Devi in 1976 and finally got to the summit on 1 September. The expedition was led by Willi Unsoeld, who climbed the West Ridge of Everest in 1963. Unsoeld's daughter, 22-year-old Nanda Devi Unsoeld, who was named after the peak, died on this expedition. Before the expedition, she had spoken about her relationship with the peak. 'I can't describe it,' she said, 'but there is something within me about this mountain ever since I was born.' She contracted stomach problems at high altitude, but refused to descend. Her father buried her somewhere near camp IV. He was philosophical. 'Nanda Devi died fulfilling her dream. There are worse ways of dying.'

CHAPTER SIX

*The Himalayan yeti. . .Hillary's insight. . .zombie
fungus. . .Bhutan's migoi. . .the Manchester plumber. . .and the
Eiger Sanction. . .crushed testicles. . .gigantopithecus. . .TV
yetis. . .a hobbit.*

'Yeti, Sahib! Yeti!' one of the Sherpas was beckoning urgently.
'Sahib!' Sir Edmund Hillary was climbing a steep pitch up to
a pass between the Ngozumpa and Khumbu glaciers in Nepal
in 1960. One of his Sherpas ahead had spotted a tuft of long
black hairs which were thick and coarse and looked more like
bristles than anything else. Hillary wrote: 'I couldn't help being
impressed by their conviction, and it did seem a strange place
to find some hair. We were well over 19,000 feet and the
Abominable Snowman was obviously no mean rock climber.'

At last we are on the trail of the original Himalayan yeti,
the creature as understood by the indigenous people of the
region. And who better to look for it than a friend of the Sherpas?
Hillary's undoubted luck in being the right man at the right
time on the successful 1953 Mount Everest expedition was
richly deserved. He was a shy man with religious convictions,
and he repaid many times the worldwide fame that climbing
the mountain had given him. He became a philanthropist,

building many schools and hospitals for Sherpa villages in his beloved Nepal. There are few climbers who would have handled the attention and the fame as gracefully and given so much back.

It is little known that he had several close shaves involving aircraft. In 1960, he was late for a flight and so just missed being killed in the TWA Flight 266 New York air disaster. Then, in 1975, his wife Louise and youngest daughter Belinda were flying out to the village of Phaphlu in Nepal where he was building a hospital when their aircraft crashed and they were both killed. In 1979, he was supposed to commentate on Air New Zealand's Flight 901 over Antarctica, but had to pull out due to other commitments in the United States and was replaced by his friend Peter Mulgrew. The aircraft crashed into the volcano Mount Erebus due to a navigational mistake, killing all 257 on board. Hillary later married Mulgrew's widow, Jane.

What Hillary brought to the yeti question was a deeper understanding of the Sherpa culture. His expedition (note that the nomenclature had now changed from 'Abominable Snowman' to 'yeti') was one of the last tolerated by the suspicious Chinese authorities. Sir Edmund took the research seriously, spending ten months in the field. His large expedition visited the Pangboche monastery and examined the dried yeti hand, not realising that Peter Byrne had already switched one of its fingers for a human digit. They were allowed to borrow the 'yeti scalp', which they sent to London, Paris and Chicago for expert examination. This time they noticed that it had curious holes around the base, rather like nail holes . . .

To confirm their suspicions, the Hillary team acquired three serow hides and set about making their own fakes, employing a lama to carve a mould from a pine log. When stretched over the wood and nailed around the base, these looked identical to the purported yeti scalp at Pangboche and another one they discovered at nearby Khumjung, except rather fresher and with a full head of hair. They then sent hair samples from their own fakes and the older, original yeti scalps to Professor Osman Hill without informing him which was which. If they proved to be from the same species, then an important argument in favour of the yeti was fatally undermined. And that is exactly what Hill concluded: 'Although it was an interesting and probably ancient relic, it was really a fake, moulded from the skin of a serow. It had certainly never held the cunning brain of the elusive Yeti.'*

The expedition also examined 'yeti pelts'. These turned out to be the skins of Himalayan brown bears, which led them to the 'very strong inference that this bear might well have been the source of much of the Yeti legend'.

Hillary's conclusions after the expedition are clear:

There is no doubt that the Sherpas accept the fact that the Yeti really exists. But then they believe just as confidently that their gods live in comfort on the summit of Mount Everest. *We found it quite impossible to divorce the Yeti from the supernatural* [author's emphasis]. To a Sherpa the ability to make himself invisible at will is just as important a part of description as his probable shape and size. Part animal, part human, part demon, the Yeti is as calmly and uncritically accepted as we accept Father Christmas as children. Pleasant though we thought it would be to believe in the existence of the Yeti, when faced with the universal collapse of the main evidence in support of this creature, the members of my expedition, doctor, scientists, zoologists and mountaineers alike, could not in all conscience view it as more than a fascinating fairy tale, born of the rare and frightening view of animals, moulded by superstition, and enthusiastically nurtured by Western expeditions.†

---

* E. Hillary and D. Doig, *High in the Thin Cold Air* (Doubleday, 1962).

† Ibid.

We may smile at the naivety of such a belief. But are we in the West so different? Imagine an alien spacecraft landing in thirteenth-century Europe. The crew disembark and roam the land in groups, examining the evidence for a legendary man, born of a virgin, executed, resurrected, and then worshipped by the populace. They too visit cathedrals and examine holy relics: the breast milk of the virgin, the blood of St Januarius, the dried hand of St Teresa, the head of St Catherine and the holy foreskin of Jesus. They, too, find it difficult to find solid evidence, even though they are impressed by the conviction of the faithful. Finally, they board their spaceship, and, climbing through the smoke of burning martyrs, ascend back to heaven convinced that medieval Europeans were quite mad.

Belief in the yeti is almost universal amongst the Bhutanese, Tibetans, Nepalese and others who inhabit the Tibetan plateau and Himalayan chain. Tibetans will swear to you that they have seen the *dremo*, which is what they call the yeti. Many Buddhist monasteries hold yeti relics and feature wall paintings. An elderly Tibetan, interviewed in 1979, told how he was herding yaks across the Tibetan plateau when a *dremo* attacked the herd. It seized a yak, grasping it by the horns and twisting the neck until it broke. 'They eat the yak meat and put the skin on the rocks. If we see a yak's skin on the rock we say a *dremo* had killed and eaten it. They live near the snowline just above the forest but move up and down according to season.'*

Bhutan has the world-famous Snowman trek, billed as the hardest walk in the world, and in 1966 a triangular Bhutanese stamp was made to honour the creature. Bhutan even has a

* See http://www.icwa.org/wp-content/uploads/2015/11/RC-12.pdf.

wildlife sanctuary dedicated to the creature, which is known locally as the *migoi*. This is the 162,000-acre Sakteng Wildlife Sanctuary, where visitors are greeted by a sign reading 'Entering Bigfoot Megoe Valley, take only pictures, leave only footprints'. The use of the name Bigfoot (and the injunction) is a nod to the many American tourists you will find there. In 2016, while I was near the Tibetan border, an expedition in three Skoda Yeti four-wheel drive vehicles arrived at the park on their own search for the *migoi*, a successful piece of product placement featured at length in the *Daily Express*.

In this park live snow leopards, red pandas, Himalayan black bear, barking deer, Himalayan red fox, and bird species including the Assamese macaw, blood pheasant, grey-backed shrike, grey-headed woodpecker, common hoopoe, rufous vented tit and dark breasted rose finch. The plant life includes Bhutan's national flower, the blue poppy, rhododendrons, primulas and gentian. And here I discovered a very good reason why the Himalayan yeti should have been spotted by now.

There are many plants here with medicinal value, including cordyceps and the 'zombie fungus', the strange caterpillar fungus which is so immensely valuable to Chinese pharmacologists. The alleged benefits are boosts to the immune system and the elimination of fatigue. It may also be useful in the treatment of cancer, as it inhibits the uncontrolled growth of cells. Researcher Dr Cornelia de Moor said: 'Our discovery will open up the possibility of investigating the range of different cancers that could be treated with cordycepin. It will be possible to predict what types of cancers might be sensitive and what other cancer drugs it may effectively combine with. It could also lay the groundwork for the design of new cancer drugs that work on the same principle.'*

What is this potential cure for cancer from the land of the yeti? The real *Cordyceps sinensis* (and there are fakes) is the

---

* See http://news.bbc.co.uk/1/hi/health/8428340.stm.

118

fungus-infected caterpillar of the bat moth, which is found only between 10,000 and 16,000 feet above sea level. It is known in Tibetan as 'yartsa gunbu' or 'summer grass, winter worm'. A family of yak herders will spend the whole summer hunting for this strange caterpillar, which is twice as valuable as gold at $80 per gram. The thitarodes moth, or the Himalayan bat moth, lays its eggs underground. When they hatch, these caterpillars spend years underground feeding and fattening until they pupate and change into a bat moth to complete their life cycle. The unlucky ones ingest spores from *Cordyceps sinensis* which then germinate within the caterpillar, with its mycelium overwhelming the host, and eventually the caterpillar dies. The fungus then sprouts from the head of the caterpillar, like a club-shaped mushroom. And I thought athlete's foot was bad. Every year the Bhutanese comb their high grasslands looking for these sprouts. They have to catch them before the sporangium matures and releases further spores, otherwise the caterpillar is too shrivelled to be worth selling.

A problem has arisen which is that indigenous Tibetans and Han Chinese are also digging across the Tibetan plateau in their thousands, excavating billions of little holes. The terrain is being damaged and of course the wild cordyceps is being hunted to extinction: a tragedy of the commons. The harvesters arrive at the Xining Cordyceps market carrying little plastic bags of their produce. Their trading system is unique, with no spoken price being agreed. Instead, market trader and gatherer hold hands under a towel, which hides their silent gestures of haggling.

The point here is that these thousands of potential witnesses are roaming the same habitat as the yeti/*migoi,* and yet not one bone, not one finger and certainly no live specimen has been collected. The value of such a thing would be clear to the cordyceps hunters.

However, our local collectors in and around the Sakteng

Wildlife Sanctuary in Bhutan are still firm believers in the *migoi*, which is thought to frequent the northern area of the park. The author of *Bhutanese Tales of the Yeti*, Kunzang Choden, said most of the encounters with the *migoi* are usually by yak herders and hunters. 'I've heard stories about the interactions between the yeti and human beings and how the yeti appears fleetingly in the lives of people here,' she reported. 'The *migoi* is known by all accounts to be a very large biped, sometimes as big as one and a half yaks. It is covered in hair that ranges in colour from reddish brown to grey-black. Its limbs are ape-like and its face is generally hairless. We are told that they communicate with each other by whistling and they exude an exceedingly foul odour that heralds their approach.'

She also writes that, unlike other wild creatures, the *migoi/* yeti is apparently not afraid of fire; in fact, it is often attracted to it and approaches porters' campfires at night seeking warmth. 'The unexpected confrontations often take place during unusually bad snow storms when the *migoi* are forced to wander around at lower altitudes, looking for food and shelter,' she said. 'From the stories we hear we know that they live in caves and make nests to keep themselves and their young warm. You must never provoke a yeti and if you encounter it you are supposed to treat it reverently. In fact, you are supposed to prostrate and show respect and leave it in peace. It is only human provocation that gets the yeti aggravated.'

Paljor Dorji, popularly known in Bhutan as Dasho Benji, is an environmental advocate and friend and advisor to Bhutan's king. He said that he believes in the yeti and pointed out the areas where there had been recent sightings. 'The yeti is something you can search for for years but you won't find it,' he said. 'But I am convinced it is there. Most people meet the yeti by chance. A friend of mine described it as an ape, but some say it is red, others say it is black but there is definitely something there.'

Dasho Benji added: 'You don't want to find a yeti as after seeing it you will get bad luck or an illness. There are often reports of people becoming very ill after seeing a yeti.'

A lama at the village, Lama Richen, said: 'There are many stories and beliefs in the Sakteng region that people are abducted by yetis. Here in Merak there was a recent time where people were lost and the last person that went missing was in 2001.'

Lama Richen had seen large footprints on the ground. He said there were a number of areas around Merak where there had been previous sightings of the beast. An old colleague and friend of Dasho Benji said he had seen a lot of yetis, which he agreed were big, almost the size of bears. 'Its eyes are cast down but its hands are big. It smelt like garlic. If you smell the garlic you should not go.' He said the beasts eat in the same way as monkeys.

So in Bhutan, the belief is alive and kicking. However, once again there seems to be no solid evidence that would satisfy a scientist or a police detective. Tall stories of sightings, abductions, footprints and chance encounters do not a yeti make. But why were there no sightings of the beast by Westerners?

Finally, after 50 years of footprints of various sizes and varieties, a sighting of the yeti by a Westerner was made. In 1970, the colourful climber and Manchester plumber Don Whillans saw strange footprints near his camp on Annapurna. Whillans was a diminutive and belligerent character. Many of his stories ended with the words '. . . and so I 'it 'im'. When pulled over for drink driving, he assaulted the police officer and it took two more sitting on his chest to restrain him. He had another go at the station. He was a hero to many climbers as he represented a break from the upper-middle-class climbers such as George Mallory and the wealthy Alpine Cub set; he and his friend Joe Brown showed that working-class Northerners could find a kind of liberation through climbing.

, For the Annapurna South Face expedition, he invented the Whillans Harness, a device rock-climbers bought in the 1970s and 80s. It was designed,, it was said, to carry a beer-gut to high altitude. If you fell very far wearing this sit harness, it could crush a testicle. Clint Eastwood wore one in his film *The Eiger Sanction*, and after one long stunt fall, enquired: 'Which side does Mr Whillans dress on?'

There were two Whillans, said Jim Perrin, his biographer: a self-caricature who drank, womanised, fought, swore and was racist and lazy when not climbing; and a careful, driven, meticulous and talented mountaineer when he was climbing. He once dropped into a pub in Calderdale on the way to a peak in South America. The other drinkers noticed that his entire luggage consisted of a plastic bag containing a bottle of whisky and a change of underwear.

At their Annapurna temporary base camp, he found and photographed footprints and later that night watched an ape-like creature about a quarter of a mile away through binoculars in bright moonlight for twenty minutes. Whillans could clearly see a powerful animal 'bounding along on all fours. . . and headed straight up the slope in the absolutely bright moonlight. It looked like an ape. I don't think it was a bear.' In the morning, he said, his stash of Mars bars had gone. The next morning, he went up to make a full reconnaissance to the permanent base camp site and he took the Sherpas along with him to gauge their reactions to the tracks.

I thought I'd see their reaction at the point where I'd photographed the tracks the day before. The tracks were so obvious that it was impossible not to make any comment, but they walked straight past and didn't indicate

122

that they'd seen them. I had already said that I had seen the Yeti, not knowing exactly what it was, but they pretended they didn't understand and ignored what I said. I am convinced that they believe the Yeti does exist, that it is some kind of sacred animal which is best left alone; that if you don't bother it, it won't bother you.*

So what exactly did he see? Disappointingly, the tracks look as if they have been made by a quadruped, and he describes a creature on all fours rather than the bipedal yeti. John Napier thought that Whillans had perhaps seen a langur, a monkey of the forested foothills, which has a long but narrow foot consistent with the tracks he photographed.

It has to be pointed out that Whillans was a notorious storyteller, and no photographs of the creature were offered as evidence. A taste for Mars bars might suggest a fellow climber rather than a hairy ape. However, there's no reason to disbelieve this particular Whillans story.

He was the author of one of the pithiest literary reviews of *The Lord of the Rings*. When stormbound in a tent at high altitude in the Himalayas, fellow climber Douglas Haston tossed him a copy of the book. Whillans opened the book, read a few lines and threw it back. 'I'm not reading that crap, it's full of fookin' fairies.'†

By the mid-1970s, Whillan's climbing days were over and he was in a descending spiral of self-destruction, drinking and smoking heavily. He had a heart attack and died in his sleep in 1985. If he had been from another class, maybe he would have been seen as a Byronic self-destructive figure. Jim Perrin characterised him by his climbs. 'You have to be positive and aggressive to get up Don's routes, but if you do crank yourself up to that pitch, then they cease to be particularly difficult.

* C. Bonington, *Annapurna South Face* (Cassell, 1971).

† J. Perrin, *The Villain: The Life of Don Whillans* (Hutchinson, 2005).

That's the adversarial nature of his climbs. You have to fight them.'

Then, in 1972, rather more convincing footprints appeared, found by American zoologist Edward W. Cronin and physician Dr Howard Emery. They were exploring the Arun valley in eastern Nepal in the company of two Sherpas. They camped in two tents at around 12,000 feet and awoke to find strange tracks which had climbed a slope of deep snow and then walked directly between the tents during the night. Being scientists, they made a comprehensive record of photographs, plaster casts and drawings. One can imagine their feelings. Like me, there would have been a mixture of fascination, speculation and trepidation.

> The prints were clearest in the middle of the depression, directly beside our trail, where some ten to fifteen prints, both left and right feet, revealed the details of the toes and general morphology of the creature's foot ... The prints measured approximately nine inches long by four and three-quarters wide. The stride, or distance between individual prints, was surprisingly short, often less than one foot, and it appeared that the creature had used a slow, cautious walk along this section ... The creature must have been exceptionally strong to ascend this slope in these conditions ... no human could have made overnight the length of tracks I could see from the top of the ridge ... we realized that whatever creature had made them was far stronger than us.*

---

* E. W. Cronin, *The Arun: A Natural History of the World's Deepest Valley* (Houghton Mifflin, 1979).

These prints had a hallux (big toe) to one side like a gorilla, but lacked the large second toe of the Shipton photographs. However, Cronin said this: 'Most impressively, their close resemblance to Shipton's prints was unmistakable.'

These prints would appear to agree with the Shipton photographs; however, his were not consistent (his trail of footprints is quite different to the 'monstrous' footprint with the giant toe). And Sir Edmund Hillary categorically stated that Shipton had hoaxed his prints. In the end, though, we have to reluctantly conclude that the Cronin–Emery footprints were only that: footprints. There was no hair, no droppings and no body.*

The cryptologists of today give the Shipton and Cronin–Emery finds much weight and have produced 'improved' plaster casts which suggest that the creature was something like *gigantopithecus*, whom we will now meet. Even scientific publications of the day took the Shipton photographs seriously. In the *New Scientist*, the '*Geminus*' editorial recorded that Mr W. Tschernezky, a technician in the Zoology Department at Queen Mary College, had written in the prestigious publication *Nature* that he had reconstructed in plaster the foot which had made Eric Shipton's print. The *New Scientist* went on: '. . . he thinks that the Abominable Snowman might well be a huge, heavily-built bipedal primate similar to the fossil *gigantopithecus*. This was the ape-like creature which combined ape and hominid features and had the largest primate molar teeth known . . .The idea of a living fossil skulking in the mountains of Tibet, a sort of land-based coelacanth, takes the whole concept of the Snowman out of the science fiction category. Tschernezky has convinced me that the Snowman must be taken seriously . . . let us hope that Sir Edmund Hillary succeeds in his attempt to find a Snowman and bring it back alive.'†

This monster, the largest ape that ever lived, was probably

---

* For the Cronin footprint, see http://cryptomundo.com/wp-content/uploads/CroninYetiTrack.jpg.

† 'It Seems To Me,' *New Scientist*, 12 May 1960, p. 1218.

the nearest thing to *King Kong* that the world has ever seen. He stood around 10 feet tall and weighed around 11,000 lb. He lived from around nine million years ago until only 100,000 years ago. His discovery was a masterpiece of intelligent field-work.

In 1935, the young German–Dutch palaeontologist Ralph von Koenigswald was hunting through a Chinese apothecary's shop in Hong Kong for the legendary 'Dragon Teeth' sometimes offered for sale. Fossilised teeth and bones are ground into powder and used in some branches of traditional Chinese medicine. 'I began to hunt for fossils in the Chinese drugstores in Java,' he later wrote. 'I discovered that I had made a grave mistake in simply inquiring about "teeth". I should have asked for "dragon teeth", since that was the name of the "drug" I sought. When I finally learned the correct name and obtained a prescription, I succeeded in finding these teeth in every Chinese drugstore in every Chinese community.' He finally struck gold by extending his search to Hong Kong.

Von Koenigswald spotted a huge molar in a dusty drawer in the Hong Kong store, saw it was an inch in diameter, and knew at once he had hit on something big. Gigantic, in fact; he named his new species *gigantopithecus*. In a fever of excitement, he continued hunting in Chinese drugstores and noticed a clue about when the apes had lived. In the shopkeepers' trays, the molars were always found mixed in with other teeth in a similar state of preservation. Von Koenigswald was very familiar with these other teeth: giant pandas, tapirs, bears and the extinct, elephant-like stegodon. This giant ape was surrounded by middle Pleistocene animals. In other words, he was about a million years old.

Then there was a strange intervention: the Japanese army arrived in Java in 1942 and Von Koenigswald was interned in a prisoner-of-war camp. This was despite his protestations that he was of dual German and Dutch nationality. The teeth he had painstakingly collected saw out the Japanese occupation in a milk bottle buried in a neighbour's garden on the island. Eventually, he was liberated and went to collect his teeth.

They caused a worldwide sensation in the palaeontological world. At first *Gigantopithecus blacki* was thought to be a close relative of an early hominid ancestor of ours, *australopithecus*, but now he is placed in the subfamily *ponginae* along with the orang-utan. Fossils of the orang-utan have been found in northern India, Pakistan, Yunnan and the western foothills of the Himalayas, so could the yeti be a memory of the orang-utan? British zoologists John Napier and Charles Stonor demonstrated that the creature could have survived in these areas possibly as late as the nineteenth century, but by 1976 their habitat was limited to the Indonesian islands of Sumatra and Borneo, where starving orang-utans now stray into the towns, their forest habitat destroyed by men searching for gold.

Returning to the hunt for *Gigantopithecus blacki*, Chinese scientists wanted to find fossils in their proper geological context and so they searched for the source of the fabled 'Dragon Teeth', eventually tracking them down to the Guangxi Zhuang area in southern China, where the rice paddy fields are found in among limestone karst mountains. The farmers, keen to keep their market, were initially secretive but eventually led the researchers to the caves set high within sheer limestone cliffs. In the Liucheng Cave, no fewer than a thousand *gigantopithecus* teeth were unearthed, with the fragments of three jawbones. But why so many teeth and no skeletons? Apparently, porcupines had been dragging the bones of the giant apes into the caves, which were once below ground level, and chewing on them to release the calcium for their spines. The teeth proved too hard to digest.

From the size of the jaws, scientists deduced the size and weight of the animal and have made a guess at his appearance. 'Even from tiny pieces of dental tissue, we learn about the diet,

Gigantopithecus.

ecology and life history,' says Kornelius Kupczik, at the Max Planck Institute for Evolutionary Anthropology in Leipzig, Germany. What is perhaps surprising is that *gigantopithecus* was a bamboo-forest-dwelling herbivore, as analysis of the fossil teeth for carbon and other trace elements reveals no hint of meat in his diet. He was a giant vegetarian.*

Unfortunately for *gigantopithecus*, at the beginning of the last of the Pleistocene ice ages about 100,000 years ago he became extinct because the climate change caused a change in the vegetation he ate.

'Due to its size, *gigantopithecus* presumably depended on a large amount of food,' explained Herve Bocherens, a researcher at Tübingen University in Germany. 'When, during the Pleistocene, more and more forested areas turned into savannah landscapes, there was simply an insufficient food supply for

---

* See http://news.nationalgeographic.com/content/dam/news/2016/01/05/01*gigantopithecus*.jpg.

the giant ape.' Presumably, his hominid cousins did rather better in the new environment, as other apes and early humans in Africa that had comparable teeth were able to survive similar transitions by eating leaves, grass and roots in the new environments.

Further research unearthed a nine-million-year-old jawbone and teeth in northern India from a smaller species confusingly named *Gigantopithecus giganteus*. Could this be the origin of the yeti myth? Again, though, we have to concede that we cannot even find a finger bone from *gigantopithecus*, nor any fossil less than 100,000 years old, let alone a corpse or a live specimen from the present day. He might look like the yeti of our nightmares, but he seems to be another giant blind alley.

Then a longer, more comprehensive account of a yeti sighting appeared. This time the witness was our greatest living mountaineer, Reinhold Messner. After being the first to climb Everest without oxygen and the first to climb all fourteen of the 8,000-metre peaks, Messner took up long journeys across the Antarctic and Greenland. In July 1986, he was trekking through Tibet when he was forced into making a dangerous river crossing. He dried himself out as well as he could and continued up the trail:

> Then, silently as a ghost, something large and dark stepped into a space thirty feet ahead among the rhododendron bushes. A yak, I thought, becoming excited at the thought of meeting some Tibetans and getting a hot meal and a place to sleep that evening. But the thing stood still. Then, noiseless and light-footed, it raced across the forest floor, disappearing, reappearing, picking up speed. Neither

branches nor ditches slowed its progress. This was not a yak. The fast-moving silhouette dashed behind a curtain of leaves and branches, only to step out into a clearing some ten yards away for a few seconds. It was as if my own shadow had been projected on to the thicket.

Messner crept forwards and discovered a gigantic footprint:

It was absolutely distinct. Even the toes were unmistakable. To see that the imprint was fresh I touched the soil next to it. It was fresh. I took a picture and checked the soil around it. My shoes didn't sink in nearly as deeply as had the creature's bare soles.

He follows more footprints, his mind whirling, thinking about Eric Shipton's yeti footprint and the many yeti legends he had heard in Sherpa households:

Sometime between dusk and midnight I came out of the forest into a clearing . . . I suddenly heard an eerie sound – a whistling noise, similar to the warning call mountain goats make. Out of the corner of my eye I saw the outline of an upright figure dart between the trees to the edge of the clearing, where low-growing thickets covered the steep slope. The figure hurried on, silent and hunched forward, disappearing behind a tree only to reappear again against the moonlight. It stopped for a moment and turned to look straight at me. Again I heard the whistle, more of an angry hiss, and for a heartbeat I saw eyes and teeth. The creature towered menacingly, its face a grey shadow, its body a black outline. Covered with hair, it stood upright on two short legs and had powerful arms that hung down almost to its knees. I guessed it to be over seven feet tall. Its body looked much heavier than that of a man of that size, but it moved with such agility and power towards the edge of the escarpment that I was both startled and relieved. Mostly I was stunned. No human would have been able to run like that in the middle of the night.

This sighting was to initiate a fourteen-year-long quest for the truth about the yeti, and resulted in his book *My Quest for the Yeti*.* To his surprise and discomfort, he was ridiculed in the West when he reported this sighting. In an interview with the *Guardian*,† he said: 'Before '86 I wrote in my books the yeti is bullshit. But then when I have seen this big animal, which I could not see exactly what it was, I understood that it was exactly matching with the legend.'

He decided to try to track down whatever he had seen, or at least discover which animal had given rise to the legends he had heard throughout the Himalayas. He knew he was demolishing a myth, but pursued the trail doggedly through Pakistan, India, Mongolia, Kazakhstan, Tibet, Bhutan, Nepal, and even Sichuan in China, employing the determination that had got him to the top of so many high mountains.

Messner had been trekking along the route he thought that the Sherpa people had taken in their flight from Tibet through Qamdo, Lhasa, Tingri and over the Himalayan chain to their present-day Khumbu territories in Nepal. (In fact, a recent study suggests that the Tibetans are the ancestors of Sherpas, and that any high-altitude adaptation comes from their ancestor's long sojourn on the high plateau.‡) He decided that the Sherpa yeti-myths arose along the way.

He, too, deduced that the name came from *yeh-teh*, a corrup-

* R. Messner, op. cit. Translated from the German and at times hard to follow, partly because of the lack of an index.

† See https://www.theguardian.com/books/2000/aug/10/travelbooks. samwollaston.

‡ See https://www.nature.com/articles/srep16249.

tion of *meh-teh*, 'man-bear'. The Tibetans also spoke of the *dzu-teh*, the cattle-bear, which is generally thought to be the Himalayan brown bear, *Ursus arctos isabellinus*, which can imitate a man by walking upon its back legs. He also discovered that the same Tibetan word was used to describe both the yeti and the Himalayan brown bear: *chemo* or *dremo*. Messner uses this word *chemo* to denote the large yak-killing yeti. The Bhutanese call it *migoi* (again, wild man), and the Chinese in various dialects call it *bai xiong* (white bear), *ma xiong* (brown bear) or *ren xiong* (man-bear). There do seem to be a lot of bears in these names. This profusion of names is a reflection of the widespread belief in the creature across so many cultures and languages.

Messner found new evidence in Bhutan. He was travelling through the recently opened country with a TV documentary team when they heard about a possible yeti pelt at Gangtey Gompa. Inside a tantric chamber in the monastery, he discovered the hide of a yeti cub that had been bewitched, killed and brought back to the monastery by the *ringpoche*, or teacher. The chamber was dark, and at first all he could see was a figure hanging on the wall above heads of elk, wild boars, tigers, black bears and sheep. He could see bones attached to the relic's hands and legs, and there was a long black hank of hair hanging from its head. As with all Bhutanese monasteries, there would be a smell of butter lamps and dust, and tiny windows would reveal the sunlit courtyard beyond.

However, in the flash of a camera he saw that the hair had been stuck on, and that little sticks supported the fingers and toes. Further investigation revealed that the hands and legs were human, probably from a child of eight or nine years. They hung from a hide that could be that of a monkey, and the face was a mask. It was a doll created to dispel bad spirits. Like the Pangboche yeti scalp and the dried hand, it was what Westerners would call a fake, but perhaps no more fake than the Father Christmas manikins of our own culture, as a reference to an invented shared myth.

After a TV documentary was broadcast, Messner received the letter from Ernst Schäfer which had suggested that there was a connection between Shipton, Smythe, Mount Everest expedition funding and yeti stories. Schäfer laid out his conclusions about the yeti:

In 1934, General Liu Hsiang, the former warlord of the province of Sichuan, had asked me to uncover the mystery of the yeti and to bring him a male and female pair of these longhaired 'Snowmen' for his zoo. The following year I had the opportunity to set out on such an expedition to the uninhabitable regions of Inner Tibet, to the source of the Yangtze River. There I shot a number of yetis, in the form of the mighty Tibetan bear.

In further correspondence, Schäfer claimed that every sighting involved a Tibetan (or Himalayan) brown bear with varying fur colour:

All these bears belong to the same species of *Ursus*, to which also the brown bear and grizzly bear belong. Early explorers, from Britain as well as from Russia, made the mistake of assuming that the colour variations of the Tibetan bear pointed to different species.

In other words, all the sightings describing various colours of yeti could be explained by the natural variation in colour of one species of bear. Young bears up to the age of three or four years can be clean white to brown. Older bears have darker fur, with patches that can be yellowish gold. The oldest bears are very dark. 'I shot most of my yetis,' Schäfer went on to write (and that is a memorable line even from the biggest of big-game hunters), 'near the sources of the Mekong, the Yangtze and the Hwang Ho, but mainly in the completely uninhabited Kunlun mountains. However, current informants who have visited these areas in the last few decades, either by jeep or by flying over them, reported that they did not spot any black bears. Tibetan nomads nowadays are often armed with automatic rifles, which might well explain things.'

One might wonder why on earth Schäfer's quite reasonable conclusions were ignored by the yeti-hunters of the 1950s. It could be that his gun-happy swashbuckling nature, combined with his German SS connections in the recent war, had discredited him. But it also wasn't what they wanted to hear. He seems to share with Messner a slightly surprised, querulous disappointment that people don't want to hear a reasonable explanation for the yeti.

In *My Quest for the Yeti*, Messner then takes us back in history and goes over much of the ground that we have covered. His unique perspective, though, is of a mountaineer who has undertaken thirty major expeditions in Nepal in the company of many Sherpa yeti-believers. He describes his travels through Tibet, arousing the suspicions of the Chinese authorities, and gives us a portrait of modern Tibet: the traffic jams, concrete barracks and kitsch shopping malls that have overwhelmed the ancient Lhasa of gilded temples and fluttering prayer flags. Tibet was, and is, a land under occupation, and Messner certainly makes us feel the weight of the Chinese yoke.

Messner succinctly paraphrases Schäfer's description of his first yeti shooting: 'The local people is [*sic*] saying to him, "Up there in the mountains is a yeti, living in a cave," and he says, "Bullshit," and he goes up with his gun and he is killing it. And he has a big Tibet bear.'[*]

Armed with Schäfer's theory, Messner himself also accompanied Tibetans to the lairs of what they called *chemos*, to find that they were indeed the dens of bears.

[*]   See https://www.theguardian.com/books/2000/aug/10/travelbooks. samwollaston.

At the end of the book, he meets the Dalai Lama, who asks him: 'Do you think that the *migio*, *chemong* and yeti might well be one and the same thing?'

'I not only think so, I am completely convinced they are,' says Messner. 'Then I put my finger to my lips, as did the Dalai Lama, as if acknowledging that this must remain our secret.'

He then goes and records the conversation in a book published for public consumption, but still, by now it is no secret what Messner's conclusions are. Messner decides that Schäfer was right all along: 'In the end I thought to myself: how could I need twelve years to come to the answer? It's so obvious.'

But surely, after so long spent hunting for the yeti, he was disappointed?

'Not for me. Because the brown bear is really a monster.' Then he gives a good explanation of how such a legend might arise. 'In the local areas they know all that; that this is an animal. But since only every ten years someone is seeing a real example, so if they speak about it, all the children and normal people that never saw one, they are imagining they are talking about something that isn't a brown bear. We should see the yeti as the sum of the legend and the zoological reality.'

After the 1960 Hillary expedition, the surge of Western yeti-hunters decreased, disillusioned by Sir Edmund's conclusions and discouraged by the CIA's antics in Tibet which had been viewed with alarm by the Chinese. No more Western-sponsored yeti-hunting expeditions would be allowed in China or Tibet. However, that didn't deter the Chinese themselves from believing in the yeti, or indeed hunting for him themselves. The *Alpine Club Journal* of 1999 carried an article by the 1954 *Daily Mail*

Snowman Expedition mountaineering leader John Angelo Jackson. He wrote:

> In November 1994 a report came out of China of a sighting that had been made of three large humanoids in a remote region of the Shennongjia National Forest Park in Hubei Province. The original report appears to have been made by a group of ten Chinese tourists, all of them engineers and well educated. They described how, whilst driving down a steep mountain road, they saw at a distance of thirty yards, three figures, tall, hairy and ape-like in appearance. When the engineers approached the creatures, they fled into the dense forest nearby, demonstrating great speed and strength. Chinese scientists hailed the sighting as a major discovery and subsequently a number of research teams revisited the area collecting samples of hair and faeces, as well as measuring the size of the footprints. It is said that analysis showed the samples to have come from a long-haired, big-footed herbivorous animal. In 1995 a Chinese expedition, including some twenty scientists, revisited the area of the Shennongjia forest, but later reported that nothing new had been discovered.

So, is there a Chinese yeti?

The 1,000-square-mile Shennongjia forest reserve of China's central Hubei province is a tangle of high mountains and deep forests: prime yeti-spotting country. The name comes from the Emperor Shennong and the word for ladder, *jia*. The emperor was supposed to have used a ladder to climb up the mountains, and these promptly transformed into a lush forest. At least a thousand different species of animal live here, including the golden snub-nosed monkey and giant salamanders. Significantly, there is also a white-furred bear that is only found in the reserve. Villagers in the area believe that the wild man, or *yeren*, lives among them.

He stands nearly seven feet tall and is covered in dark grey hair. He also leaves size-12 footprints, most unusual in China.

A shepherd near the reserve had seen a pair of the creatures: 'They had hairy faces, eyes like black holes, prominent noses and dishevelled hair, with faces that resembled both a man's and a monkey's,' said Zhang Jianong. There is even a sign outside the reserve warning of the presence of the *yeren*, and at the bottom in English: 'Beware of Bigfoot!'

However, there is some scepticism from the authorities: 'I simply want to put an end to the argument that it exists,' said Wang Shancai, at the Hubei Relics and Archaeology Institute, when he set out to find the *yeren* in 2010. And Zhou Guoxing, a palaeontologist and one-time director of the Beijing Museum of Natural History, has poured scorn on the idea that there may be a Chinese yeti. 'There is no Wild Man in this world,' he said, in 2002. 'I've visited every place where the Wild Man was reported in China. I've studied everything related to the Wild Man including hair, skulls and specimens. All of them are dyed human hair or come from monkeys and bears.'

He claimed the local government in Hubei was trying to drum up tourist revenue. Sure enough, the Shennongjia National Nature Reserve has signed agreements with Beijing to help promote package holidays to the area for nature lovers . . . and yeti-hunters.

In the 1990s, along came a whole new breed of yeti-hunter, propelled by the rise of Western technology in the form of cheap jet travel and lightweight video cameras. Suddenly, TV companies could afford to send small crews out to the Himalayas and elsewhere to look for the yeti. In 1996, a couple trekking in the Himalayas came back with footage that was broadcast by Paramount's UPN TV show, *Paranormal Borderland*. The film was presented as genuine and shows a huge, hairy biped walking slowly uphill in deep snow. Three of the top yeti/Bigfoot researchers, Dr Jeff Meldrum, Dmitri Bayanov and Igor Bourstev, examined the film closely and pronounced it real:

Meldrum: 'I am quite confident in my estimate of scale, which was derived from the witnesses' snowshoe trackway. Using that trackway as a scale, the subject had to be in excess of 9 feet tall. When you are confident of the size in excess of 9 feet, you have to ask, 'where did they find an actor to fill that costume?'*

Bayanov: 'The footage is very impressive, very, very impressive because the creature that it shows has all the characteristic features of a relic hominoid – such as the cone-shaped head, hairy body, very massive limbs and trunk and torso.'†

Bourstev: (badly translated from Russian) 'It's not possible, it's not a man.'‡

The footage became known as the Snow Walker video, a reference to a Canadian snow survival drama, and the yeti/Bigfoot community was gripped by it and convinced. However, Jeff Meldrum investigated the film further and became suspicious of the reactions he was getting from the TV producers. He pursued the matter doggedly with UPN. When the show *Paranormal Borderland* was cancelled, the producers admitted that the Snow Walker was a hoax and explained how it was

* See http://bigfoot101.proboards.com/thread/131/snow-walker-video-hoax-1996.

† See Yeti episode, *Fortean TV*, Series2 (Rapido TV, 1998).

‡ See http://squatchopedia.com/index.php/Snow_Walker.

done.* Presumably to maximise viewers and income, the show was recycled by the same network in a programme called *The World's Greatest Hoaxes: Secrets Finally Revealed.*

If you watch the video† in the spirit of scientific enquiry you might wonder how a creature whose habitat is snow-clad mountain slopes manages to fall over backwards.

When invited by old friends to join an expedition to the north of Kangchenjunga in Sikkim, northern India, I kept my ears open. I knew that this was yeti territory from the stories by Tilman and Hunt, back in the 1930s. One night around the campfire, I got talking about the yeti with our Indian expedition leader, Anindya Mukherjee (Raja), a highly educated young man with an interest in natural history. He seemed embarrassed about the subject, and said that the large yeti was indeed probably a bear. When pressed, he said that there were persistent rumours among the local people about a small yeti, known as the *Bon Manchi* (yet another local name for the yeti!). He eventually admitted that, when camping one night, in one of the many unexplored high valleys that surrounded us, he himself had heard the characteristic whistling calls of the *Bon Manchi*. On investigating in the morning, he found tracks of a small bipedal hominid 'like the footprints of a small child'.

The simple explanation is that these footprints were exactly that: the footprints of a small child. However, the 2003 discovery of the small hominid *Homo floresiensis,* a 3-foot 7-inch hominid nicknamed 'the hobbit' which survived until relatively recently

* Loxton and Prothero, op. cit.

† See http://bigfootevidence.blogspot.co.uk/2012/02/snow-walker-bigfoot-hoax-video.html.

Raja and his tracks in Sikkim.

in geological terms, makes it just possible that there is a distant relative to humans surviving in the high valleys of the Himalayas. The legends of Ebu Gogo, a mythical small creature among the Nage people of Flores, might just be a surviving memory of *Homo floresiensis*.

In 2003, a joint Australian–Indonesian expedition of archaeologists excavated caves in the Indonesian island of Flores, hoping to find evidence of human migration to Australia. Instead, to their surprise and delight they discovered a new species of hominid. They found nine partial skeletons of the creature, and a 2017 study concluded that *Homo floresiensis* and *Homo sapiens* (humans) are separate species. The most recent specimen died around 50,000 years ago, which is around the time that modern humans reached Flores, and there is speculation that the hobbit was exterminated by our ancestors. The size of the hobbit would have corresponded to Raja's description of the *Bon Manchi*.

In 2011, I helped Malcolm Walker, the CEO of Iceland Foods, to learn to climb in the Alps and on Kilimanjaro, and then acted as deputy expedition leader on his attempt on the North Ridge route on Mount Everest. There had been much talk of the yeti before the trip, and one morning at advanced base camp Malcolm rather surprised me dressed in a yeti costume. (What was interesting about Malcolm's suit is that the colour is white in line with the Western image of the yeti as an Abominable Snowman, instead of the orangey-brown colour of what I have called the Himalayan yeti.)

I decided to look for the yeti on the very next chance I had, but knew that, if found, he would be unlikely to benefit from contact with *Homo sapiens*. The next expedition, described in

The Iceland man Malcolm Walker dressed to kill. But what made the giant footprints behind him?

the Introduction of this book, was the one on which I found the footprints. It arose from a walk through England following the progress of the spring of 2015. My girlfriend Gina and I had walked from Christchurch on the South Coast to Gretna Green.* We hiked down into Wooton-under-Edge, where an old friend was picking us up and putting us up for the night. Steve Berry is another mountaineering pal and was clearly excited about something to do with a recent trip. When we arrived at his home, he led us up to his study, filled with Bhutanese memorabilia. Steve runs Mountain Kingdoms, the foremost trekking company working in the Himalayas. He told us that he had spotted yeti tracks on Gangkar Punsum, Bhutan's highest mountain (and still unclimbed to this day). We studied his images of indisputably bipedal tracks in the snow. What Steve felt particularly significant was the jump made by the creature from the rock. A quadruped would have landed on all fours, but this creature seemed to stride off on two legs: so *one, two,* instead of *one, two, three, four.* Gazing at the image, I wondered what these fabled creatures might do in spring. Would they retreat from humans up into the icy Himalayas? Or hide in leafy forests?

These tracks were to lead to the expedition with Steve to look for the yeti in 2016 and to the events described at the beginning of Chapter One, which brings us up to date. I was bewildered by the footprints that I saw and really couldn't make my mind up. When I got home, I decided that it was now time for me to take stock and look at all the evidence I could find.

We have traced the rise of the Western yeti from the very first accounts, and there is a total lack of solid evidence. Initially the reports are of footprints, and the Westerner witnesses Waddell, Howard-Bury and Smythe all conclude that what they were seeing were bear tracks. The water was then muddied by Shipton and Tilman, first of all by a running gag and then

---

* G. Hoyland, *Walking Through Spring* (William Collins, 2016).

what I think was a deliberate hoax perpetrated by Shipton, faking a footprint with the aim of increasing public interest in another Mount Everest expedition. In that he was spectacularly successful. Schäfer, irritated by the yeti stories, made it his business to track down several bears and kill them to prove to his porters that these were yetis. Hillary spent ten months in the field, taking alleged yeti scalps and hairs for analysis, and came up with the same conclusion: yetis are bears.

After nearly a century of footprints, faked footprints and dubious sightings, we reluctantly have to conclude that the Western yeti does not exist. There has been no living specimen, no haplotype, no scalps, fingers, dung or even hair evidence worth a damn. Even DNA evidence, which was the great hope of the cryptozoologists, has always come back with a negative for a large unknown primate. To the believers who will no doubt come up with more sightings of the yeti, I say: 'Lovely. Show me the body.' Then I'll believe in it.

How about the single line of tracks that Steve Berry saw at high altitude in Bhutan? In a letter to *Country Life* magazine, 23 July 1970, John Pollard wrote to the editor with an observation he made in the Austrian Tyrol of Alpine choughs, a bird often seen at high altitude in the Himalayas (a friend of mine saw one fly over the summit of Everest). Pollard, looking down from a high peak, saw a line of what appeared to be human steps traversing a cornice of steeply angled snow. As he watched, two Alpine choughs landed and hopped along the cornice breast-deep, leaving behind them a row of what looked like human footprints.[*]

What about the two footprints I saw that inspired this book? Several friends told me later that they didn't like to point out that the prints looked just like a pair of gloved hands pressed, chest wide, into the snow. There are even signs of a jacket cuff. The witness who pointed them out to the rest of the trekking group was impossible to question as, although he is a helpful

[*] Reported by John Napier in *Bigfoot*, op. cit.

and intelligent young man, he is also deaf and mute. Unfortunately, my sighting also has to go in the 'uncertain' drawer.

The Himalayan yeti is a different matter. Many indigenous people in the Himalayas have seen the creature and believe in it firmly. To them and to some Westerners who are attuned to a Himalayan way of thinking, the beast exists as powerfully as Father Christmas or God exists to some of us. As Messner said, we should see the yeti as the sum of the legend and the zoological reality. He wasn't concerned that his book would destroy the legend of the yeti 'The Tibetans won't read it. Even if they could read it. And for us in the West it was important for me to show that this wasn't just some tall tale. The yeti, you see, is a monster created in the people's heads from the reality. I am sure: the yeti will never die.'*

But are there beasts like the yeti in other countries?

* See http://www.independent.co.uk/news/people/profiles/you-aint-seen-nothing-yeti-637632.html.

CHAPTER SEVEN

A Russian Bigfoot. . .Zana, a Russian wild woman. . .Rawicz and his long walk. . . a French Spy. . .more Yogi than yeti. . .An English yeti. . .Piltdown Man. . .A Scottish yeti. . .the Big Grey Man of Ben Macdui. . .Am Fear Liath Mór. . .a fictional yeti.

In 2012, I joined a ski expedition to Mount Elbrus in the Russian Caucasus. While we were in the village below the mountain, we heard the story of Zana, a Russian 'wild woman' from the area who was captured by hunters in the 1870s. She was said to be large, powerful and dark-skinned, with a great tolerance of cold. She was thought to be an Almasty, a legendary human-like bipedal animal up to six-and-a-half feet tall, the body covered with reddish-brown hair, with anthropomorphic facial features including a pronounced brow ridge and a flat nose.* Zana did not communicate with human speech. At first, she was aggressive towards her captors and had to be kept in a cage, but later she became socialised and performed simple tasks such as grinding corn. She even had four children by her captor. These children looked much like any other Russians,

---

* M. Newton, *'Almas/Almasti' Encyclopedia of Cryptozoology: A Global Guide* (McFarland & Company, 2005), p. 19.

and had their own descendants who are alive today. Zana died in 1890. Was she a Russian yeti?

If that wasn't strange enough, we then heard the tale of the Long Walk through Russia. This was more familiar, as I had read the book. During the Second World War, the Polish cavalry officer Sławomir Rawicz escaped from a gulag camp in Siberia and managed to walk 4,000 miles south to freedom. With six companions, he marched through Outer Mongolia, across the Gobi desert, through Tibet, and after crossing the Himalayas finally arrived in Calcutta where he rejoined the Allied forces in British India. On the way, he had this extraordinary experience:

In all our wanderings through the Himalayan region we had encountered no other creatures than man, dogs, and sheep. It was with quickening interest, therefore, that in the early stages of our descent of this last mountain Kolemenos drew our attention to two moving black specks against the snow about a quarter of a mile below us. We thought of animals and immediately of food, but as we set off down to investigate we had no great hopes that they would await our arrival. The contours of the mountain temporarily hid them from view as we approached nearer, but when we halted on the edge of a bluff we found they were still there, twelve feet or so below us and about a hundred yards away.

Two points struck me immediately. They were enormous and they walked on their hind legs. The picture is clear in my mind, fixed there indelibly by a solid two hours of observation. We just could not believe what we saw at first, so we stayed to watch. Somebody talked about dropping down to their level to get a close-up view.

Zaro said, 'They look strong enough to eat us.' We stayed where we were. We weren't too sure of unknown creatures which refused to run away at the approach of us.

146

I set myself to estimating their height on the basis of my military training for artillery observation. They could not have been much less than eight feet tall. One was a few inches taller than the other, in the relation of the average man to the average woman. They were shuffling quietly round on a flattish shelf which formed part of the obvious route for us to continue our descent. We thought that if we waited long enough they would go away and clear the way for us. It was obvious they had seen us, and it was equally apparent they had no fear of us.

The American said that eventually he was sure we should see them drop on all fours like bears. But they never did.

Their faces I could not see in detail, but the heads were squarish and the ears must lie close to the skull because there was no projection from the silhouette against the snow. The shoulders sloped sharply down to a powerful chest. The arms were long and the wrists reached the level of the knees. Seen in profile, the back of the head was a straight line from the crown into the shoulders – 'like a damned Prussian,' as Paluchowicz put it.

We decided unanimously that we were examining a type of creature of which we had no previous experience in the wild, in zoos or literature. It would have been easy to have seen them waddle off at a distance and dismissed them as either bear or big ape of the orang-utan species. At close range they defied description. There was something both of the bear and the ape about their general shape but they could not be mistaken for either. The colour was a rusty kind of brown. They appeared to be covered by two distinct kinds of hair – the reddish hair which gave them their characteristic colour forming a tight, close fur against the body, mingling with which were long, loose, straight hairs, hanging downwards, which had a slight greyish tinge as the light caught them.

Dangling our feet over the edge of the rock, we kept them closely under observation for about an hour. They were doing nothing but move around slowly together, occasionally stopping to look around them like people admiring a view. Their heads turned towards us now and again, but their interest in us seemed to be the slightest.

Then Zaro stood up. 'We can't wait all day for them to make up their minds to move. I am going to shift them.'

He went off into a pantomime of arm waving, Red Indian war dancing, bawling and shrieking. The things did not even turn. Zaro scratched around and came up with half-a-dozen pieces of ice about a quarter-inch thick. One after another he pitched them down towards the pair, but they skimmed erratically and lost direction. One missile kicked up a little powder of snow about twenty yards from them, but if they saw it they gave no sign. Zaro sat down again, panting.

We gave them another hour, but they seemed content to stay where they were. I got the uncomfortable feeling they were challenging us to continue our descent across their ground.

'I think they are laughing at us,' said Zaro.

Mister Smith stood up. 'It occurs to me they might take it into their heads to come up and investigate us. It is obvious they are not afraid of us. I think we had better go while we are safe.'

We pushed off around the rock and directly away from them. I looked back and the pair were standing still, arms swinging slightly, as though listening intently. What were they? For years they remained a mystery to me, but since recently I have read of scientific expeditions to discover the Abominable Snowman of the Himalayas and studied descriptions of the creature given by native hillmen, I believe that the five of us that day may have met two of the animals. If so, I think recent estimates of their height as about five feet are wrong. The creatures we saw must have been at least seven feet.*

When I read *The Long Walk*, I was gripped by the tale until this description of the yetis. Everything in the book seemed so tragic, romantic and uplifting. There was even a love interest: the 17-year-old Polish girl, Kristina, who (spoiler alert) sadly dies en route, as do three other companions. But the yeti description seemed a little far-fetched, as did the claim that the party drank no water in the Gobi desert for thirteen days. This prompted me to do some digging.

The Long Walk had caused controversy as soon as it was published. Eric Shipton saw many inconsistencies about the mileages claimed in the book, and another Himalayan explorer, Peter Fleming (brother of Ian Fleming), called the whole thing a hoax. Then this article appeared in *The Spectator* in 1956:

The main reason why *The Long Walk,* as well as being widely read, is being widely discussed centres on the question of its veracity. This has been called in question. None of the three other survivors has been traced or has come forward to identify himself. Still more inexplicably – for all three might have died – none of the British troops with whom Rawicz and his companions shared a hospital ward for several weeks in Calcutta has had his memory jogged by the publicity which the book has attracted. The doctors and nurses who looked after him, the officers who interrogated him or studied the reports of his interrogation have remained silent. Both the then Director of Military Intelligence in India and his principal subordinate in Calcutta have no recollection of an incident which might have been expected, even after fourteen years, to leave

* S. Rawicz, *The Long Walk: The True Story of a Trek to Freedom* (Constable, 1956).

some impression on their minds . . . It is only when you read it a second or a third time, with an atlas open beside you, that strange omissions and daunting improbabilities begin to appear.*

Over these gaps and obstacles, the *Spectator* readers did their best to help Rawicz. It is not possible, they pointed out, to arrive in Tibet from Outer Mongolia without at some point crossing the main highway from Lanchow to Urumchi; it was carrying a lot of traffic in 1941, and the party, even if they failed to notice a somewhat primitive caravan-cum-lorry road, must surely have noticed the telegraph wires? Rawicz remembered no telegraph poles: he had also forgotten the mountain barrier, 20,000 feet high, which he must soon afterwards have scaled to gain the Tibetan plateau. Yet in writing of this stage of the journey, he describes in great detail the apparel of an old shepherd whom they met; 'in a leather-bound wooden sheath he carried a horn-handled knife which I later observed was double-edged and of good workmanship'. Memory plays strange tricks; but can you forget a main road and a mountain range, both of which directly affected your chances of reaching freedom, and remember the knife of an old man with whom you spent a few hours? Throughout the walk, he had seen, he told Shipton, only a few stunted trees.

One fact is known with certainty about Rawicz's movements in 1941–42, and it is curious that no one should have noticed how gravely this single grain of truth, which research has ascertained since his book was published, impairs his credit as a dealer in facts. Polish Army records show that he joined a transit camp in Iraq on 10 April 1942.

In contrast, readers of *The Long Walk* will remember that 'towards the end of March 1942' his party was still on the wrong side of the Himalayas, facing 'the tallest and most forbidding

* *The Spectator*, 12 July 1956.

peaks we had yet seen.' The chronology is difficult to follow after this, but it seems to have been at least twenty days later that they met a British patrol in the foothills on the other side.

They spent 'a few days' recuperating before making a 'long' train journey to Calcutta. Here, Rawicz was unconscious in hospital for a month. After convalescence (length unspecified), he went by bus to a transit camp 'where I was to await a troopship to the Middle East'. In the summer of 1942, the Japanese Navy dominated the Bay of Bengal, and I doubt whether any troops were embarked from Calcutta for the Middle East. But even if I am wrong, Rawicz could hardly, on his own showing, have reached Iraq before July or August; and we know that he was there on 10 April.

One is regretfully forced to the conclusion that the whole of this excellent book is moonshine. It is extremely probable that Rawicz was in prison in Russia, whence many thousands of his compatriots, released under the terms of the Anglo-Russian alliance, were transported via Persia to the Middle East in 1942. The story of his escape through Outer Mongolia and points south must be either wholly true or wholly false. He could not have done half the journey and not the other half; he could not, for instance, have crossed the Gobi in September 1941, and reached Iraq in April 1942, without following some route almost as remarkable as the one he describes. The answer is, I fear, that he did not do the journey at all.

Is his strangely compelling story the product of some kind of hallucination? An ordinary impostor would surely have done a little more homework. He would not, as Rawicz did on the Sunday, deny all knowledge of tsamba, the staple food of Tibet; it was like a man who claims that he has begged his way from John o'Groats to Land's End, saying that he never heard of a cup of tea.

In fact, Sławomir Rawicz (born 1 September 1915, died 5 April 2004) was a real person, a Polish Army lieutenant who was imprisoned for the killing of an NKVD officer in the defence of his country, after the German–Soviet invasion of Poland. After the war he moved to Nottingham, England. But Rawicz met fierce critics at a lecture in London 1956 when he gave a talk about his book to a group of Polish ex-servicemen. While he was speaking, several men stood up and claimed they had known the author before and during the war, that he had been in the infantry and was never a cavalry officer. His whole story was fabricated, they said. Rawicz claimed the hecklers were communist agents.

It then transpired that Rawicz had signed a document stating that he had been freed in Russia, transported to Persia, and that he had never been in India. It was also found that Rawicz had been freed from the Soviet gulag camp in 1942, when he supposedly was making his Long Walk. So what was the truth?

Rawicz's story had been faked by a *Daily Mail* journalist, Ronald Downing, who was his ghostwriter. Downing had been tasked by his editor with finding further evidence of yetis to support the *Daily Mail* Snowman expedition of 1954, which of course had been prompted by the faked Shipton footprints. Downing heard that Rawicz had a tale to tell, travelled to Nottingham to see him, and the result was the book. If he hadn't been so sloppy with the love interest, the lack of water, the yetis, the distances, the road, the telegraph poles and the historical facts, then suspicions might not have been aroused. In the event, the book sold more than half a million copies and was translated into 25 languages. It even inspired the Hollywood movie *The Way Back*. One wonders how it would have sold had it been represented as it was: a novel.

Downing's version of Rawicz's story was fictional, yet the credulous still to this day believe this yarn. On the front cover is a quote by Benedict Allen: 'A classic of triumph over despair, of beauty found in the void.' One of the many five-star reviewers on Amazon writes: 'This is a true story, you won't believe what these people went through . . .' [no, I don't] and 'Every time I put this book aside, I felt almost as if I was also drained by the endless adversity this stoic band had to endure.' [I know how you feel.]

There is a strange postscript to the tale. A British intelligence officer, Rupert Mayne, said he interrogated three emaciated men in Calcutta in 1942 who claimed they had escaped from Siberia. He couldn't remember their names. So perhaps someone else had done the Long Walk.

Poor yeti. Once again stories had been exaggerated, lies had been told and he had been mis-represented.

What about Zana, our Russian wild woman? In November 2013, Channel 4 broadcast an Icon Films programme about the Almasty which concentrated on Zana. Here, surely, was the best evidence yet for a Russian yeti: a female who was captured, imprisoned and who even gave birth. With modern DNA sampling, her descendants could be tracked down and tested. Was she in fact a surviving Neanderthal? And is that what the yeti really is?

The film examined the work of Bryan Sykes, Professor of Human Genetics at the University of Oxford, who has undertaken a worldwide study of alleged yeti, Almasty and Bigfoot samples. He carried out DNA tests on saliva samples taken from Zana's descendants.

Sykes's predecessor in the field of serious scientific study of Bigfoot and the yeti was our old friend John Napier, who once said: 'It is hardly surprising that scientists prefer to investigate the probable rather than beat their heads against the wall of the faintly possible.' Scientists such as Sykes and Napier also risk the opprobrium of their colleagues who feel that crypto-zoology is not a serious subject of study.

Russian researchers have been looking for proof of living Neanderthals in the Caucasus for over 50 years. Dmitri Baynov, aged 81, Michael Trachtengerts, 76, and Igor Burtsev, 73, have together put in a combined 130 years of effort. They belong to Moscow's Relict Hominoid Society (the name refers to the creatures, not the age of the members). They still meet regularly at Moscow's Darwin museum, where there are many Neanderthal specimens, a species which most scientists believe died out over 30,000 years ago. But could small groups have survived in the remote regions of the Caucasus – the very regions where large concentrations of Neanderthal fossils have been found?

Abkhazia is a remote breakaway state within the Republic of Georgia which once belonged to the Ottoman Empire. Zana was captured and beaten into submission by two hunters in a lonely forest in the 1870s, tied up and sold to a local landowner named Edgi Genaba in Tkhina. Here, she was imprisoned in a cage and had four children by rape. She was described by local villagers as huge and strong, with a hair-covered body. She had, they said, a short neck and a protruding jaw.

Her family tree has been painstakingly researched by Almasty hunters, as Zana was seen as the strongest proof of their theories. Professor Sykes was able to obtain DNA samples from many of her descendants, who look much like other residents of the area. Researchers even exhumed Zana's son, Khwit, who was so strong he could pick up a table in his teeth and hold it at head height. The DNA in one of those remaining teeth was tested.

The results were intriguing. Zana *did* indeed have Neanderthal DNA: just about as much as you or me. Asians and Europeans have between 2 and 4 per cent of this type of DNA, probably as a result of interbreeding. What was surprising is that the saliva tests on her surviving descendants show that Zana's DNA was African, not Caucasian; and that her maternal ancestry was sub-Saharan African.

Professor Sykes had this reaction: 'The most obvious solution that springs to mind is that Zana or her ancestors were brought from Africa to Abkhazia as slaves, when it was part of the slave-trading Ottoman Empire, to work as servants or labourers. While the Russians ended slavery when they took over the region in the late 1850s, some Africans remained behind. Was Zana one of them, who were living wild in the forest when she was captured?'*

But how did this explain Zana's extraordinary features? Her son, too, had very wide eye sockets, an elevated brow ridge and perhaps an extra skull bone that suggest ancient origins.

There is an even more intriguing alternative theory. Having carefully studied the skull of Zana's son, Khwit, Professor Sykes believes that these features could suggest ancient, as opposed to modern, human origins. Sykes thinks it is possible that Zana's ancestors were part of an unknown human tribe forming part of an earlier African migration tens of thousands of years ago. This tribe could have found refuge in remote regions of the Caucasus from the later waves of modern humans pouring out of Africa.

The sad truth of Zana's tragic life is that she was as human as you or me, and the victim of an appalling kind of racism. This poor African woman was beaten, kidnapped, imprisoned, raped and treated as a monster. Perhaps the villagers knew the shameful truth of her kidnapping, that she was a human woman, and embellished her 'otherness' with stories of a wild appearance.

So human ignorance and gullibility were eventually trumped by modern science, but too late for Zana. It brings

---

* B. Sykes, *The Nature of the Beast: The First Scientific Evidence on the Survival of Apemen into Modern Times* (Coronet, 2015).

to mind the villagers of Hartlepool, who, according to local legend, hanged a monkey as a French spy. During the Napoleonic Wars, a French ship was wrecked upon the coast of northeast England. The one survivor was a monkey, supposedly wearing a French uniform as a kind of mascot for the French crew. The creature was put on trial. It refused to answer questions and wouldn't sign a confession. Because the inhabitants of Hartlepool had seen neither a Frenchman nor a monkey, the villagers concluded that it was a spy. The poor creature was sentenced to death and hanged there and then on the beach.

While our expedition was climbing Mount Elbrus in the Caucasus, another mountainous part of Russia was in the grip of yeti-mania. For three years, there had been sightings of a tall, long-haired creature at loose in the Mount Shoria region of southern Siberia. The monster had shed its black and grey fur in the caves where it had been living. This had been collected and was on its way to Professor Bryan Sykes, who was running the worldwide genetic research programme studying possible Bigfoot samples.

Shortly after this, an 11-year-old boy and his friends filmed a yeti in the Kemerovo region of southern Siberia, not so far from the Mount Shoria sightings. Yevgeny Anisimov was with two friends in a snow-filled wood about 18 miles from the coal-mining city of Leninsk-Kuznetsky. They saw large footprints ahead of them: 'They got very inquisitive about the tracks and followed the trail, filming them on the mobile-phone camera,' said Igor Burtsev. 'They continued walking for a bit and got closer to the bushes where suddenly they saw a yeti, some 50 metres away from them. It noticed them as well, sharply moved, bent down, then to the left, and ran left. The boys, scared, ran in the opposite direction.'

The mobile-phone footage, filmed through branches, shows a hair-covered bipedal creature turning suddenly towards them. Yevgeny yelled: 'I'm the nearest, I'm going to be eaten!' and started running. His friends started swearing, which later got them into trouble with their families. The footage certainly impressed the authorities. Burtsev claimed he had checked the footage with experts and it was genuine. 'It is a first time in Russian modern history that someone manages to film the yeti so clearly,' he said. 'I don't doubt it was a yeti. It stood in a typical pose with its back slightly bent, and its long arms down.'

Meanwhile, the Mount Shoria hair-sample DNA results had come back from Professor Sykes. The *Sun* newspaper had the best headline on the morning of 3 February 2013: 'Bigfoot: It's Yogi not Yeti.' Professor Sykes's tests showed that one long thick hair came from a rare type of black bear from North America, *Ursus americanus,* which can reach a height of seven feet. The other hairs cames from a horse and a raccoon. 'The hairs did not come from a yeti,' said the professor. 'The American black bear result was highly unusual. An explanation could be an animal escaped from a circus, zoo or private collection, but it is extraordinary.'

An American bear at loose in Russia. Was it a spy? Sometimes, truth is stranger than fiction and is just too implausible to find suitable explanations.

As for the boys' mobile-phone footage, it is surely relevant that their location is not far from the Mount Shoria sightings, which the boys (and their fathers) may have heard about. The footprints are large and well defined, with a curious two-toed shape unlike the Shipton prints. On the video soundtrack, the boys are laughing in that excited way children do when they know a jape is in progress; it's not fearful, nervous laughter. And when we see him, the figure in the video looks awfully like a man in a gorilla suit. But hoaxes are very hard to disprove.

Now we turn to the English yeti. Ever since 1859 when Charles Darwin published *On the Origins of Species*, scientists had been hunting for a particular kind of fossil. Thomas Henry Huxley (grandfather of Frank Smythe's biologist Julian Huxley) had applied Darwin's ideas to humans and shown the connection between apes and man. Neanderthal fossils had already been found in Germany three years before Darwin's book, and Cro-Magnon man was discovered in France in 1868. But neither of these seemed to fit the bill, being early modern humans. The world of science was filled with excitement: there had to be a missing link between apes and man, and he was down there somewhere. The sound of frantic digging filled the air. However, English palaeontologists failed to turn up anything significant. They were derisively dismissed by one French scientist as nothing but pebble hunters: *chasseurs de cailloux*. There was a huge thirst for an Early English Man. There was a more philosophical reason, too. Religious writers such as G. K. Chesterton wanted the missing link to stay missing as he provided a firewall between men and brutes, ensuring the divine right of man: 'All we know of the Missing Link is that he is missing – and he won't be missed either.'

Then, in 1908, Charles Dawson, a somewhat rotund lawyer and amateur archaeologist, was strolling past some labourers after dinner one evening at Barkham Manor in the Sussex village of Piltdown. He glanced down at the flint-strewn road-works and hailed one of the workmen. Had they found any ancient flint arrowheads in the gravel pit? No, sir, but he had something better. The man produced from his pocket 'a portion of human cranium . . . of immense thickness'. The men had smashed it up, believing it to be a fossilised coconut. There were also some iron-stained flints. The labourer's name, the true discoverer, was never recorded.

Dawson appropriated the skull and later did some digging himself. Finally, he wrote a letter to a friend at the Natural History Museum, Arthur Smith Woodward. First, he passed on some gossip about a mutual acquaintance, Sir Arthur Conan Doyle, who lived near Piltdown and who, strangely enough, was writing his prehistory novel *The Lost World*. Then Dawson revealed his find. Woodward was interested in the story and joined Dawson at the site. Although the two men worked together between June and September 1912, it was Dawson working alone who found further skull fragments and half of the lower jawbone. The skull given to Dawson was the only piece discovered *in situ*; most of the other pieces were found in the gravel pit spoil-heaps. There were further discoveries: fragments of bone and even the teeth of hippopotamuses that once luxuriated in the tropical swamps of early Sussex.

When the pieces of human skull were wired together by Woodward back at the Natural History Museum in London, it looked like a modern human's skull with an ape-like lower jaw. At last, here was the missing link. They couldn't keep the find secret any more: on 21 November 1912, the *Manchester Guardian*'s headlines trumpeted: 'The Earliest Man: Remarkable Discovery in Sussex.' The skull was revealed at a special meeting of the Geological Society in London in 1912 and immediately named *Eoanthropus dawsoni* after Dawson. 'Dawson's Dawn-man' was declared to be around 500,000 years old and England was declared to be the birthplace of mankind. Woodward's book was proudly entitled *The Earliest Englishman*.

This bombshell burst in the world of palaeontology and turned the tide of opinion. Woodward showed how the skull was similar to a modern human but had a brain capacity of around two-thirds the size. He indicated that the jaw had two molar teeth very similar to a human's, but mounted in a jawbone similar to that of a modern chimpanzee. He concluded that Piltdown Man was the missing evolutionary link between apes and man, as the combination of a human-like cranium combined with an ape-like jaw confirmed the English palae-ontologist's prevailing belief that human evolution was driven by the possession of a large brain, preceding our omnivorous diet. Exciting drawings of *Eoanthropus dawsoni* appeared, showing a satisfactorily robust-looking chap clutching a spear while modestly hiding his missing link. Venerable scientists were said to be able to enumerate the hairs on his head. Further excavations by Father Teilhard de Chardin, who later became one of the twentieth century's most influential Jesuit scholars and philosophers, turned up a canine tooth, another skull and a large elephant bone shaped into a cricket bat. So, *the Earliest Englishman* even played cricket!

There were some murmurings from foreign sceptics in the scientific community that the skull looked like a modern human's with a chimpanzee's jawbone wired to it, but these were ignored. Then in South Africa, in 1924, Australian anato-mist Raymond Arthur Dart discovered the Taung Child fossilised skull of an ape-like man with human-like teeth, but as this contradicted the brain-first theory he was ignored. British scientists dismissed the find as an ape. Further finds abroad which cast doubt on Piltdown Man were also ignored, possibly for nationalistic reasons. More and more fossils were discovered that differed from *the Earliest Englishman*, but for 40 years British palaeontologists maintained that Piltdown Man was part of human evolution. God might not have been an Englishman, but at least Man was.

However, doubts grew over the years, modern techniques of fossil dating were introduced, and in 1948 Dr Kenneth Oakley, a member of staff at Natural History Museum, decided to test the skull and jaws. To his horror, he discovered that they were modern. He urgently contacted Professor Joe Weiner and Sir Wilfrid Le Gros Clark from Oxford and together they applied stringent tests to all the Piltdown artefacts. They found that the human-like wear patterns on the teeth had been made by filing down teeth from an orang-utan jaw. The skull itself had come from an unusually thick-boned medieval human. The mammal fossils found at both sites had come from all over the world but had been stained with iron solution and chromic acid to look the same age as the skull. The scientists called the fake 'extraordinarily skilful' and the hoax 'so entirely unscrupulous and inexplicable as to find no parallel in the history of palaeontological discovery'.

In November 1953, *Time* magazine published their conclusions that Piltdown Man was a forgery composed of a medieval human skull, the lower jaw of an orang-utan and filed-down teeth. The cricket bat had been carved with a knife. Every one of the 40 finds was a fake.

The newspapers had a field day: 'Fossil Hoax Makes Monkeys Out of Scientists!' Piltdown Man was, quite simply, the greatest scientific hoax ever perpetuated, and certainly the most embarrassing for the English scientific establishment.

But there was a more serious point. The consequences of this fraud were long-lasting, as the belief that modern humans evolved in Britain persisted falsely for 40 years. Most scientists dismissed the real archaic human fossil, the Taung Child, when it was found in South Africa in 1924. And the hoax weakened the public's trust in science. Creationists still point to Piltdown Man to justify their suspicion of evolution: to them there is still a divine gap between brute and man. What might seem amusing, like Eric Shipton's faked footprint, actually had consequences, like Himmler's fake Nazi science.

The hunt was now on for the guilty party. It was like the

plot of one of Conan Doyle's Sherlock Holmes cases, whose protagonist once mused: 'What one man can invent another can discover.'* Or perhaps an English country-house murder mystery. After all, there was a skull; there was a small rural village stocked with upper middle-class characters; and there were clues galore. But who was the villain?

The suspects were Charles Dawson, the Rotund Lawyer, and Arthur Woodward, the Eager Scientist. But then there was Martin Hinton, a Jealous Colleague of Woodward's, the Jesuit Priest, Father Teilhard de Chardin, and the World-Famous Writer, Sir Arthur Conan Doyle. Suspicion at first fell on Conan Doyle. He was once a medical doctor and thus knew about anatomy and perhaps even had access to human bones. He collected fossils. He lived near Piltdown, knew Dawson and occasionally gave him a lift in his car when playing golf there. So he had the opportunity. At the time, he was writing a relevant novel, *The Lost World*, in which another of his characters says: 'If you are clever and know your business you can fake a bone as easily as you can a photograph.' He also had a motive. His belief in spiritualism had been derided by the scientific establishment and he may have wanted to humiliate his persecutors. But surely he would have revealed his hoax, therefore collecting his revenge?

The Rotund Lawyer had done well out of the dead Piltdown man: he would have been knighted, as were Woodward and his colleague Keith, if he hadn't died of septicaemia in 1916. The Jealous Colleague Hinton left a trunk in storage at the Natural History Museum in London stamped with his initials. In 1970, this was found to contain animal bones and teeth carved and stained in the same way as the carving and staining on the Piltdown finds. More clues. The revelation of a hoax would have embarrassed Woodward and elevated Hinton. The Eager Scientist Woodward had a

* A. Conan Doyle, *The Adventure of the Dancing Men* (Dover, 2003).

162

motive, he gained enormous international prestige and was knighted. And then the Jesuit Priest, Father Teilhard de Chardin, has been fingered by the South African palaeontologist Francis Thackeray. 'I think Teilhard did it as a joke,' says Thackeray. 'Just after Piltdown's first announcement, he wrote to a colleague to say he thought palaeontology deserved to be the subject of jokes. He was also known to be a joker.' Perhaps like Eric Shipton, Teilhard might have expected the prank to be spotted immediately, but once it gained ground he would have kept quiet. Perhaps the cricket bat was a deliberately ludicrous construct, a hint that the cricketing Piltdown Man was at silly point.

So, who was it? We can first dismiss the World-Famous Writer, Arthur Conan Doyle. Given his extraordinary credulity over the matter of the Cottingley faked photographs, when he was duped by a pair of little girls with pictures of fairies, he was more likely to have fallen for the Piltdown hoax than to have perpetrated it. He didn't have sufficient motive, either. But any of the others could have 'dunnit'. For help, we can turn to Miles Russell, who wrote a book about the whole hoax, *Piltdown Man: The Secret Life of Charles Dawson.** He presents a masterly case and reveals that the Rotund Lawyer Charles Dawson was our man. Russell analysed Dawson's collection and found that at least 38 of his specimens were fakes. Significantly for our case, there were the teeth of a reptile-mammal hybrid, *Plagiaulax dawsoni*, found by Dawson in 1891 (and named after him) and whose teeth had been filed down in the same way that the teeth of Piltdown Man were. There was also the Bulverhythe Hammer, a piece of antler shaped with an iron knife in the same way as the Piltdown cricket bat. Russell wrote: 'Piltdown was not a "one-off" hoax, more the culmination of a life's work.' Furthermore, Harry Morris, an

---

* M. Russell, *Piltdown Man: The Secret Life of Charles Dawson* (The History Press, 2003).

acquaintance of Dawson, had acquired one of the flints supposedly found by Dawson at the Piltdown gravel pit. Morris wrote that he suspected that it had been artificially aged, 'stained by C. Dawson with intent to defraud'.

Miles Russell shows that Dawson spent a lifetime making uncannily lucky finds and reaping huge rewards – eventually. In 1909, he wrote to Smith Woodward: 'I have been waiting for the big "find" which never seems to come along.' Why did Woodward not smell a rat? Because Piltdown Man satisfied his theories and he wanted him to be found. When the big 'find' did come, the British Museum gave Dawson the title of Honorary Collector. He was also elected a fellow of the Geological Society and a fellow of the Society of Antiquaries of London. He almost certainly would have been knighted for his efforts had he not died prematurely. Russell said that Dawson's whole academic career was 'one built upon deceit, sleight of hand, fraud and deception, the ultimate gain being international recognition'.*

To make absolutely certain that Dawson was the perpetuator, a further DNA sequencing and spectroscopic study was undertaken by palaeontology researchers in 2016. They reported† to the Royal Society that they had discovered that the jaw and teeth all came from one orang-utan, even the teeth Dawson claimed were from the second site miles away. 'The story originated with him,' the authors wrote. 'Nothing was ever found at the site when Dawson was not there, he is the only known person directly associated with the supposed finds at the second Piltdown site, the exact whereabouts of which he never revealed, and no further significant fossils,

* M. Russell, *The Piltdown Man Hoax: Case Closed* (The History Press, 2012).

† I. De Groote et al., 'New genetic and morphological evidence suggests a single hoaxer created "Piltdown man"', http://rsos.royalsocietypublishing.org/content/3/8/160328.

mammal or human, were discovered in the localities after his death in 1916.'

The team reserve their most damning criticism for the scientists who believed Dawson. 'Solving the Piltdown hoax is still important now. It stands as a cautionary tale to scientists not to see what they want to see, but to remain objective and to subject even their own findings to the strongest scientific scrutiny.'

Let that be a lesson to us all.

As Piltdown Man was a cricket-playing English yeti, we should mention the Scottish yeti, which I have seen. In 1890, the Scottish climber Professor J. N. Collie had this terrifying experience while alone in fog near the summit of Ben Macdui in the Cairngorms: 'I began to think I heard something else than merely the noise of my own footsteps. For every few steps I took I heard a crunch, and then another crunch as if someone was walking after me but taking steps three or four times the length of my own . . . As the eerie crunch, crunch, sounded behind me, I was seized with terror and took to my heels, staggering blindly among the boulders for four or five miles.' Collie recounted his experience at the 1925 Annual General Meeting of the Cairngorm Club, and soon afterwards received a letter from the noted Scottish explorer Dr Alexander Kellas, the first man to recognise the value of Sherpas in summit climbs.* Kellas said that he and his brother Henry were approaching the summit of Ben

* For an appreciation of this unsung Himalayan hero, see G. Rodway and I. R. Mitchell, *Prelude to Everest: Alexander Kellas, Himalayan Mountaineer* (Luath Press, 2011).

Macdui when they saw a giant figure approaching. It disappeared into a dip but frightened the men so much that they retreated before seeing if it would reappear. This Scottish McBigfoot is also known as the Big Grey Man of Ben Macdui, or Am Fear Liath Mòr. There have been other reports of him on this intimidating mountain, the second highest in Scotland. During the Second World War, the Big Grey Man was even shot at by the experienced mountaineer and naturalist Alexander Tewnion:

> In October 1943 I spent a ten-day leave climbing alone in the Cairngorms . . . One afternoon, just as I reached the summit cairn of Ben Macdui, mist swirled across the Lairig Ghru and enveloped the mountain. The atmosphere became dark and oppressive, a fierce, bitter wind whisked among the boulders, and . . . an odd sound echoed through the mist – a loud footstep, it seemed. Then another, and another . . . I peered about in the mist here rent and tattered by eddies of wind. A strange shape loomed up, receded, came charging at me! Without hesitation I whipped out the revolver and fired three times at the figure. When it still came on I turned and hared down the path, reaching Glen Derry in a time that I have never bettered. You may ask was it really the Fear Liath Mòr? Frankly, I think it was.[*]

If only more climbers were armed, we might have more luck in collecting a specimen.

I, too, have seen the Big Grey Man in Scotland. Climbing with my father along the narrow and rocky Castles Ridge on the Isle of Arran in the 1960s, I became aware of a fast-moving vertical screen of fog lifting out of the valley below. The air around us was clear. The sun was behind us, and all of a

---

[*] *The Scots Magazine*, June 1958.

sudden we were confronted by a huge grey shape marching out of the fog. It must have been ten feet high and in our case was surrounded by a huge circular rainbow with a diameter of perhaps 30 feet. The effect was stunning and terrifying.

'Brocken Spectre!' shouted my father. He grabbed my arm and explained that when the sun is behind the viewer, the breath condensing around the head refracts the light and produces the rainbow. The huge figure is your own shadow cast on the fog screen. I proved this by waving my arm. The 'monster' waved his arm in reply. My father went on to say that because of one's point of view only one figure is seen, even if two climbers stand shoulder to shoulder. This had disturbed one climbing companion of his on a previous occasion so much that he was convinced one of them was going to die shortly. It was first recorded, he said, on the Brocken, the highest peak in the Harz mountains. The effect is also known to aircraft pilots, who call it a 'Glory', an effect sometimes noticed by observant passengers who will see a shadow of the aeroplane cast on cloud contained within a circular rainbow.

He said that the poet Samuel Taylor Coleridge had seen one, too:

And art thou nothing? Such thou art, as when
The woodman winding westward up the glen,
At wintry dawn, where o'er the sheep-track's maze,
The viewless snow-mist weaves a glist'ning haze,
Sees full before him, gliding without tread,
An image with a glory round its head;
The enamoured rustic worships its fair hues,
Nor knows he makes the shadow he pursues!*

* S. Taylor Coleridge, 'Constancy to an Ideal Object,' *The Collected Works of Samuel Taylor Coleridge* (Princeton University Press, 1981).

Note that Coleridge's woodman has the sun behind him at dawn as he walks westward and sees his own shadow cast on the morning's snow-mist. With all the sightings of the Fear Liath Mòr, the clue is in the fog.

Frank Smythe, the eternal yeti-sceptic, also reported that he had seen his own shadow thrown in exactly this way on the clouds of Ben Macdui.*

The Western yeti has had a long and vigorous life in the world of letters. The assiduous Jim Perrin, perhaps exhausted by the tyranny of mountaineering biography, finally turned his hand to fiction and told us a story about the real yetis. In his collection of short stories, *Snow Goose*, there is the tale of two mountaineers who attempt a technically difficult mountain in Nepal. One of them is Joe Rigby, a mendacious self-publicist whose lack of climbing ability becomes dangerously and painfully obvious.† *After the Fall* is the title of this utopian fantasy, and after the long slide from the summit ridge the two men find they have tumbled into a community of men who live an ideal life. They are referred to as yetis by the Nepalese hill tribes. The protagonist Erasmus Moss finds that, instead of being frightening, these people are telepathic, peaceable, benign and nearly immortal. As in H. G. Wells' 1904 novella *The Country of the Blind*, which Perrin discusses in his notes, and James Hilton's *Lost Horizon*, this is an ideal Himalayan society being run on socialist lines. Rigby is swiftly dismissed by

---

* F. Smythe, *Behold the Mountains: Climbing with a Colour Camera* (Chanticleer Press, 1949), p. 55.

† This character is a touching portrait of a well-known British climbing writer.

attempting to escape and drowning in the rapids, but Moss decides to stay in the community for good. Perrin's descriptions of the climbing are as gripping and authentic as always, and his notion of the yeti community gives him a vehicle for describing an ideal society.

In his notes, he says 'if ever there were the perfect icon for human credulity, it's the cypto-zoological oddity the Yeti – created out of the Sherpa sense of fun and polished by the drolleries and mutual teasing of the great Himalayan explorers Eric Shipton and H.W. Tilman.'

CHAPTER EIGHT

Bigfoot. . .Windwalkers. . .Denali. . .Sasquatch. . .cannibal wildmen. . .a curious interest in bulldozers. . .The Bigfoot film. . .the Minnesota Iceman. . .Cripplefoot. . .the Grolar bear. . .eating people is wrong. . .magical realism.

In the late 1990s, I travelled through Alaska with a film crew on the way to attempt the highest mountain in North America, Mount McKinley (or Denali). We were filming the disabled and blinded Royal Marine Alan 'Reggie' Perrin who was trying to climb the mountain. I learned from Reg how comradely banter and the Blind Veterans charity got him through the worst of times after a grenade exploded in his face. He suffered on the mountain but got through the trip. He pointed out to me quietly one day that we're all disabled at high altitude.

At a barbecue in Anchorage, we heard stories about Bigfoot, America's version of the yeti. Apparently, these 'Windwalkers' were terrorising cabin owners in the snowy Denali National Park at that time. They were described as hairy bipeds, but (as befitting Americans) much bigger than the yeti: up to 10 feet tall. Their footprints were bigger, too: up to two feet long.

There is a considerable backstory. In April 1840, Elkanah

Walker, a missionary to the Spokane tribe of northern Washington state, reported that his flock had a strange belief:

> They believe in the existence of a race of giants which inhabit a certain mountain off to the west of us. This mountain is covered with perpetual snow. They inhabit its top. They . . . cannot see in the daytime. They hunt and do all of their work in the night. They are men-stealers. They come to the people's lodges in the night when the people are asleep and take them, and put them under their skins and take them to their place of abode without even waking. When they wake in the morning they are wholly lost, not knowing in what direction their home is. The account that they give of these Giants will in some measure correspond with the Bible account of this race of beings. They say their track is about a foot and a half long. They will carry two or three beams upon their back at once. They frequently come in the night and steal their salmon from their nets and eat them raw. If the people are awake they always know when they are coming very near, by their strong smell, which is most intolerable. It is not uncommon for them to come in the night and give three whistles and then the stones will begin to hit their houses. The people believe that they are still troubled with their nocturnal visits.

These men-stealers are reminiscent of the monster Grendel in the epic Old English poem *Beowulf*.

In 1847, the Irish-born Canadian painter Paul Kane travelled through the area making portraits of the aboriginal inhabitants. He reported their legends of what they called 'Skoocooms', clearly the same creatures described by Elkanah Walker: a race of cannibal wildmen who lived on the peak of Mount St Helens. In Canada, there were similar stories,

171

and in the 1920s the journalist J. W. Burns compiled the local legends for a series for a Canadian newspaper, coining the term 'Sasquatch' in the process. The term entered the public mind, and even today, just before the North American eclipse of August 2017, an e-map was published named 'Sunsquatch', showing the path of totality plotted with all known Bigfoot sightings within it, so you could share the darkness with a furry friend.

One of the Native American Lakota chieftains killed at the battle of Wounded Knee in 1890 was called Big Foot. His name was probably the inspiration for later press stories about two giant grizzly bears named Bigfoot who raided sheep flocks in California.

The stage was set for a sighting, with a name ready to hand. And along it came on 27 August 1958, at the height of yeti-mania in the Himalayas. A bulldozer driver, Jerry Crew, was making a new trail near Bluff Creek in the forests of Humboldt County, northwest California. Returning to work in the morning, he found enormous footprints 16 inches long completely encircling his machine. The paces were correspondingly large: up to 60 inches, twice his own length of stride. These footprints disappeared into the woods. Jerry thought it was a hoax until the same pattern of footprints appeared three days running, together with a giant pile of faeces 'of absolutely monumental proportions'. He was ready with plaster on the third occasion and made casts of the left and right footprints, then took them (but not the dung) to the local newspaper, the *Humboldt Times* of Eureka. Their story took off and went around the world, making another pile of monumental proportions. But what to call the beast? Jerry looked at the enormous plaster casts and said 'Bigfoot'.

Then Bigfoot reappeared the night before Jerry's boss Ray Wallace returned from a business trip. Wallace was concerned that he might lose vital employees from a difficult location because of these sightings. He brought in two trackers with dogs who caught sight of the beast itself, squatting by the side of the road. In appearance it was like an enormous human, covered with six-inch-long hair. In two bounds, it leapt the 20-foot-wide road and disappeared into the night. One middle-aged Hoopa Indian tribe member was quoted as saying: 'Good Lord, have the white men finally got round to that?'

One Bigfoot hunter in particular, Roger Patterson, was excited by a *True Magazine* article about Bigfoot which appeared in December 1959. It was written by our old friend Ivan T. Sanderson. Patterson travelled to Bluff Creek, spoke with fellow Bigfoot hunters and drove with a timber-man to Laird Meadows where they found fresh tracks.

Patterson spent years of his time and thousands of dollars in his own searches, and self-published a book about the available evidence so far. It was entitled *Do Abominable Snowmen of America Really Exist?* (rhetorical questions like these usually invite the answer 'No'). By then he was suffering from cancer and only had five years to live. In May 1967, he decided to make a pseudo-documentary film about a fictional Bigfoot hunt. In this film, he had a fake Indian guide and volunteers to play cowboys. Presumably, he would have had a suit made to represent the object of the hunt, unless he could recruit a real Bigfoot from the Actors Guild.

Then, to everyone's amazement, Patterson and his friend Robert Gimlin returned with footage which they said was real. They had been riding up Bluff Creek on horseback and disturbed a creature which they filmed. The footage shows a large ape-like bipedal figure with short brownish hair covering its body. The creature walks away, looking back at the camera, and disappears. It was the first moving pictures of Bigfoot anyone had seen.

The short film created a sensation. Although serious scientists declined offers to view it, cryptozoologist Ivan T. Sanderson (whom we keep encountering, even more often than Bigfoot) promoted it enthusiastically and, in 1974, CBS made a film about the Loch Ness monster and Bigfoot, including Patterson's film, titled *Mysterious Monsters*. It got 60 million viewers.

So what did Jerry Crew see? When Jerry's boss Ray Wallace died in 2002, his son Michael revealed that among his father's possessions was a large pair of poorly made wooden feet. The family admitted that Ray, his brother Wilbur and nephew Mack McKinnley used the feet to make footprints around the logging trails of northern California. Ray would hang off the back of the truck, which would then drive along slowly, giving him the ability to make giant paces. He left hair samples from bison and personally created the huge piles of faeces which he left around to hoax his employees.

'This wasn't a well-planned plot or anything,' said Michael Wallace. 'It's weird because it was just a joke, and then it took on such a life of its own that, even now, we can't stop it.'

It wasn't the only prank Ray Wallace was involved in. One favourite was to wrap a firecracker in a damp newspaper, climb onto the roof of a logging bunkhouse and drop it down the chimney into the wood stove. He would then re-enter the bunkhouse and sit down just in time for the wood stove to explode. 'He'd say it must be the firewood,' Michael reported. 'The guy could act.' He was obviously an unusual employer.

And the Patterson film? Unfortunately, in 2002, 35 years after the film was shot, a Philip Morris came forward. He was the owner of a North Carolina costume and prop-making company. He said that he had made a gorilla costume for Roger Patterson and sent it to him by mail order in 1967. Patterson said it was for 'a prank'. Morris had been reluctant to speak up before, because revealing a performer's secrets would have been bad for his theatrical business.

When scientists hear stories about Bigfoot sightings, they have an irritating habit of saying something along the lines of: 'That's nice. Show me the body.' This was dealt with at length by Michael Shermer in an article under the same title in the *Scientific American*.* He explains how scientists need a holotype or type specimen from which a detailed description can be made, photographs taken, models cast and a professional scientific analysis prepared. Regarding eyewitness accounts, he quotes the words of social scientist Frank J. Sulloway: 'Anecdotes do not make a science. Ten anecdotes are no better than one, and a hundred anecdotes are no better than ten.' So, a body was what was required.

At last, along came a Bigfoot holotype. In 1969, Ivan T. Sanderson got a tip-off about the finding of a corpse of a Bigfoot in Minnesota. In an article for the men's magazine *Argosy*, headlined 'Is This The Missing Link Between Man and the Apes?', Sanderson describes what happened:

I was sitting at my typewriter and staring at nothing . . . when the phone rang. The caller was a Minneapolis man who introduced himself as a zoologist and owner of an animal import-export business specializing in reptiles . . . After a general chat, this fellow told me he had just returned from Chicago where he had visited the famous annual Stock Fair. While there, he had inspected a side show which consisted of a single large coffin in a trailer- truck. In this

* M. Shermer, 'Show me the Body,' *Scientific American*, May 2003.

coffin, which was glass-covered and brightly lit with strip lights, there was a huge block of ice, about half of it as clear as the air in the room, the rest frosty or darkly opaque. In the ice was the corpse of a large, powerfully built man, or 'man-thing', completely clothed in dark, stiff hair about three inches long. My informant urged me to go take a look at it, since he, being a real student of what we call ABSMery (abominable-snowman-related information) and having read everything available on the subject, felt that it was the real thing, despite it being a mystery.

Staying with Sanderson at the time was Bernard Heuvelmans, the zoologist he had inspired in his 1948 *Saturday Evening Post* article 'There Could Be Dinosaurs'. Terrifically excited, they travelled to Frank D. Hansen's farm in deepest Minnesota near the town of Winona. Their feelings as they stepped into Hansen's trailer can only be imagined, because before them was an insulated coffin with a plate-glass cover, and beneath it, frozen into a block of ice, was the body of a previously undescribed creature. It was Bigfoot. As Sanderson reported:

> I must admit that even I, who have spent most of my life in this search, am filled with wonder as I report the following. There is a comparatively fresh corpse, preserved in ice, of a specimen of at least one kind of ultra-primitive, fully-haired man-thing, that displays so many heretofore unexpected and non-human characteristics as to warrant our dubbing it a 'missing link' . . .

Sanderson and Heuvelmans spent two days studying the monster. It was so cramped in the trailer that they had to lie on the glass lid face to face with the Bigfoot to make drawings. Sanderson later described the smell of putrefaction, which nauseated him. After their vigil, Heuvelmans published a description of what they saw in the February 1969 *Bulletin of the Royal Belgian Institute of Natural Sciences:*[*]

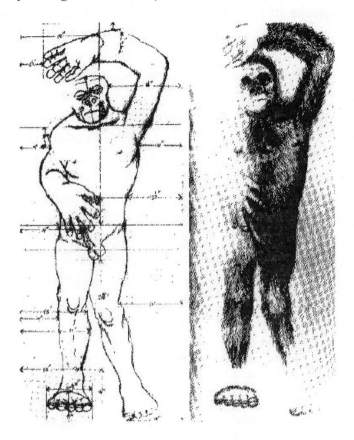

The Minnesota Iceman

General appearance. The body is lying on its back, right arm across the lower abdomen and the left arm crooked above the head; the knees are slightly bent. The torso appears long and massive giving the impression of flowing into the thighs, an appearance which is due presumably to

[*] B. Heuvelmans, 'Notice on a specimen preserved in ice of an unknown form of living hominid: Homo pongoides,' *Bulletin of the Royal Belgian Institute of Natural Sciences*, February 1969.

177

the absence of any outward swelling at the hips. The length of the creature is about six feet. The body apart from the face, palms of the hands and sides is covered with fairly long, dark-colored, coarse hair, the roots of which are widely separated from each other. The hair shows an agouti pattern.

Face. The creature is somewhat pug-faced, the tip of the nose turning upwards revealing wide, flaring, thick-walled nostrils; on the septum between the nostrils is a narrow band of hair. The forehead is sloping but the top of the head is lost in the depth of the ice. The face is broad and the mouth is slit-like, lacking the everted lips of modern man. The eye-sockets are large and, according to Sanderson, empty, but Heuvelmans asserts that the left eyeball is dislocated and is lying on the left cheek. In Heuvelmans's opinion the creature had been shot by a high velocity bullet through the right eye, blowing out the back of the skull. It has been stated by Hansen, the lessee, that this area is badly smashed. The explosion dislocated the left eye from its socket. The condition of the left forearm would be consistent with such an injury supposing that the creature had raised its left arm to cover its face from frontal assault.

Arms and hands. The arms appear to be long and excessively hairy. The left forearm is apparently fractured about midway along its length and the flesh is seen to be gaping at the site of the wound. The hands are gross, disproportionately large with long, slender, tapering thumbs. On the palm of the left hand, the bare skin on the inner side (ulnar side) extends backwards on to the wrist to form a sort of 'heel' to the hand, precisely as one might find in the hand of a monkey but certainly not of an ape or a man.

Legs and feet. Compared with the arms the legs are rather short but very 'human' in appearance; they are also extremely hairy. The feet are tremendously broad and spatulate, the big toe is aligned alongside the second toe (a human characteristic) and the nails are blunt and straight-edged. The big toe is not excessively 'big' relative to the small toes.

The genitalia. The penis is long, slender and tapering, and the scrotum rather small: when erect the penis would certainly not have been particularly striking in its dimensions.

Frank D. Hansen, the proprietor, explained how he had come into possession of the Iceman. It had, he said, been found floating in a block of ice in the Sea of Okhotsk by a party of Russian sealers. This sea is between eastern Siberia and the Kamchatka peninsula. The Iceman, after tortuous dealings with customs officials, ended up in a Chinese dealer's shop in Hong Kong, where an anonymous wealthy American living on the West Coast of the United States purchased it. It was then rented to Hansen, who proceeded to exhibit the creature around the carnival circuits of the United States for two years under the title 'Siberskoye Creature frozen and preserved forever in a coffin of ice.' He charged 35 cents per viewing.

Giving the Iceman the Latin name of *Homo pongoides* (ape-like man) was a bold step which immediately raised questions in the minds of mainstream scientists. Heuvelmans wrote a book about the Iceman story and in 1974 published *L'Homme Néanderthal est Toujours Vivant (Neanderthal Man is Still Alive)*. This was not published in English until 2016. A large part of the story concerns Heuvelmans' theory that the Iceman had been shot and killed during the Vietnam War. He argues that it was unlikely that the Iceman had been found drifting at sea frozen in ice or shot in the Minnesota woods (a later suggestion from Hansen), and then postulates that in a 'cloak and dagger' operation (his own term) the body was smuggled out of Vietnam along a drug-smuggling route, then brought to the USA by its guardian, Frank Hansen. Furthermore, quoting the

1972 book *The Politics of Heroin in Southeast Asia,** he suggests that the Iceman smuggling operation actually established this same drug route. This book alleged that the CIA was complicit in initiating aid to the Southeast Asian opium/heroin trade, and here, once again, is the curious connection between the Agency and a cryptid. It is only fair to point out that the CIA angrily denied these allegations. If we wonder where this tale could have come from, remember that Heuvelmans' colleague Ivan T. Sanderson had friends in the Office of Strategic Services, the predecessor of the CIA, and the sheer implausibility of this tale has all the hallmarks of a Sanderson conspiracy story.

Heuvelmans' thesis was that the Iceman was a modern-day Neanderthal descended from the Neanderthals of the Pleistocene, a representative of a relict population hiding in woods and mountains from their murderous cousin *Homo sapiens*. He maintained that this species had evolved with the apes from *Homo sapiens*, not the other way round.

It should be pointed out that Heuvelmans had a great number of supporters. The naturalist Gerald Durrell, the author of *My Family and Other Animals*, wrote an introduction to Heuvelmans' *On the Track of Unknown Animals* in which he writes: 'In this book Dr Bernard Heuvelmans has marshalled an astonishing parade of unknown animals and he has done so with great skill and scientific detachment, resisting the temptation to sensationalise.'

John Napier, the primatologist who was the first mainstream scientist to take Bigfoot seriously, tells the story of his part in the Minnesota Iceman analysis in his book *Bigfoot*. (This is the book, incidentally, in which he states: 'I am convinced that the Sasquatch exists.') Napier at the time was Director of the Primate Biology Program at the Smithsonian Institution, a prestigious position. He first heard about the Iceman from Ivan

---

* A.W. McCoy, *The Politics of Heroin in Southeast Asia* (Harper & Row, 1972).

Sanderson in February 1969 and he studied the drawings he had made. He writes in *Bigfoot* that his first impression was that the Iceman combined the worst features of apes and humans and none of the best features which made the two groups so successful in their respective environments. The Iceman's foot was neither adapted for climbing (as in a chimpanzee) nor for two-footed walking (as in man). The hands were neither typical of apes nor of man but were a ridiculous compromise between the two. The limbs seemed to be another compromise between humans and apes. Another feature bothered Napier: the agouti pattern of hairs. 'Agouti is a condition where the hairs are composed of alternating bands of light and dark and is probably familiar to most people as the fur pattern of squirrels . . . It is seen in the monkeys of both the New and Old Worlds; but at the higher levels of primate evolution – amongst the apes and man – it is completely unknown. That the Iceman should possess agouti-patterned hairs is a zoological improbability of the highest order.'

Sanderson suggested that Napier might interest the Smithsonian in the specimen, as he was keen to have official approval for the creature. Napier's boss S. Dillon Ripley wrote to Frank Hansen and got an evasive reply along the lines that the owner had removed the original Iceman, and so it was no longer in his possession. Meanwhile, Heuvelmans had opined that the Iceman was an unknown species of man. As a result, the apparent bullet wounds could indicate murder had been committed. So Ripley (who was obviously well connected) then wrote to J. Edgar Hoover, head of the FBI, requesting help for tracing the exhibit. Hoover was unhelpful: no law had been broken as the creature was not proven to be fully human.

Under questioning at a press conference he held at his ranch in April 1969, Hansen said that the Iceman now in his possession was man-made, a latex model of the real original. The real one had been returned to the owner, he said. Heuvelmans disagreed: 'There was only one point on which my views diverged from Sanderson's, as well as from all others who had looked into the matter, and that was on the nature of the specimen exhibited by Hansen after 20 April (1969). I was the only one to believe that *it was still the actual corpse* [author's italics]. True, I had a definite advantage over everyone else – I was the only one to have many excellent photos of the original exhibit . . . I had been sent a few colour slides of Hansen's new exhibit. After a comparison with my own, I had to agree with the evidence: *it was the same and only specimen*' [author's italics].

Then, on 30 June 1969, a headline appeared in the *National Bulletin*: 'I Was Raped By The Abominable Snowman.' A young woman, Helen Westring, told how she was on a solo hunting trip near Bemidji, Minnesota, when she encountered an 'Abominable Snowman'. It raped her, she said, and then she shot it through the right eye. That's how the Minnesota Iceman met his end, she claimed. Frank Hansen re-emerged and, in an article in *Saga* magazine in the following year, he contradicted her story and claimed that it was *he* who had shot the creature in the same woods. He had shot and wounded a deer and followed the drops of blood into a swamp. When he came up with it, he found three hairy creatures tearing the doe to pieces and drinking its blood. One jumped up and attacked Hansen, who shot it in the eye, killing it instantly. He fled in terror, but returned a couple of months later to retrieve the frozen body, which he put in his wife's chest freezer.

Napier meanwhile was making his own enquiries. Working with a colleague at the Smithsonian, he made an investigation of Hansen's affairs and found that he had commissioned the creation of the Iceman from a West Coast company in 1967, leading Napier to conclude that 'The Smithsonian Institution . . . is satisfied that the creature is simply a carnival exhibit made of latex rubber and hair . . . the "original" model and the present so-called "substitute" are one and the same.'*

In short, Frank D. Hansen was a con artist of the top rank, and he had taken in Sanderson and Heuvelmans, who were desperate to find a real Bigfoot. Napier theorised that Hansen had thought up the idea of a monster encased in ice, and had commissioned a latex model from a model maker in Hollywood, an expensive glass-lidded coffin and a trailer to transport it between fairground exhibitions. It was a classic fairground gaff, but an expensive one: it probably cost around $50,000, and Hansen had failed to get his money back, as he admitted to journalists in 1969. He decided that he must do something else to drum up business; he knew of Sanderson's books about the Abominable Snowman and decided to try to hook him in. By sheer luck, Heuvelmans was staying with Sanderson, and with the two men no doubt whipping each other up into a frenzy of excitement, Hansen managed to catch two suckers hook, line and sinker.

Napier points out that Hansen's real talent was the quality of his slippery replies to questions. 'I take my hat off to Frank Hansen, not because he glorified the monster myth (in my opinion he helped to debase it) but because he showed supreme skill in his chosen profession. I don't believe he ever told a lie – he simply talked his way around every issue.'

The latex model is still doing the rounds. The *Daily Mail* of 29 June 2013 ran a story about Hansen's model which had been bought by the proprietor of the Museum of the Weird in Austin, Texas. The headline was: 'Hairy 6ft beast shot in the 1960s and kept in a Minnesota freezer to go on display in Texas. Is this Bigfoot?' Once again, a rhetorical question; once again the same answer: No.

---

* D. J. Daegling, *Bigfoot Exposed: An Anthropologist Examines America's Enduring Legend* (Altamira Press, 2004), p. 77.

Bernard Heuvelmans fell out with his friend, mentor and colleague Ivan Sanderson over the Minnesota Iceman affair. Heuvelmans stated in his book about the Iceman that he felt that Sanderson tried to whip up the mystery by exaggerated statements. He also objected to the way Sanderson had tried to force through official acceptance of the specimen by the scientific elite. In fact, Sanderson was doing what he always did: making money selling stories about mystery monsters. He never seemed particularly concerned about scientific accuracy. Darren Naish, in his excellent analysis of the scandal, wrote: 'There are good reasons for thinking that Sanderson was playing this whole episode like a showman because, basically, that's what he was – I've gradually come to the conclusion that he deliberately engaged in mystery-mongering and hype because that's how he made a living; he was never interested in any of this stuff for honest, scientific reasons.'*

However, Heuvelmans, the so-called 'father of cryptozoology', believed to his death bed that the Iceman was the real thing. He was a character who is worth studying as he combined a training in formal zoology with a decidedly credulous bent. To learn more about him, I travelled to the village in the Dordogne where he established his centre for cryptozoology. His library here had 2,500 volumes, with 800 on the subject of cryptid beasts. Nearby were the caves of Rouffignac in the Vézère valley where ice-age Cro-Magnon artists depicted strange creatures on the ceilings. Born in France but raised in Belgium, Heuvelmans had been influenced by Jules Verne's and Conan Doyle's fictional books about present-day encounters with dinosaurs. After taking a

---

* D. Naish, *Hunting Monsters: Cryptozoology and the Reality Behind the Myths* (Arcturus, 2016).

degree in zoology, he escaped from a Nazi prison camp during the war and then earned a living as a showman himself, as a jazz singer in Paris. After his conversion to cryptology by Sanderson's 1948 *Saturday Evening Post* article, 'There Could Be Dinosaurs', he began to inhabit a strange intellectual landscape in which he held strong beliefs about the existence of multiple cryptids, fuelled by anger at the way he felt he was being treated by mainstream scientists. He genuinely believed in the existence of around 140 unknown large animal species (in fact, it is estimated that we have still to identify millions of species, but few are likely to be large primates running around the woods of Minnesota). His writing style is fast-paced and angry: he makes big claims, such as his own book *On the Track of Unknown Animals* being 'the greatest success in zoological literature since Darwin', and he clearly resented 'the constant disbelief of certain individuals'. However, the book, although heavily researched, presents many pictures of the author posed with an artist's impressions of the mystery creatures he promoted, and he makes extravagant claims that leave any sceptical reader unimpressed.

Cripplefoot

A particularly clever hoax was perpetrated in the November after the Minnesota Iceman phenomenon. This one fooled even John Napier, who had so quickly proved the fakery of the Minnesota Iceman. In the tiny town of Bossburg, Stevens County, in Washington state just south of the Canadian border, Bigfoot tracks were found by a well-known Bigfoot hunter Ivan Marx, just after he moved to the town. These ones were unusual in that while the left foot looked much like a normal human foot, apart from the fact that it measured seventeen-and-a-half inches long, the right foot was a club-foot. The forepart of the foot was twisted inwards, the third toe was squeezed out of alignment and there was possibly dislocation of the bones on the outer border.

Napier, the primate footprint expert, was convinced. 'I conclude that the deformity was the result of a crushing injury to the foot in early childhood. It is very difficult to conceive of a hoaxer so subtle, so knowledgeable – and so sick – who would deliberately fake a footprint of this nature. I suppose it is possible, but it is so unlikely that I am prepared to discount it.'*

Bigfoot believers were convinced, too, and descended on Bossburg in droves. Then Marx claimed that he had full-colour film footage of Bigfoot. He showed it to many enthusiasts, who were convinced. Peter Byrne, Tom Slick's yeti-hunter, turned up, examined the film, and gave Marx the promise of $25,000 if the film turned out to be authentic. Marx gave him a sealed film can containing the master copy and a viewing copy which Byre showed to a local family. He was listening when a child in the room, Stephen Byington, whispered that he knew where Mr Marx had been filming. When Byrne examined the location, he found a number of inconsistencies. A tree branch under which the 'eight-foot tall' Bigfoot in the film had walked was found to be only six feet high, making the man in the gorilla suit around five feet ten inches tall. Then he noticed that the shadows on the film and a still shot, allegedly taken at the same time as the moving footage, were significantly different, showing that the Bigfoot actor had worked with Marx for some time. Marx had also been reported as buying pieces of fur locally. When Byrne went to challenge Marx at his tar-paper cabin, he found that he had disappeared from the area. On opening the sealed film can, it was found to contain 100 feet of black-and-white Mickey Mouse film footage.† For some reason, Napier failed to relate this exposé in his 1973 book in which he states his belief in the existence of the Sasquatch: 'Will the real Sasquatch please stand up! . . . my money is on

* Napier, *Bigfoot*, op. cit.

† See http://www.bigfootencounters.com/hoaxes/marx_footage.htm.

the Bossburg tracks.' It is just possible that he hadn't heard about the exposure of the fraud three years before publication (this was all happening before the Internet), but it undermines the only piece of evidence in his book that he presents as incontrovertible.

As a postscript, Napier then relates the story of Ray Pickens, a self-confessed hoaxer who made three sets of wooden feet for his family and happily made thousands of tracks in the woods near Bossburg just to show how easily it could be done. Napier then airily writes: 'I have on my files a further set of tracks which were clearly made by a hinged, wooden contraption which wouldn't fool the village idiot.' But Napier himself had been fooled by Marx's faked tracks, not to mention Shipton's faked footprint. So, who's he calling an idiot?

Far from daunted, Bigfoot hunters still continued to hunt for a specimen, but now they were heavily armed. It wasn't going to be a live specimen this time. Sightings of Bigfoot seemed to take a dip, so maybe all those guys with gorilla suits stopped going for walks in their local woods. Then, in 2010, the Internet was filled with stories about a Bigfoot shooting. On one of the many Bigfoot sites* we meet Justin Smeja, who claimed to have shot two Bigfoot (Bigfeet?) in Plumas County, California, in October 2010. He was in a car on a forest track when he and his companion saw two figures: one standing between seven and eight feet tall, and an infant. He raised his rifle and shot both of them. The adult escaped into the undergrowth, but the baby lay still. When he ran up to it, it was clearly dying.

---

* 'Bigfoot Evidence: The World's Only 24/7 Bigfoot News Blog,' see http://bigfootevidence.blogspot.co.uk/.

He said he looked into its eyes, which had whites like a human. Still in shock and assuming he had committed a crime, Smeja buried the infant Bigfoot. After several days, he returned and dug it up. He cut off a sample of skin and hair, which became known as the Bigfoot steak.

This was passed on to veterinarian Melba Ketchum, who had been conducting a Bigfoot DNA study in her laboratory in Texas. There was a leak of some preliminary findings, forcing her to come out with a press release about her Bigfoot DNA study on 25 November 2012. 'A team of scientists can verify that their 5-year-long DNA study, currently under peer review, confirms the existence of a novel hominin hybrid species, commonly called "Bigfoot" or "Sasquatch", living in North America. Researchers' extensive DNA sequencing suggests that the legendary Sasquatch is a human relative that arose approximately 15,000 years ago as a hybrid cross of modern *Homo sapiens* with an unknown primate species.'

So, was it proved? Unfortunately, it seems that there are different levels of reliability in the world of DNA sequencing. Science by press release is not impressive, and this one came with no data and no published paper. When a paper was eventually published after three months, it made no sense to established scientists, being evolutionarily dubious and lacking any credible peer review.

The paper titled 'Novel North American Hominins, Next Generation Sequencing of Three Whole Genomes and Associated Studies,' which analysed DNA from a total of 111 samples submitted from across the continent, appeared in the inaugural issue of *DeNovo: Journal of Science*. This appeared to be a new website with only one paper.* There were question marks over the laboratory and its owner; unusually for a scientist in her position, Melba Ketchum had not completed a PhD. The samples included a toenail, blood from a smashed PVC

---

* See http://www.denovojournal.com.

pipe, and flesh from the remains of Smeja's Bigfoot steak. But it was not clear that all the samples were collected properly, and they may have been contaminated. In the end, the work was not credibly peer-reviewed.

However, some of Smeja's Bigfoot steak was sent to Professor Bryan Sykes and he analysed hairs. The results were published in his paper 'Genetic Analysis of Hair Samples Attributed to Yeti, Bigfoot and Other Anomalous Primates', which then appeared in the *Proceedings of the Royal Society* in August 2014. Most scientists agreed that this was the first legitimate large-scale DNA survey of anomalous primate evidence. And the answer? A black bear.

If ever you meet a black bear, be very careful. A cameraman friend of mine once encountered a grizzly mother and cubs in the woods at very close range, usually a dangerous combination. He immediately lay down and played dead. The mother slowly approached, and he smelled her foul breath as she nuzzled his ear. She then ambled away. It is not a technique I would recommend if pursued by a bunch of angry taxidermists.

If Bigfoot and yetis are essentially bear sightings, what kind of bear was it? And can science help? Climate change is causing the emergence of a new type of bear in the Arctic. A specimen recently shot in Canada is believed to be a 'grolar', a polar bear-grizzly hybrid, a consequence of the increasing interactions between the two bear species. Grizzly bears found in Alaska and Canada appear to be moving north as their environment warms, bringing them into contact with their polar bear cousins nearer the coastline. Meanwhile, polar bears are moving south, spending more time on land as the ice melts. And they're hungry.

'The combination of warmer temperatures and vegetation growth means there is more overlap between the species and I'd expect that overlap to increase,' Chris Servheen, a grizzly bear expert at the University of Montana, reports.

These hybrids are dangerous because they take after their polar bear daddies: they like the taste of human. So, could the grolar be a new, man-eating Bigfoot?

What is interesting about this interbreeding is that it supports a theory that this hybrid is already present in the Himalayas, left over from the last ice age. Professor Sykes analysed hairs from two unknown animals, one found in Ladakh (the *tengmo*) in the western Himalayas and one from Bhutan at the other end of the Himalayas (the *migou*). He said that he had a match with a sample from an ancient polar bear jawbone found in the Svalbard archipelago to the north of Norway that dates back at least 40,000 years, a time when the polar bear and closely related brown bear were separating as different species. Professor Sykes believes that the Himalayan animal hairs are from hybrids, crosses between polar bears and brown bears. The species are closely related and are known to interbreed where their territories overlap.

'This is an exciting and completely unexpected result that gave us all a surprise,' says Sykes. 'There's more work to be done on interpreting the results. I don't think it means there are ancient polar bears wandering around the Himalayas. But we can speculate on what the possible explanation might be. It could mean there is a subspecies of brown bear in the High Himalayas descended from the bear that was the ancestor of the polar bear. Or it could mean there has been more recent hybrid-isation between the brown bear and the descendant of the ancient polar bear.'

However, there were doubts in scientific circles. In late 2017, a DNA study at the University of Buffalo* reported that they had tested nine samples from purported yetis. They included hair found by nomadic herdsmen, bones collected by a spiritual healer, and a tooth from Ernst Schäfer's stuffed 'yeti' at Messner's Mountain Museum.

'Of those nine samples, eight of them matched local bears that are found in the region today,' said Dr Charlotte Lindqvist, who is an expert on bear genomics and a co-author of the research. 'The purported yetis from the Tibetan plateau matched Tibetan brown bears, the ones from the western Himalayan mountains matched the Himalayan brown bear, and then, at possibly slightly lower altitude, were Asian black bears.'

So, all of these alleged yeti samples were discovered to be from bears, except for the tooth which was from . . . a dog. I wondered if it had died under Schäfer's gun.

Television companies have expended much time and money on the hunt for the yeti and its American cousin Bigfoot. Yet I was told quite explicitly by a producer who shall be nameless: 'They don't want you to actually *find* it. They want to keep the viewers for another season.' The fact is that TV programmes involving searches for the Bigfoot/yeti are enduringly popular, and any conclusion that the creature was, say, a bear would dry up the dollars.

Finding Bigfoot is a documentary television series on the Animal Planet channel which after nine seasons has so far

---

* T. Lan, S. Gill, E. Bellemain, R. Bischof, Muhammad Ali Nawaz and C. Lindqvist, 'Evolutionary history of enigmatic bears in the Tibetan Plateau–Himalaya region and the identity of the yeti,' *Proceedings of the Royal Society B*, 29 November 2017.

failed to live up to its name. Some enthusiasts prefer to call it *Not Finding Bigfoot*. The series premiered in May 2011 and began its ninth season in January 2017, with over 100 shows so far, and still no find. The programme follows researchers and explorers investigating evidence. Notable cast members include Matt Moneymaker. 'I'm not saying it was Bigfoot. But it was Bigfoot' – a quote which neatly encapsulates the show's appeal. Then there's Cliff Barackman, who claims 'there's maybe 10,000 individuals, give or take a few thousand'. It's just that you can't take a picture of even one, Cliff.

While the *Finding Bigfoot* team have not yet captured filmed evidence of the creature's existence, the show continues in production because of high ratings and it is a big earner for Animal Planet. In fact, *not* finding Bigfoot is essential to the programme's survival.

Another programme, *$10 million Bigfoot Bounty*, is a TV reality show which followed nine teams of Bigfoot hunters into the wilderness of the Northwest, the area where most Bigfoot/Sasquatch sightings are reported. Patrick Kevin Day of the *LA Times* reviewed it thus: 'Not surprisingly, the series, which premieres Jan. 10, hasn't attracted a whole lot of what you would call studious, academic types. Instead, you get a whole lot of angry, sexist rednecks yelling at each other in the woods. What better way to attract a notoriously camera-shy, quite probably mythical creature, than to have a bunch of people arguing in the woods?'*

So, what's in it for the viewer? Simply this: the possibility that there *might* be an unknown giant hominid living in the woods.

---

* *LA Times*, 5 December 2013.

Magical Realism is a literary genre usually associated with Latin America and Gabriel García Márquez, whose novel *One Hundred Years of Solitude* won him a Nobel Prize for literature. Magical events occur in otherwise normal settings. García Márquez said: 'My most important problem was destroying the line of demarcation that separates what seems real from what seems fantastic.' The genre was not entirely new, as Gothic novels show similar features, but it was new to the twentieth century.

Bigfoot helped to kick-start the rise of a Pacific Northwest magical realism in the novels of Tom Robbins and now Sharma Shields. Her *The Sasquatch Hunter's Almanac** introduces a Bigfoot character named Mr Krantz to a little boy, Eli, who meets:

> an enormous ape crushed into a filthy pin-striped suit. He remembered a book from school about exotic beasts, the giant apes who lived in the savage countries of the world, and the guest resembled those creatures: deep hooded brow, small blank eyes, thin-lipped mouth like a long pink gash. And the hair! The guest was so hairy that Eli was unsure of the color of his skin: Beneath the thick brown fur, his flesh—tough and charred, like strips of dried deer meat—appeared red in some places, purple in others. The guest even smelled of hair, badly, like a musty bearskin rug singed with a lit match.

Eli's mother Vanessa runs away with Mr Krantz to become his bride, abandoning her own little boy. 'They hastened into the woods together, extinguished by the trees.' Krantz offers her an

---

* S. Shields, *The Sasquatch Hunter's Almanac* (Holt McDougal, 2015).

animal's experience of the wild that we humans have lost, and that is maybe the key to understanding our eternal fascination with Bigfoot and the yeti. He is part man, part beast.

CHAPTER NINE

An uneasy night's sleep. . .Loch Ness. . .a brave Saint. . .
Nessie. . .the beast. . .a Jurassic jaywalker. . .a big-game
hunter. . .the Surgeon's photograph. . .a Knight and a
dragon. . .Greenland sharks. . .satellites.

One night in the 1980s, I was camping alone on the shores of Loch Ness and my mind was filled with thoughts of the monster as I drifted off to sleep. A sudden crunch on the shingle woke me with a start and I imagined great, wet webbed feet plodding up the beach towards the tent, and then jaws closing on my face through the thin canvas walls. I trembled, and cautiously unzipped the door. It was pitch black and I could see nothing. Sleep wouldn't come but I could do nothing until the morning, when I peered out again and saw what the monster was: an empty aluminium beer keg crunching on the shingle in the waves. The point is that I was *expecting* a monster. And so my feverish brain provided one.

Loch Ness is a 23-mile-long freshwater lake which lies along the Great Glen in the Highlands of Scotland. Underneath it lies the Great Glen fault, a long 'strike-slip' geological fault that continues across Ireland and the North Atlantic to North America. The fault dates from when Europe and America together formed a supercontinent. Occasional earth tremors have still been observed over the last couple of centuries. The Great Glen, a U-shaped valley, runs for 63 miles between Fort William in the southwest and Inverness in the northeast through dramatic mountain scenery. There is a string of lesser lochs along the way. The Glen is a line of weakness through the Scottish Highlands and as a result has been used for centuries as a main thoroughfare. This was recognised during the Jacobite rebellions in the eighteenth century by the strategic construction of forts at the two settlements at either end, and this enabled the largely English garrisons to control the movement of the Scottish Highland clans. The course of the Caledonian Canal runs through Loch Ness, which lies 52 feet above sea level, and so the canal requires flights of locks at either end of its 60-mile length to gain the height of the loch. Unusually, Scotland is therefore a nation bisected by a single canal, like Panama. Queen Victoria travelled through the canal in 1873, and afterwards trips became hugely popular, with thousands of sightseers passing through Loch Ness on steamers every year. The modern A82 road was improved in the 1930s, and as a result thousands more witnesses gazed at Loch Ness through the windows of charabancs and coaches. Loch Ness is thus one of the most intensively observed stretches of water on the planet.

Some Scottish friends of mine, Jimmy and Louise, were driving along the loch side when they noticed a coach-load of tourists pointing and taking pictures of something in the water. They jumped out of the car, leaving their young children on the back seat, and hastened to the waterside. What they saw was 'a floating object with fins following a boat'. They are honourable people, and I do not doubt for a moment that they believed what they think they saw: the monster. Like me, they *expected* to see Nessie.

Loch Ness is by volume the largest freshwater lake in the British Isles, partly because of its great depth. It is also extremely cold. One summer, I was helping my brother to sail his old wooden yacht through the loch when we were hit by ferocious headwinds and choppy waves, so we ducked into an inlet for a rest. Somehow, we managed to get a rope around the propeller and I was volunteered to go over the side with a kitchen knife to cut the rope away. All I remember is that it was ballachingly cold, and as a warm-blooded mammal I couldn't wait to get out. Once again, I imagined a great shape swirling through the water towards me and teeth sinking into my legs.

There is a huge amount of evidence from witnesses, photographs, sonar scans and satellite images to support the hypothesis that a large creature, perhaps a surviving Jurassic-era dinosaur, is living in the loch. The evidence goes back to St Columba, who in AD 565 was reported as defending one of his followers against 'a water beast' who attacked him with 'great roaring' after having killed a local man. And there is a long tradition in Scotland of kelpies, malevolent shape-shifting demons associated with running water and appearing as water-horses or handsome young men.

In 1852, a local newspaper, the *Inverness Courier*, reported that a large group of people gathered on the loch side armed with scythes, pitchforks and guns prepared to repel a couple of 'sea serpents' that had been observed swimming steadily towards them across the loch. Then, in 1930, another newspaper, the *Northern Chronicle*, reported that three young anglers from Inverness were fishing for trout in the loch one August morning when they were disturbed by 'a great commotion' which looked like a creature swimming towards them. It turned sharply away when 300 yards from the boat, but caused a wave two-and-a-half feet high.

Then, on 2 May 1933, the *Inverness Courier* published an article on the front page under the headline: 'Strange Spectacle on Loch Ness: What Was It?' It reported that on 14 April 1933, Mrs Aldie Mackay, manageress of the Drumnadrochit hotel, had seen a whale-like creature in the loch: 'the creature disported itself, rolling and plunging for fully a minute, its body resembling that of a whale.'

But it was the sight of a dinosaur crossing the loch-side road which really kicked off the Loch Ness monster craze. The original sighting which prompted all our camera-happy hopes was reported in a letter to the *Inverness Courier* on 4 August 1933 by a Mr George Spicer, a director of the tailors Todhouse, Reynard & Co. Ltd, who was touring Scotland on holiday from London. In the letter, he recounted how he and his wife were driving along the south shores of the loch when 'I saw the nearest approach to a dragon or prehistoric animal that I have ever seen in my life. It crossed my road about fifty yards ahead and appeared to be carrying a small lamb or animal of some kind. It seemed to have a long neck which moved up and down, in the manner of a scenic railway, and the body was fairly big, with a high back.'

Lieutenant-Commander Rupert Gould of the Royal Navy had already written a treatise on the sea serpent. He was a serious observer, an expert navigator, and had been entrusted with the restoration of one of Harrison's chronometers. He became interested in the Spicers' story and toured Loch Ness by motorcycle, making his own observations. He suspected a hoax and interviewed the Spicers, then transcribed their story for his own book on the subject. He left their house convinced that their story was true:

They had passed through Dores, and were on their way towards Foyers when, as the car was climbing a slight rise, an extraordinary-looking creature crossed the road ahead of them, from left to right, in a series of jerks. When on the road, it took up practically the whole width of it. He saw no definite head, but this was across the road before he had time to take the whole thing in properly – it was in sight for a few seconds. The creature was of a loathsome-looking greyish colour, like a dirty elephant or a rhinoceros. It had a very long and thin neck, which undulated up and down, and was contorted into a series of half hoops. The body was much thicker, and moved across the road, as already stated, in a series of jerks. He saw no indications of any legs, or of a tail – but in front of the body, where this sloped down to the neck, he saw something flopping up and down which, on reflection, he thought might have been the end of a long tail swung round to the far side of the body. The latter stood some 4–5 feet above the road. The whole looked like a huge snail with a long neck.*

On reaching the point where the creature had lurched across [writes Gould], they could not see whether the loch was disturbed, and he had heard no splash but the sound of his car would have covered any other noise. I can concur with these sentiments, adding that I was watching the loch between Dores and Foyers this July and can say that the waters were particularly choppy and noisy in this area compared to further south.†

So, in other words the Spicers had seen a Jurassic-era dinosaur crossing the road, a lamb hanging from its jaws, in 1930s Britain. If this were true and if a specimen could be secured, this would shake the world of science to its foundations.

The Spicers' experience struck a chord with the public, and more reports of past and present sightings poured in. These events provoked a fever of excitement. Later in 1933, the *Daily Mail* decided to get to the bottom of the Loch Ness mystery. They despatched a celebrated big-game hunter, Marmaduke Wetherell, to the shores of the Loch, where he almost imme-

* See http://lochnessmystery.blogspot.co.uk/2010/08/classic-sightings-spicers.html.

† R. T. Gould, *Loch Ness Monster* (Geoffrey Bles, 1934).

diately found the tracks of the monster near the shore. 'You may imagine my great surprise,' he said in a BBC interview, 'when on a small patch of loose earth I found fresh spoor, or footprints, about nine inches wide, of a four-toed animal. Its prints were very much like those of a hippo.' Wetherell took plaster-cast impressions of the four-toed footprints, which he estimated were made by a creature around twenty feet long. The plaster casts were sent to the Natural History Museum, and the *Daily Mail* splashed the story. As a result, hundreds more monster hunters turned up at the loch side.

Then the *Daily Mail*, the very next year, provided us with the iconic picture of Nessie which still remains in the public imagination, rather as Eric Shipton's photograph of the yeti footprint became the iconic image of that creature. On 21 April 1934, they published a black-and-white picture, now referred to as 'The Surgeon's Photograph', which appeared to show a creature in the loch looking much like a plesiosaur with a long snake-like neck and head. It was said to have been taken by a man named Robert Kenneth Wilson, a prominent London gynaecologist who did not want to have his name associated with it, hence the picture's nickname. It showed the head and neck of the creature raised above the waves on the loch, but no body or legs were visible. Wilson claimed to have been walking by the loch when he saw the creature break the surface. He hurriedly took four photos, only two of which came out; the second showed a similar head and neck in diving position, but was rather blurred. On seeing this photograph in the *Daily Mail*, Sir Edward Mortimer Mountain, an insurance millionaire, recruited twenty unemployed men from the Inverness labour exchange at the sum of £2 a week. He armed them with binoculars and cameras and placed them as observers around the loch in strategic positions for five weeks beginning on 13 July 1934. He offered the reward of ten guineas to any man who came back with a picture of the monster. A correspondent to the Editor of *The Field* in November 1934 complained that not enough was being done: 'Had a quarter of the existing evidence for the Loch Ness monster been available for the presence of some rare animal in a lake in Central Africa, more than one expedition would already have set out in the sacred cause of science.'

By April 1938, the author Virginia Woolf was writing to her sister, Vanessa Bell, about a 'charming couple' she had met at a Loch Ness hotel 'who were in touch . . . with the Monster. They had seen him. He is like several broken telegraph posts and swims at immense speed. He has no head. He is constantly seen.' By now, even the authorities were becoming worried about the way events were shaping up. A question had been tabled in the House of Commons asking for an investigation, and William Fraser, chief constable of Inverness-shire in Scotland, became so concerned for the public's safety that he wrote to the Scottish Office on 15 August 1938. He reported that a twenty-strong hunting party, led by a Londoner called Peter Kent, accompanied by a Miss Marion Stirling and armed with a specially made harpoon, had arrived at Fort Augustus intent on capturing the monster 'dead or alive'. His letter concluded: 'That there is a strange creature in Loch Ness seems now beyond doubt, but that police have power to protect it is doubtful. I have, however, caused Mr Peter Kent to be warned of the desirability of having the creature left alone but whether my warning will have the desired effect or not remains to be seen.*

So even the police had 'no doubt' that a strange creature lived in the loch, but Britain was going to be preoccupied with other monsters soon. It wasn't until December 1954 that a fishing boat, *Rival III*, was passing through the loch with its newfangled sonar apparatus switched on. This technology, essentially radar for water, had been intensively developed

* See http://www.scottisharchivesforschools.org/naturalScotland/Nessie. asp.

during the war against German U-boat submarines. The operator observed a large object keeping pace underneath the vessel at a depth of 479 feet. The creature, or whatever it was, kept up with the fishing vessel for half a mile.

Sir Peter Markham Scott, CH, CBE, DSC and Bar, FRS, FZS and son of Robert Scott, the South Pole explorer, was an eminent naturalist and war hero who founded the world conservation movement World Wide Fund for Nature. He also designed its giant panda logo. Scott was quoted as saying: 'I have for a long time thought it more than probable that an undescribed animal lives in Loch Ness', and he resolved to search for it. In May 1960, he contacted Buckingham Palace for permission to name it after the Queen: *Elizabethia nessiae*. A friend of his, the Palace official Martin Charteris, the Queen's then assistant private secretary, wrote back to the impressively well-connected Scott to say there was enthusiasm in the Palace for the project, adding it would be 'a great day in the zoological world if it can be proved that a hitherto unknown animal exists'. However, he injected a note of courtierly caution: 'If there is any suggestion of naming the animal after the Queen, there must of course be absolutely irrefutable evidence of its existence. It would be most regrettable to connect Her Majesty in any way with something which ultimately turned out to be a hoax. Even if the animal does prove to exist I am not at all sure that it will be generally very appropriate to name it after Her Majesty since it has for so many years been known as "The Monster".'

Far from daunted, Scott set up the Loch Ness Phenomena Investigations Bureau (LNPIB) in 1962 with the help of his wartime comrade David James, a Conservative MP who was also a friend of the Duke of Edinburgh, the Queen's husband. The LNPIB persuaded the Ministry of Defence to lend them a photo-reconnaissance unit to examine photographs and also searchlights to look for the monster at night. The LNPIB boasted over 1,000 members by 1969, and their permanent camp and observation deck eventually attracted over 50,000 visitors a year.

During a visit in 1972, an intellectual property lawyer and sonar expert named Robert Rines reported a sighting of the monster. He said he saw 'a large, darkish hump, covered . . . with rough, mottled skin, like the back of an elephant'. Thus encouraged, Rines mounted repeated expeditions to the loch over the next 35 years (this strikes a chord, as the finding of George Mallory's body on Everest in 1999 led to at least six further expeditions searching for his camera). Leading a group of fellow researchers from the Academy of Applied Science, he scanned the murky waters of the loch with sonar and underwater cameras of his own design. If sonar detected movement, floodlights would be turned on and the cameras triggered. Rines employed a local mystical diviner who claimed to have seen the monster on repeated occasions. She directed the placement of the camera that eventually produced the best images. Two underwater photographs were obtained, both appearing to show a rhomboid, or diamond-shaped, flipper.

Peter Scott was knighted in 1973. In the same year, he came up with a new suggestion for Nessie's official name, *Nessiteras rhombopteryx*, which translates roughly as 'Ness monster with the diamond-shaped fin'. This was based on Rines's underwater photographs. The idea was that Scott could register Nessie as an endangered species and presumably Loch Ness could then be declared a nature reserve. Rather unkindly, the *Daily Telegraph* pointed out that the name was an anagram of 'Monster hoax by Sir Peter S'. They obviously had far too much time on their hands. Rines, who had provided the pictures, leapt to Sir Peter's rescue by pointing out that the letters could also be read as an anagram for 'Yes, both pix are monsters, R'. The two men contributed to a paper for *Nature** which showed that at least some scientists were taking the subject seriously. With the might of the British establishment and the military on the hunt, surely it had to be only a matter of time before the real monster surfaced with her flippers held up in surrender?

Nessie was never found, though sightings regularly roll in up to the time of writing. In 1987, twenty-four small vessels were specially equipped with the latest echo sounder equipment donated by sonar expert Darrell Lowrance, founder of Lowrance Electronics. In 'Operation Deepscan', the boats deployed in a line across the width of the loch, rather in the manner of beaters on a grouse moor. Movement was detected, and after examining a sonar return indicating a large, moving object at a depth of 590 feet near Urquhart Bay, Lowrance said: 'There's something here that we don't understand, and there's something here that's larger than a fish, maybe some species that hasn't been detected before.'

In 2016, one observer entered the *Guinness Book of Records* for the longest continuous monster-hunting vigil on Loch Ness. Steve Feltham had been watching for Nessie for no less than 25 years, living in a converted mobile library in a pub car park at Dores. Feltham, who began his vigil in 1991 and has been fascinated by the mystery since a Highland holiday in childhood, said: 'I look at 25 years as a good halfway mark in trying to solve this. I am willing to dedicate another

---

* Sir P. Scott and R. H. Rines, 'Naming the Loch Ness Monster', *Nature* vol. 258, 11 December 1975.

25 years. Hopefully it will only take another few weeks. Who knows? When I first came here I had no clear idea how long I would need. But I thought I would see something in three years.' Two years into his vigil, he saw the monster but didn't have his camera on him at the time: 'I was sitting on the shore near the Fort Augustus end of the loch when something went past the bay, through the water. It was like a torpedo shot and it had some weight behind it, hitting through the waves. Nothing in Loch Ness could create a disturbance like that, apart from Nessie. I just sat there in amazement.' He saw something. But what?

Nessie from space

Satellites might solve the problem of finding the Loch Ness monster. There was a gap in sightings between 2012 and 2014, and then a 100-foot-long shape that looked as though it was swimming just below the surface was filmed from space from a satellite. This was accessed by Apple's satellite map app by two users who reported it to the Official Loch Ness monster Fan Club. It looks like a giant catfish with two enormous fins, cruising just a few feet below the surface. One of the observers, Andrew Dixon, said: 'It was a total fluke that I found it. I was looking at satellite images of my town and then just thought I'd have a look at Loch Ness. The first thing that came into my head when I saw it was, "That's the Loch Ness monster". It was the shape of it; I thought it had to be something more than a shadow.' The chairman of the club, Gary Campbell, a chartered accountant who lives in Inverness, said: 'Now that we have spies in the skies above Loch Ness, maybe we will get more sightings which will whet the appetite of more down-to-earth Nessie hunters to come north. Furthermore, the use of satellite tech- nology means that if Nessie is just swimming below the surface like in this case, we can still pick her up . . . Last year was the first time in almost 90 years that Nessie wasn't seen at all. After

Nessie "going missing" for 18 months, it's great to see her back.'
And the *Daily Mail* ran yet another Nessie headline: 'Have Apple
Maps Found the Loch Ness Monster? Satellite Image Reveals
Mysterious Shape Lurking in the Scottish Highlands'* alongside
an Apple Maps satellite picture of the creature.†

So where is the Loch Ness monster? Here we have a large body
of calm, cold fresh water which is observed by thousands of
camera-wielding tourists every year. Google Street View has
mounted cameras on and in Loch Ness and webcams monitor
the water night and day. And of course, we all want to take a
picture of Nessie. Where is her family, her body, bones, DNA
or at least a clear photograph?

Let's now follow Nessie's monstrous footprints back in time
and try to disentangle truth from fiction.

St Columba saw Nessie

The Loch Ness monster's fans maintain that the story has been
going strong since AD 565, when St Columba prevented a 'water
beast' from attacking his follower Luigne moccu Min by making
the sign of the cross. Here is a translation of the account. It
was written by Adomnán, the ninth abbot of Iona Abbey:

> Concerning a certain water beast driven away by the power
> of the blessed man's prayer . . . when the blessed man was

---

* See http://www.dailymail.co.uk/news/article-2607667/Is-THIS-Loch-
Ness-Monster-Apples-Maps-satellite-image-Nessie.html.

† See http://i.telegraph.co.uk/multimedia/archive/02887/loch-ness_
2887190b.jpg.

for a number of days in the province of the Picts, he had
to cross the river Ness. When he reached its bank, he saw
a poor fellow being buried by other inhabitants; and the
buriers said that, while swimming not long before, he had
been seized and most savagely bitten by a water beast.
Some men, going to his rescue in a wooden boat, though
too late, had put out hooks and caught hold of his
wretched corpse. When the blessed man heard this, he
ordered notwithstanding that one of his companions
should swim out and bring back to him, by sailing, a boat
that stood on the opposite bank. Hearing this order of
the holy and memorable man, Luigne moccu Min obeyed
without delay, and putting off his clothes, excepting his
tunic, plunged into the water. But the monster, whose
appetite had earlier been not so much sated as whetted
for prey, lurked in the depth of the river. Feeling the water
above disturbed by Luigne's swimming, it suddenly swam
up to the surface, and with gaping mouth and with great
roaring rushed towards the man swimming in the middle
of the stream. While all that were there, barbarians and
even the brothers, were struck down with extreme terror,
the blessed man, who was watching, raised his holy hand
and drew the saving sign of the cross in the empty air;
and then, invoking the name of God, he commanded the
savage beast, and said: 'You will go no further. Do not
touch the man; turn back speedily.' Then, hearing this
command of the saint, the beast, as if pulled back with
ropes, fled terrified in swift retreat; although it had before
approached so close to Luigne as he swam that there was
no more than the length of one short pole between man
and beast. Then seeing that the beast had withdrawn and
that their fellow soldier Luigne had returned to them
unharmed and safe, in the boat, the brothers with great
amazement glorified God in the blessed man. And also

the pagan barbarians who were there at the time, impelled by the magnitude of this miracle that they themselves had seen, magnified the God of the Christians.

Let's examine this evidence. Firstly, this is not an eyewitness account but a hearsay story written down 100 years later. Adomnán never met St Columba and was writing about an event a century after it was supposed to have happened. Secondly, this incident was reported as having occurred in the River Ness, not the loch, but the story was appropriated by later monster-makers in the 1930s who had already settled Nessie in Loch Ness. Thirdly, a 'great roaring' was also observed: *cum ingenti fremitu*. As an Italian geologist has suggested, this could point to an earthquake or the release of gas through a fault, and of course Loch Ness lies on the Great Glen Fault.

Fourthly, this story is designed, as the writer himself states, to magnify 'the God of the Christians'. Miraculous stories are commonplace in hagiographies of Christian saints, often with hundreds of witnesses, far more than the average Nessie sighting. For a well-attested example, take St Joseph of Cupertino (1603–63), who it was said was able to enter a religious trance and levitate himself into the air. Even sticking pins in him and burning him with embers wouldn't stop his flying antics, and he would only land when his superiors ordered him down. This flying saint was said to have performed the feat in front of Pope Urban VIII, and Joseph is now the patron saint of pilots. Michael Grosso, in his absorbing account of the Flying Saint,[*] collects 150 cases and says that the numbers of witnesses were in the thousands. The eyewitness accounts were given under oath. What did they see? During Holy Mass, St Joseph would rise up in the air during the Elevation of the Host, his

---

[*] M. Grosso, *The Man Who Could Fly: St Joseph of Cupertino and the Mystery of Levitation* (Rowman & Littlefield, 2015).

toes lightly touching the ground. He was also said to float to the ceiling of his cell, and once he ended up in an olive tree and was unable to get down without a ladder:

> Fr Antonio Chiarello, while walking with Padre Giuseppe through the orchard of the convent, at a certain point gazed up into the heavens. 'Padre Giuseppe, what a beautiful sky God has made!' These words seemed like an invitation for Padre Giuseppe to fly up into the sky, and so he did, letting out a loud cry and bounding from the ground to fly up to the top of an olive tree where he landed on his knees on a branch that kept shaking. One reads in the processi that it was as though a bird were perched on a branch. Padre Giuseppe stayed up there about a half an hour and finally came back to himself, asking the priest how to get down from the tree. The priest had to get a ladder and in that way he descended from the olive tree.[*]

St Joseph was a public figure for 35 years throughout Italy, and his levitations, spontaneous and unpredictable, occurred throughout this period. When he got in trouble with the Inquisition, who thought this was witchcraft or annoyingly ostentatious sanctity on his part, his flights only ceased temporarily. Grosso points out that the witnesses were impeccable: the Inquisitors from Rome and Naples, clerics, artists, pilgrims, surgeons, kings, cardinals and popes. Some were so disturbed by what they saw that they ran away, gripped by fear. Others, like a Lutheran duke from Germany, were beset by religious doubt.

Now, much as we want to believe Grosso, is the story likely? So far, humanity has not mastered the art of (survivable) flight without a large amount of modern technology. The sceptics suggest there are other possible explanations. One is that the witnesses exaggerated their stories, or testified years after St

[*] D. Bernini, *Vita del Giuseppe* chap. 22.

Joseph's death and just embroidered their stories. Robert Smith* suggested that St Joseph was actually performing high jumps like a modern gymnast. His alleged levitations 'originate from a leap, and not from a prone or simple standing or kneeling position; the witnesses mistook a leap of a very agile man for levitation.' St Joseph was prone to outbursts of anger and ecstatic states during flight, emitting piercing screams or cries, so perhaps his gymnastic leaps were involuntary and unconscious.

If we are amazed by St Joseph's aerial manoeuvres, don't forget the Natural Law Party, founded in the United Kingdom in 1992. They promised world peace through transcendental meditation and yogic flying. Their party-political video featured a number of gentlemen squatting on mattresses with their eyes closed and legs crossed. These practitioners of the Natural Law then hopped across the room in the manner of giant frogs.† This could not by any stretch of the imagination be called levitation. A group of yogic flyers had apparently already reduced crime in Merseyside by 60 per cent, presumably by reducing potential criminals to helpless laughter. This was not levitation; it was what science would call bouncing on cushions. Still, ex-Beatles guitarist George Harrison performed a benefit concert for the party in 1992, and had they won the General Election their key appointments would have been tycoon Sir James Goldsmith as Chancellor, Sir Paul Condon, Commissioner of the Metropolitan Police, as Home Secretary, and Anita Roddick of Body Shop as Foreign Secretary. Who says the great and the good don't have a sense of humour?

The phenomenon of levitation was clearly being believed by sober, modern-day witnesses, so it is not so unexpected that St Joseph had his believers. The point here is that hagiography is filled with seemingly plausible miracles, but somehow there is never any solid evidence which would satisfy a scientist. To return to our monster-bothering St Columba:

* R. Smith, *Comparative Miracles* (B. Herder Book Company, 1965).

† See https://www.youtube.com/watch?v=438UKM1Av1g.

On the appointed day as he had intended the Saint came to the long lake of the river Ness, followed by a large crowd. Then the magicians began to exalt, because they saw a great mist brought up, and a stormy adverse wind . . . so our Columba, seeing that the elements were being roused to fury against him, called upon Christ the Lord. He entered the boat, and while the sailors hesitated, he himself, more steadfast, ordered the sail to be raised against the wind. When this was done, and with the whole crowd looking on, the ship moved with extraordinary speed, sailing against the contrary wind.

Now, I really have to take issue with this. As a sailor of cranky old sailing boats, I know that the only way they sail against a contrary wind is by the application of power from a diesel engine. So I just don't believe this story.

Nessie seen by over a thousand witnesses

Yes, over a thousand sightings have been recorded. But what did they see? To take the most famous sightings consecutively:

The Three Anglers

The young men didn't actually see a monster, only a 'great commotion'. They described a wave two and a half feet high, and 'we have no idea what it was, but we are quite positive it could not have been a salmon'.

Mrs Aldie Mackay

Let's try to work out exactly what this witness saw in 1933. Alex Campbell was a water bailiff at Fort Augustus and a part-time journalist for the *Inverness Courier*. He happened to be a friend of the Mackays and this is what he wrote:

Loch Ness has for generations been credited with being the home of a fearsome-looking monster, but, somehow or other, the 'water kelpie', as this legendary creature is called, has always been regarded as a myth, if not a joke.

Now, however, comes the news that the beast has been seen once more, for on Friday of last week, a well-known businessman who lives in Inverness, and his wife (a University graduate), when motoring along the north shore of the loch, not far from Abriachan pier, were startled to see a tremendous upheaval on the loch, which, previously, had been as calm as the proverbial millpond. The lady was the first to notice the disturbance, which occurred fully three-quarters of a mile from the shore, and it was her sudden cries to stop that drew her husband's attention to the water.

There, the creature disported itself, rolling and plunging for fully a minute, its body resembling that of a whale, and the water cascading and churning like a simmering cauldron. Soon, however, it disappeared in a boiling mass of foam. Both onlookers confessed that there was something uncanny about the whole thing, for they realised that here was no ordinary denizen of the depths, because, apart from its enormous size, the beast, in taking the final plunge, sent out waves that were big enough to have been caused by a passing steamer. The watchers waited for almost half an hour in the hope that the monster (if such it was) would come to the surface again; but they had seen the last of it.

Questioned as to the length of the beast, the lady stated that, judging by the state of the water in the affected area, it seemed to be many feet long.

It will be remembered that a few years ago, a party of Inverness anglers reported that, when crossing the loch in a rowing boat, they encountered an unknown creature, whose bulk, movements, and the amount of water displaced at once suggested that it was either a very large seal, a porpoise, or, indeed, the monster itself!

But the story, which duly appeared in the press, received scant attention, and less credence. In fact, most of those people who aired their views on the matter did so in a manner that bespoke feelings of the utmost scepticism. [It should be mentioned that, so far as is known, neither seals nor porpoises have ever been known to enter Loch Ness. Indeed, in the case of the latter, it would be utterly impossible for them to do so, and, as to the seals, it is the fact that though they have on rare occasions been seen in the River Ness, their presence in Loch Ness has never been definitely established.]*

Aldie Mackay was clearly uneasy about Alex Campbell's treatment of her story. For a start, only she had sight of the object; her husband only saw splashing. A year after her sighting she admitted to Rupert Gould, the first Loch Ness researcher, that the article had been somewhat exaggerated. In fact, she actually 'thought at first that it was caused by two ducks fighting', although later she decided on reflection that 'the splashing was far too extensive to be caused that way'. Also, whereas Campbell's newspaper report had reported one body 'resembling that of a whale', instead she had actually seen two humps with a total length of around twenty feet. This could describe two otters.

Alternatively, it could describe a peculiar form of standing wave often observed in Loch Ness on calm days. Let's look at the evidence again. It was a sunny and calm day on Loch Ness with good visibility when Aldie Mackay and her husband John were driving back to the hotel from Inverness to Drumnadrochit. They were on the A82, near the seven-mile marker stone just beyond Lochend at the narrow, north end of Loch Ness. Aldie was looking out across the calm water, when she saw a disturbance in the water. She yelled for her husband to stop the car.

* *Inverness Courier*, 2 May 1933.

In a rare interview years later, Aldie Mackay described the moment to marine biologist and founder of The Loch Ness Project, Adrian Shine. 'She said it was black, wet, with the water rolling off it,' he said. 'It went in a circle, round and down. She yelled at her husband "Stop! The beast!" but, by the time he had done so, all he could see were ripples.'* It was later reported in the *Scotsman*† that, as the commotion subsided, a big wake spread across the water towards Aldourie pier on the opposite shore. Then, about halfway across, two black humps emerged, moving in line, the rear one somewhat larger than the front one. They moved forward in a rolling motion like whales or porpoises, but with no fins visible, rising and sinking in an undulating manner. Then the objects turned sharply to the left and, after describing a half-circle, suddenly sank with considerable commotion. *If* this is a more accurate description of what Aldie Mackay saw, 'two black humps' and a 'rolling motion' suggest waves rather than monsters.

Because of its long straight shape and its alignment with the prevailing wind direction, Loch Ness is prone to an unusual wave formation caused by the water 'piling up' at one end of the loch and then oscillating back and forth. The effect is called a *seiche*, a Swiss–French dialect word meaning 'to sway back and forth', and it was first used to describe the effect in Lake Geneva. The natural frequency in Loch Ness is thirty-one and a half minutes. There was another cause of odd waves in the loch: just two years before Aldie Mackay's sighting, the ice-breaking tug *Scot II* had been built at the Henry Robb shipyards in Leith, in 1931. The *Scot II* operated on the Caledonian Canal from her home berth at Fort Augustus, initially to keep the canal clear and later as a passenger cruiser. Dan Clark, the son of her skipper James Clark, said during

---

* See http://www.bbc.co.uk/news/uk-scotland-22125981.

† See http://www.*scotsman*.com/heritage/people-places/steuart-campbell-say-goodbye-to-loch-ness-mystery-1-2893334.

the *Scot II*'s time as a cruiser that she was often credited with provoking sightings of the Loch Ness monster due to the bow wave that her heavy blunt hull created. 'Twenty minutes after the *Scot II* passed, her waves were still on the loch and many people mistook that for the Loch Ness monster.' In the article, Campbell describes 'waves that were big enough to have been caused by a passing steamer'. I would suggest that's exactly what they were. Unfortunately, the Mackays didn't manage to take a photograph, which may have supported this explanation.

It's interesting that Aldie Mackay shouted 'stop!' and 'beast!' which (as long as she wasn't referring to her husband) suggests that 'a beast' was already in her mind in connection with the loch. That is significant, as many Loch Ness witnesses seem to see things they expect to see.

Alex Campbell's article has come in for a fair amount of criticism for its exaggeration and downright embroidery. As Daniel Loxton points out in his sceptical book on cryptozoology,* Campbell turned the three anglers' account into a sighting of 'the monster itself!' Ten days after this, the first Loch Ness monster article, the editor of the *Inverness Courier* at last turned to an expert, Captain John Macdonald, who over fifty years had commanded several steamers that had plied the waters of the loch. He was critical of Alex Campbell's story:

> In the first case it is news to me to learn, as your correspondent states, that 'for generations the Loch has been credited with being the home of a fearsome monster.' I have sailed on the Loch Ness for fifty years, and in this time have made no fewer than 20,000 trips up and down Loch Ness. During that half-century of almost daily intercourse with Loch Ness I have never seen such a 'monster' as described by your correspondent.

* Loxton and Prothero, op. cit.

Captain Macdonald had seen what might be described as a 'tremendous upheaval in the Loch', but this 'very ordinary occurrence' was more likely to be 'sporting salmon in lively mood, who, by their leaping out of the water, and racing about, created a great commotion in the calm waters, and certainly looked strange and perhaps fearsome when viewed some distance from the scene.' He had seen this hundreds of times.

A part-time journalist had exaggerated a dubious story, and so the Mackay sighting has to be put in the 'uncertain' file. Note how much hype had been added by Campbell, and ponder what might possibly benefit the proprietors of a hotel more than coach-loads of tourists?

The George Spicer sighting of a Jurassic-era dinosaur

The Loch Ness monster was born in the 1930s with a couple of exaggerated stories which rapidly escalated into a torrent. The Three Anglers, the Mackays and then this, the Spicers' sighting of an actual living dinosaur, were thrilling. However, the idea of Jurassic-era creatures living in the present day was nothing new. In fact, science and popular fiction had made the idea widespread.

The French naturalist George Cuvier had demonstrated that fossils were the remains of fantastical creatures that no longer roamed the earth, but it was Mary Anning's discoveries along the coast of Dorset that brought home the fact that southern England once was filled with giant monsters more strange and terrible than the wildest dream. Somewhat unfairly, she gained scant credit for her achievement in her own short lifetime. Mary Anning was eventually acknowledged by the Royal Society as one of the ten British women who most influenced the history of science, but her background was one of poverty and her education was meagre. Her home, Lyme Regis, had become a holiday destination for the English middle classes, after the outbreak of revolution in France in 1792 had made the continent too dangerous to visit. To scratch a living, Mary Anning's poverty-stricken father dug strange-shaped rocks out of the crumbling cliffs nearby and sold them to the tourists.

Mary Anning's parents had ten children, but only two survived to adulthood. She herself was struck by lightning aged fifteen months, appeared to be dead but was resuscitated by immersion in a warm bath. After that event, which a local doctor thought was miraculous, she seemed to blossom. She helped her father in the family business of collecting fossils. These were known locally as curios, and they had names such as 'snake stone' for the coiled-up ammonites and 'devil's fingers' for belemnites. The cliffs they came from were composed of alternating layers of limestone and clay and are part of the Blue Lias geological formation from the later Triassic and earlier Jurassic times, between 195 and 200 million years ago. The area is now a World Heritage Site known as the Jurassic Coast. The cliffs are unstable, and during the winter they regularly collapse, revealing more fossils. This season was when Anning did most of her work.

This work was dangerous. Her father eventually died partly due to injuries sustained from a fall from a cliff, and she herself was nearly swept away in a landslide that killed her pet dog Tray. 'Perhaps you will laugh when I say that the death of my old faithful dog has quite upset me, the cliff that fell upon him and killed him in a moment before my eyes, and close to my feet . . . it was but a moment between me and the same fate.' However, she persevered and her discoveries began to attract the notice of the gentlemen of science. In a find important to students of the Loch Ness monster, on 10 December 1823 she found the first complete *Plesiosaurus*, an eleven-foot-long marine reptile with a long neck and small head. This was very much like the creature the Spicers described as crossing the road next to Loch Ness. Anning's discovery aroused huge excitement in the scientific community, which in England was largely composed of God-fearing Anglican clergymen.

Plesiosaurus was one of the first reptiles to be discovered from the 'antediluvian' or Pre-Flood period described in the Bible. The name meant 'near lizard' to show that it was more like a modern reptile than *Ichthyosaurus*, the complete specimen of which Mary Anning had also found in the same rock strata just a few years earlier. The significance of her discovery was that as a creature with no living representative, *Plesiosaurus* provided evidence for the new theory of extinction. This theory contributed to some of Charles Darwin's ideas about evolution.

Tourists started to come to Lyme Regis to see Mary Anning at work. Lady Harriet Sylvester visited her on 17 September 1824 and noted in her diary:

> The extraordinary thing in this young woman is that she has made herself so thoroughly acquainted with the science that the moment she finds any bones she knows to what tribe they belong. She fixes the bones on a frame with cement and then makes drawings and has them engraved . . . It is certainly a wonderful instance of divine favour – that this poor, ignorant girl should be so blessed, for by reading and application she has arrived to that degree of knowledge as to be in the habit of writing and talking with professors and other clever men on the subject, and they all acknowledge that she understands more of the science than anyone else in this kingdom.

Mary Anning also demonstrated a rigorous attitude towards scientific truth. She noticed that one of the fossil collectors, Thomas Hawkins, was 'improving' some of the finds: 'He is such an enthusiast that he makes things as he imagines they ought to be; and not as they are really found.' Hawkins was later found to have added faked fossil bones to make some ichthyosaur skeletons seem complete and had then sold them on to the British Museum without declaring his additions. In this he was certainly not as egregious a faker as Charles Dawson, the Piltdown Man hoaxer, but truthfulness is the very foundation of scientific knowledge and Anning understood this.

Mary Anning died of breast cancer at the age of 47. Towards the end of her brief life, she did gain plaudits from the geological community and was granted a small pension, but she suffered from her poverty and her gender. It is interesting to imagine what she could have done in our times.

The idea of a world swarming with monsters proved irresistible to writers of fiction. Jules Verne, the 'father of science fiction', published his novel *Journey to the Centre of the Earth* in 1863. In it, a German professor, Otto Lidenbrock, is studying an Icelandic runic manuscript and comes across a coded description of a secret passage that descends into the bowels of the earth from the volcano Snæfell in Iceland. Taking his nephew Axel and the eiderdown duck-hunting guide Hans, they identify the correct crater and descend. Eventually, after terrifying adventures they come into a vast continent-sized cavern lit by electrical discharges and filled with a huge ocean. They build a raft, embark on a voyage across the sea and then witness a fight to the death between two Jurassic-era monsters: a giant *ichthyosaurus* (the first specimen that was found by Mary Anning) and a *plesiosaurus*:

Two monsters only were creating all this commotion; and before my eyes are two reptiles of the primitive world. I can distinguish the eye of the *ichthyosaurus* glowing like a red-hot coal, and as large as a man's head. Nature has endowed it with an optical apparatus of extreme power, and capable of resisting the pressure of the great volume of water in the depths it inhabits. It has been appropriately called the saurian whale, for it has both the swiftness and the rapid movements of this monster of our own day. This one is not less than a hundred feet long, and I can judge of its size when it sweeps over the waters the vertical coils of its tail. Its jaw is enormous, and according to naturalists it is armed with no less than one hundred and eighty-two teeth. The *plesiosaurus*, a serpent with a cylindrical body and a short tail, has four flappers or paddles to act like oars. Its body is entirely covered with a thick armour of scales, and its neck, as flexible as a swan's, rises thirty feet above the waves.

Those huge creatures attacked each other with the greatest animosity. They heaved around them liquid mountains, which rolled even to our raft and rocked it perilously. Twenty times we were near capsizing. Hissings of prodigious force are heard. The two beasts are fast locked together; I cannot distinguish the one from the other. The probable rage of the conqueror inspires us with intense fear.*

In this novel, Jules Verne demonstrates his fascination for the submarine world, which he so brilliantly described in *Twenty Thousand Leagues Under the Sea*. Verne is unfairly dismissed as a children's writer in English-speaking nations, as his works published in English were usually abridged translations, but in Francophone countries he gets his full credit as a major literary figure.

Our next work of fiction to describe a present-day Jurassic menagerie was *The Lost World* by our old friend Sir Arthur Conan Doyle, the creator of Sherlock Holmes and the world-famous novelist of Piltdown. His 1912 novel concerns an expedition to a high plateau in South America where the members are attacked by pterodactyls and assorted dinosaurs.

---

* J. Verne, *Journey to the Centre of the Earth* (Griffith and Farran, 1863).

Once again, plesiosaurs and ichthyosaurs wallow in the swamps and threaten to kill and eat the puny humans.

The public appetite for dinosaurs was insatiable. In 1915, the Russian academician Vladimir Obruchev published his *Plutonia*, presenting a lost subterranean world north of Alaska, rather like Verne's, and stocked with Jurassic-era dinosaurs like Conan Doyle's. Then the American novelist and Tarzan originator Edgar Rice Burroughs took the borrowing to new heights in *The Land That Time Forgot*, published in book form in 1924. Once again, the hero accepts adventure to impress the woman he loves (like *Journey to the Centre of the Earth* featuring Gräuben, and *The Lost World*'s Gladys), except this time her name is Lys La Rue. Once again, a secret land is filled with rampaging dinosaurs. Rudyard Kipling gave the Tarzan writer a backhanded compliment when he wrote about fictional animals: 'My *Jungle Books* begat Zoos of them. But the genius of all the genii was one who wrote a series called *Tarzan of the Apes*. I read it, but regret I never saw it on the films, where it rages most successfully. He had "jazzed" the motif of the *Jungle Books* and, I imagine, had thoroughly enjoyed himself. He was reported to have said that he wanted to find out how bad a book he could write and "get away with", which is a legitimate ambition.'

Now Hollywood got into the act with the immortal 1933 film *King Kong*. Jungle films such as *Tarzan of the Apes* and *Stark Mad* had been popular, and then Conan Doyle's *The Lost World* was successfully filmed in 1925 using pioneering stop-motion special effects by Willis O'Brien to realise the prehistoric monsters. Once again, a range of creatures is seen, from flying pteranodons to a tyrannosaurus. A captured brontosaurus is taken back to London, causes Tower Bridge to collapse and swims off down the Thames. Audiences clearly had an appetite for more of this stuff and in *King Kong* they got it in spades.

King Kong was released on 2 March 1933 to greedy anticipation. The film features a frightening giant ape that falls in love with Ann, a beautiful young woman (actress Fay Wray) whom he tries to possess. The special effects were so horrifying that the audiences screamed and screamed in their seats. The film has been ranked as the greatest horror film of all time by the Rotten Tomatoes site. It begins with a ship chartered by a wildlife film-maker heading for a secret tropical destination. There is the usual band of hardy characters, but this time they take the love-interest Ann with them. The destination is revealed to be Skull Island, where there is rumoured to exist a giant ape. On arrival, the local villagers kidnap Ann, tie her to an altar and offer her as sacrifice to King Kong, the giant ape, who duly turns up but falls in love with her. Kong releases her and carries her off to his jungle lair. The band of adventurers set out to rescue Ann and build a raft on which to cross a lake in the interior of the island. They find to their horror that the island is filled with prehistoric monsters. They are attacked by a stegosaurus which they manage to kill. Then through swirling mist they see the long dark neck looming above them. It disappears, and the men strain their eyes into the gloom. Suddenly, it attacks again and the raft is capsized, throwing the men into the water. The creature seizes some of the men and kills them. Those that survive swim to the shore, climb out of the water and think they're safe: after all, it's a water monster, isn't it? To their horror, the creature lumbers out of the water and pursues the men across the screen from left to right. It isn't a water-bound plesiosaur, it's more like a land-trampling diplodocus.

Freeze the film! For this moment exactly replicates George Spicer's sighting of the Loch Ness monster in 1933, just weeks after the release of the film in London. Daniel Loxton* demonstrates that both Spicer's verbal description and the drawing he oversaw correspond directly with the scene from the film. Just as Spicer's beast 'seemed to have a long neck which moved up and down, in the manner of a scenic railway, and the body was

* Loxton and Prothero, op. cit.

fairly big, with a high back,' so did the film's diplodocus. Just as the film's monster had a dirty grey skin, so too did Spicer's: 'The creature was of a loathsome-looking greyish colour, like a dirty elephant or a rhinoceros.' And just as George Spicer 'saw no indications of any legs, or of a tail', so too did the film-makers hide the legs of their monster behind bushes to make their animation easier. Finally, Spicer's lamb hanging from the monster's mouth exactly replicates the man hanging from the mouth of the *King Kong* film's diplodocus when it snatches him out of a tree.

This may seem far-fetched, but Loxton explains that he wasn't the first to notice the strange correspondences between the film and the sighting. While discussing his story with George Spicer, his first interlocutor Rupert Gould had raised the subject of the film: 'I happened to refer to the diplodocus-like dinosaur in *King Kong*: a film which I discovered we had both seen. He told me that the creature he had seen much resembled this, except in his case no legs were visible, while the neck was much larger and more visible.' So Spicer had seen *King Kong* just weeks before his Scottish tour where he sees a monster that exactly replicates one in the film.

It is incontrovertible that the birth of the Loch Ness monster happened at the same time as the release of the *King Kong* film in London on 10 April 1933: the sighting by the Mackays of the disturbance in the loch occurred just four days later, and Spicer's sighting came just weeks after the release. Is it too much of a coincidence that the beginning of the 'long-necked' sightings should also correspond with a similar depiction in a popular film?

Loxton does not claim to be particularly original in this insight, although he argues it closely in his book. He refers to an e-mail from a fellow researcher, Adrian Shine, whom he quotes: 'I believe personally that *King Kong* was the main influence behind the "Jurassic Park" hypothesis at Loch Ness

. . . Before Spicer's sighting there were no long-neck reports at all, and it was the long neck that was so critical.'

Loxton then refers to the positive feedback loop that investigators of paranormal happenings see again and again: legends feed into popular entertainment which feeds into paranormal belief which feeds round again, escalating all the time. This was particularly evident at Loch Ness, where the Ealing Studios feature film, *The Secret of the Loch*, was released less than a year after the Spicers' eventful drive.

So what did George Spicer and his wife really see? Modern research tells us humans are prone to apophenia, or seeing patterns within random data. Car drivers at night might see a bush suddenly appear as a pedestrian. We have also learned in recent years that eyewitnesses are notoriously unreliable, and the so-called 'forgetting curve' starts within twenty minutes.* A tight group of deer crossing the road, half-seenthen re-imagined as a monster like the one seen recently in the *King Kong* film, seems more likely than a surviving plesiosaur. This would explain the movement being described as 'in a series of jerks'. While researching for this book, I recently drove along the same stretch of road, which is narrow and heavily wooded on either side. The deer hypothesis seemed highly likely.

If Loch Ness monster supporters take issue with the 'it all came from the *King Kong* film' theory, then let's carry on through the evidence adduced by believers and examine it carefully.

The Marmaduke Wetherell footprints

The *Daily Mail* sent Marmaduke Wetherell, whom they described as a big-game hunter, to search for evidence of the Loch Ness monster. With impressive speed, Wetherell said he had discovered the monster's footprints and had even taken plaster casts

* M. P. Gerrie, M. Garry and E. F. Loftus, *Psychology and Law: An Empirical Perspective* (Guilford Press, 2005).

of them. He said they had been made by something like a hippopotamus, which was half right. The paper splashed the story under the headline: 'Monster of Loch Ness Is Not Legend But a Fact', and the plaster casts were sent to the Natural History Museum where they were examined by the Head of the Department of Zoology.

The first feature of the plaster casts that the experts noted was that all the footprints were made by the same foot. Was Nessie hopping on one leg? Further work at the museum led to their conclusion that the footprints were indeed those of a hippopotamus: after comparing the casts with those of a live hippo at London Zoo, the museum concluded that the impressions had been made by a dried, mounted specimen, possibly an umbrella stand.

Rival newspapers enjoyed the *Daily Mail*'s discomfort, but the paper, nothing daunted, retorted with the headline: 'Monster Mystery Deepens.' However, Wetherell was dismissed and publicly humiliated. The BBC interview was conducted by Peter Fleming (the adventurous brother of James Bond creator, Ian Fleming). In *The Spectator*,* he described his encounter with Wetherell and his assistant: 'For some strange reason I was then doing a short tour of duty at the BBC, and it fell to my lot to "produce" this pair of (as even I could see) transparent rogues.' Pilt (as he calls Wetherell) was 'a dense, fruity pachydermatous man in pepper-and-salt tweeds; Down (as he calls the assistant) was the brains of the enterprise.' In this, Fleming was possibly the first BBC producer to use a fruit cake (or perhaps a Scottish clootie dumpling) to insult a contributor. It turned out that Wetherell was a British–South African part-time actor and director of mediocre films, an eccentric but likeable rogue and another attention seeker. He left the *Daily Mail*'s employ humiliated, angry – and vengeful.

---

* *The Spectator*, 5 April 1957.

The Surgeon's Photograph

Undaunted by the derision from other newspapers over the hippo's-foot debacle, just four months later, on 21 April 1934, the *Daily Mail* published their 'Surgeon's Photograph' of the Loch Ness monster itself, allegedly taken by that most reliable of witnesses, the London gynaecologist Robert Kenneth Wilson. The blurry black-and-white photograph shows the head and neck of an undoubted Jurassic-era plesiosaur and it has come to be the archetype of the Loch Ness monster. It was chosen by the US magazine, *Time*, in 2016 as one of the 100 most influential images of all time.

However, it's a fake. The *Sunday Telegraph* outed the forgers of the Surgeon's Photograph as hoaxers on 7 December 1975. For some curious reason, the writer, Philip Purser, of 'Sunday Morning with Mandrake' fame, failed to connect his revelation with the well-known photograph itself, and so the full story did not appear until 1999 when authors David Martin and Alastair Boyd published *Nessie: The Surgeon's Photograph Exposed*.* In it they reveal a tale of treachery, humiliation, cunning and revenge fit for *Macbeth*: 'It's not a genuine photograph. It's a load of codswallop and always has been.' The

---

* D. Martin and A. Boyd, *Nessie: The Surgeon's Photograph Exposed* (Thorne, 1999).

speaker was Christian Spurling, Marmaduke Wetherell's son-in-law. The author David Martin had tracked him down through the *Sunday Telegraph* article, and met him at his home in February 1991. It turned out that the hippo's footprints had been made by a stuffed hippo foot, into which a silver cigarette ashtray had been mounted. This was still in the family's possession. Wetherell, filled with rage at his public humiliation by the *Daily Mail*, decided to have his revenge. 'All right, we'll give them their monster!' he was reported to have said.

Christian Spurling, a sculptor, modified a toy submarine bought at Woolworth's department store by Wetherell's son, Ian. He added a long neck and head modelled out of linseed oil putty. This took eight days to dry. After tests on a pond, the hoaxers travelled to Loch Ness and launched their model monster near what is now the Alsaigh Youth Hostel. A friend, Maurice Chambers, an insurance agent, came along for the fun. They took a few shots and then they heard the ominous crunch of a water bailiff's feet approaching on the gravel beach. To avoid detection, Marmaduke Wetherell stuck his foot on the model to sink it and it is 'presumably still somewhere in Loch Ness'. Chambers passed the negatives on to the surgeon Wilson, who had said that he enjoyed a good practical joke. He had them developed by Ogston's, an Inverness chemist, and sold the first photo to the *Daily Mail*. The rest is history.

Or is it? In the original *Sunday Telegraph* article, Ian Wetherell told how his fellow conspirators: 'found an inlet where the tiny ripples would look like full-size waves out on the loch, and with the actual scenery in the background. Then it was just a matter of winding up the sub and getting it to dive just below the surface so the neck and head drew a proper little V in the water.' However, in the photograph the model is clearly stopped in the water, with no V. In the uncropped version of the photograph, still held by the *Daily Mail*, it is clear that the scale of the model is tiny compared to the waves, so the picture editor surely must have realised that the paper was being defrauded. Furthermore, if the whole plot was intended to embarrass the *Daily Mail*, why didn't Wetherell make the most of it in the five years he had left to live? Loch Ness monster evidence, just like yeti and Bigfoot evidence, seems to disappear down endless Alice in Wonderland rabbit holes. In the end, though, the Surgeon's Photograph turned out to be a well-per-petrated hoax.

The monster only visits occasionally

This theory proposes that Nessie swims up underwater passages connected with the sea and appears just long enough to provoke more searches. Then she returns to her natural habitat, the North Sea. The only problem is this: the loch is 52 feet above sea level, so Nessie would be shot down the tunnel like a bullet out of a rifle. And then the loch would empty into the sea.

It's a Greenland shark

This extraordinary creature, as long as a great white shark, lives at great depths in extreme cold and is the longest living vertebrate, coming to maturity at a sprightly 150 years old, and living to at least 270 years, and possibly up to 500 years. This is because it lives down near the seabed at near-freezing temper-atures of around 2 degrees Celcius and as a result has a slow metabolism. For this reason, it is the slowest moving of the sharks. It can reach up to 24 feet in length and more than 3,100 lb in weight. It eats fish, seals, and just possibly humans. In 2013, Icon Films produced a *River Monsters* programme featuring the extreme angler Jeremy Wade in which he suggests that the Greenland shark could be the cause of non-'long-necked' Loch Ness sightings, as its rounded body and small dorsal fins make it appear like an upturned boat, like many sightings (which are probably of upturned boats). This species usually lives down to 7,200 feet in sea water, although these sharks have been observed in the St Lawrence River. Two relevant sightings have been reported: in 1940 a wildlife officer told how he was stalked by a Greenland shark while walking on pack ice at Basques Island in the St Lawrence in behaviour consistent with a seal predator, and in 1859 a human leg was reportedly found in the stomach of a Greenland shark caught at Pond Inlet, on Baffin Island.*

Some scientists maintain that Greenland sharks do not have the ability to osmo-regulate, meaning that, like most saltwater fish, they cannot live in freshwater. If a specimen did somehow get into the freshwater Loch Ness, it would hyper-hydrate and die within hours from electrolyte imbalance. This does not accord with the St Lawrence River sightings, though. Furthermore, it swims exceedingly slowly and could not make it up the River Ness due to the shallow rapids. Waiting patiently in the locks of the canal, a yachtsman might just notice a Greenland shark accompanying their boat. Little is known about this shark, but there is a faint possibility that one might have found its way into Loch Ness. It is not known for crossing roads, though; nor for having a long neck.

It's an elephant

In 2006, there was a suggestion that travelling circuses might allow elephants to bathe in Loch Ness, with the trunk of the entirely submerged elephant perceived as the head and neck. A quick look at a picture of a swimming elephant will show that the 'head' of the monster is missing. No sensible elephant, or plesiosaur for that matter, would get into the loch, which is extremely cold.

---

* See http://www.geerg.ca/greenland-shark.html.

It's a plesiosaur

After the Spicers' sighting, it was suggested that the monster was the plesiosaur, which had been thought to have become extinct during the Cretaceous–Paleogene extinction event. It is unclear whether plesiosaurs were cold-blooded reptiles requiring warm tropical waters; if so, Loch Ness is too cold. If the plesiosaurs were warm-blooded, they would require a food supply beyond the 22 tonnes of biomass provided by Loch Ness: a predator could be expected to weigh no more than a tenth of this, around 2.2 tonnes. So where is the rest of Nessie's family? In his book *Why Big Fierce Animals Are Rare*, Paul Colinvaux explains that it is the calorie supply available in a habitat that limits the numbers of big predators at the top of what is called the Eltonian pyramid. 'At each successive level of the pyramid, the animals have to make do with the fuel (food) that can be extorted from the level below . . . energy (is) degraded step by step as it flows down food chains, losing its power to do work and pouring steadily away to the sink of heat. The grand pattern of life that Elton had seen on Spitzbergen . . . was clearly and directly a consequence of the second law of thermodynamics.'*

Furthermore, in October 2006 the *New Scientist* ran an article entitled 'Why the Loch Ness Monster Is No Plesiosaur.' In it, Leslie Noè, of the Sedgwick Museum in Cambridge, wrote: 'The osteology of the neck makes it absolutely certain that the plesiosaur could not lift its head up swan-like out of the water.' Also, Loch Ness is only about 10,000 years old, dating to the end of the last ice age. Before then it was frozen, with thousands of feet of ice above it for around 20,000 years, so any air-breathing creature would expire. Lastly, an air-breathing creature such as the plesiosaur would need to surface regularly and would therefore be easily spotted.

---

* P. Colinvaux, *Why Big Fierce Animals Are Rare: An Ecologist's Perspective* (Allen and Unwin, 1978).

It's a tree

In the 1980s, the *New Scientist* ran a series of articles about Loch Ness,[*] and in one of them Maurice Burton, the enviably titled Curator of Sponges at the British Museum of Natural History, suggested that sightings of the monster could be caused by decaying pine trees lying on the bottom of the loch. He suggested that gases generated by the process of decay could not escape initially because of a plug of resin on the broken stump. The rise in pressure would eventually burst this seal and the trunk of the tree would be propelled to the surface in the manner of a breaching whale, then cruise along the surface for a while before sinking again. According to the zoologist and popular science writer Burton, the shape of these decaying trees, with their arching roots, could easily resemble the descriptions of the monster. This ingenious suggestion is one of my favourites. Why not?

It's a mis-identification

In 1852, the *Inverness Courier* had reported that a large group of people had gathered on the loch side ready to repel a couple of 'sea serpents' that had been observed swimming steadily towards them across the loch. As the two creatures approached the shore, one elderly man exclaimed and put down his gun. Then two Highland ponies scrambled ashore, having swum from the opposite shore. If local people can be deceived like this, then diving birds, otters, eels and swimming deer could all be responsible for sightings made by people unfamiliar with the surroundings. Furthermore, the newspaper referred to the legends of 'kelpies', or the phantom water horses that were generic to all Scottish bodies of water. These legends served a practical purpose of keeping children away from

[*] M. Burton, 'The Loch Ness Saga,' *New Scientist*, 1982, 24 June, p. 872;1 July, pp. 41–42; 8 July, pp. 112–113.

dangerous stretches of water and perhaps warning young women about the perils of handsome young men. The newspaper did not refer to a specific Loch Ness monster.

What about a giant catfish?

Apple maps appeared to show a giant catfish cruising underwater. A little adjustment of highlighting shows the image to be that of a vessel transiting the loch.*

It's the tourist industry

In 2013, the *Inverness Courier* reported on a celebration on the loch commemorating 80 years since Aldie Mackay's sighting. Willie Cameron, of Loch Ness Marketing, said: 'The report in the *Courier* about the strange spectacle in Loch Ness started the ball rolling and the rest is history. From the start of tourism, to my mind, there is no greater story in the UK – effectively creating a tourist industry in the middle of nowhere. It has become a worldwide phenomenon attracting a million tourists a year and worth £25 million to the local economy.'

Then, on 14 April 2013, the BBC website ran a story: 'Loch Ness Monster: Is Nessie Just a Tourist Conspiracy?' It quoted Dr Charles Paxton, a research fellow and statistical ecologist at St Andrew's University, who had sifted through the 1,000 recorded sightings. He pointed out that a sizeable number came from café and hotel proprietors, including Mrs Mackay herself.

Malcolm Roughhead, chief executive of Visit Scotland, said it all: 'It would be difficult to overstate the importance of Mrs Mackay's sighting of the Loch Ness Monster to tourism in Scotland. There are few places in the world where people haven't heard of the phenomenon and the 80th anniversary is sure to

---

* See https://www.metabunk.org/debunked-photo-of-nessie-in-apple-maps-satellite-image-of-loch-ness-boat.t3474/.

spark renewed interest and encourage even more visitors to come here and see if they can spot Nessie for themselves.'

Since the 1930s, when the legend gained currency, guesthouse owners and bar-owners have been deeply grateful for the hordes of sightseers. This was summarised by a headline from the *Express* on 24 April 1934: 'Monster Bobs Up Again. Hotels Doing Fine.'

CHAPTER TEN

*A brontosaurus babe. . .one who stops rivers. . .a German
baron. . .Sanderson again. . .creationists. . .Destination:
Untruth. . .the Giant of Kandahar. . .the Devil's Footprints. . .a
balloon. . .Ockham's Razor. . .Bertrand Russell's teapot. . .flying
saucers. . .Crop circles. . .a Devil Mower. . .hoaxers and the
hoaxed. . .the power of belief. . .UFOs.*

Now we turn to a darker chapter in the curious discipline of
cryptozoology: the Mokèlé-mbèmbé. The hunt for this beast
reveals some of the dangers of seeking cryptids.

Mokèlé-mbèmbé is a legendary elephant-sized surviving
dinosaur resembling a sauropod which is supposed to live in
the lakes of the Congo River basin. Cryptozoologists say it has
the long neck, long tail, small head and four stout legs familiar
to us from imagined pictures of dinosaurs such as the brontosaurus (the old name for apatosaurus). Sauropods lived in
the Triassic and Jurassic periods around 200 to 150 million
years ago and were remarkable for their huge size: supersaurus
was no less than 108 feet long, which is around the length of
three buses parked nose to tail. What could be more wonderful
than finding one of these creatures still living in an African
swamp?

Fortunately, sauropods were vegetarian, but they could still cause immense damage just by sitting around. Mokèlé-mbèmbé means 'The one who stops rivers' in the local Lingala language. And Mokèlé-mbèmbé is still supposed to live in Lake Tele, a near-circular body of water about 3.5 miles across, located in the equatorial forest of Central Africa. All the early signs of a mystery beast such as the gorilla or yeti are there: legends about a spectacular creature, eyewitness accounts from local people, and footprints. The French missionary Liévin-Bonaventure Proyart claimed to have seen gigantic prints in the region. In his 1776 book, *History of Loango, Kakonga, and Other Kingdoms in Africa*, he wrote that the creature that made them 'must have been monstrous: the marks of the claws were noted on the ground, and these formed a print about three feet in circumference.'

Then an eyewitness report came in from a Westerner elsewhere in Africa. A German officer named Baron Ludwig Freiherr von Stein zu Lausnitz was said by the cryptozoologist Willy Ley to have seen a brontosaurus-like creature in 1914 when he was exploring the interior of Cameroon:

The animal is said to be of a brownish-grey colour with a smooth skin, its size is approximately that of an elephant; at least that of a hippopotamus. It is said to have a long and very flexible neck and only one tooth but a very long one; some say it is a horn. A few spoke about a long muscular tail like that of an alligator. Canoes coming near it are said to be doomed; the animal is said to attack the vessels at once and to kill the crews but without eating the bodies. The creature is said to live in the caves that have been washed out by the river in the clay of the shores at the sharp bends. It is said to climb the shores even in daytime in search of food; its diet is said to be entirely vegetable.

Then, in 1919, *The Times* in London ran a story from a Mr LePage in the Belgian Congo, who reported a 24-foot-long

235

creature with a huge pointed snout, tusks and a horn on the end of the nose. Apparently, it had horse-like front hooves, with cloven back hooves. It had apparently rampaged through the village of Fungwrame, killing native villagers. This was followed up with another report from a big-game hunter in the same area, a Mr Gapelle, who saw a similar animal, this time with scales and a kangaroo-like tail. He fired shots at it and the beast dived deep into a swamp.

Readers were agog: this was Conan Doyle's *Lost World* come to life. Together with murderous attacks on humans! Then Ivan Sanderson claimed to have seen one of these murderous beasts on an expedition to Cameroon in 1932. He spotted a huge creature's back, as big as a hippopotamus, breaking the surface of a lake. Filled with trepidation, he then followed back into the jungle 'vast, hippo-like tracks', which he said could be identified as those of a sauropod, and eventually found a large fruit with huge toothmarks grazed into it.

Roy Mackal, an American zoologist who had become fascinated by the Loch Ness monster, also got involved. Mackal was the third pillar of the cryptozoological establishment along with Ivan Sanderson and Bernard Heuvelmans, and he helped to found the International Society for Cryptozoology, which was created in 1982 at the National Museum of Natural History in Washington DC, in the hope of bringing a degree of respectability to a pseudoscience. Mackal travelled to the Congo, and although he never saw the creature himself, he collected numerous eyewitness accounts and recorded them in his book, *A Living Dinosaur? In Search of Mokèlé-Mbèmbé.*

These accounts kicked off the stories of dinosaurs in African swamps that are still current. Eventually, the film industry became interested, and in 1985 the Hollywood film *Baby: Secret of the Lost Legend* told the story of a cute baby brontosaurus and its parents found by a palaeontologist searching for the Mokèlé-mbèmbé in Central Africa. This film was not a success but it helped to pave the way for the blockbuster *Jurassic Park* series. Creationists, in particular, seemed fascinated by the stories and sent repeated expeditions to the Congo to try to produce evidence for the creature. No specimen has yet been produced.

Can we do any better? A cursory look at the evidence throws up a few problems:

1. Baron Ludwig Freiherr von Stein zu Lausnitz's report should be significant as it is the first account. However, there is no original document provided and all we have is a translation from Ley. Also, it becomes obvious that this is a third-hand report, with a great deal of 'said to be' and 'some say' and 'it is said to'.

2. The LePage and Gapelle accounts do not describe sauropods, and the actions they describe are set over a thousand miles from where explorers now seek the Mokèlé-mbèmbé. It turns out that David LePage was a notorious local joker who told his story to a missionary who swallowed it whole. Gapelle is a partial anagram of LePage and was a name invented by a second joker. These stories caused much amusement in the towns concerned. However, these corrections were not given any prominence by the press and before long the first of many expeditions set out to find the monster. Newspapers soon reported that the big-game hunter Captain Lester Stevens had left with his dog Laddie in search of the giant reptile, which he believed lived in a subterranean lake.

3. Ivan Sanderson is not a credible witness. His colleague Roy Mackal saw no creature and produced no specimen.

4. Dozens of expeditions have set out in pursuit of this creature, but so far no specimen has been produced.

University of Queensland scientists Diana Fisher and Simon Blomberg made a study of thought-to-be extinct animals and found that species that still survived were often found after three to six searches, but if more than eleven searches were made with no result, as is the case for the Tasmanian tiger and Yangtze river dolphin, then the species is probably *really* extinct.

5. There is no trace of sauropods in the fossil record in the 65 million years since the mass extinction that wiped them out.

6. The imagined creature is based on an outdated idea of what sauropods were. The old nineteenth-century reconstructions of sauropods as swamp-dwelling animals have proved to be incorrect. So too were the imaginative paintings of Charles R. Knight and Zdeněk Burian. Recent research has established that sauropods' bodies were filled with air sacs which would have made it impossible for them to submerge, and made them prone to instability on the surface. Indeed, they have been described as 'tipsy punters' by one palaeontologist.

What is disturbing is that some creationists interested in cryptozoology have latched onto the Mokèlé-mbèmbé as proof of their belief that the earth is only a few thousand years old. They believe that finding such a creature would disprove evolutionary theory. The finding of such a living animal would not do any such thing, of course; it would just show that one particular species survived longer than was thought. The enormous fossil record would continue to show the earth as billions of years old. One such creationist is William Gibbons, who has undertaken several searches for the creature. He writes:

In case there is any doubt about our motivation for this work, I should tell you that we feel that the discovery of any of these creatures will be an earthshaking event. It is our belief that eliminating common objections regarding why the Bible can't be trusted, and demonstrating the historical and scientific accuracy of Scripture will naturally lead people to the next logical step in thinking: If the Bible is true in other respects, what does that tell us about its spiritual ramifications? When the evolution hypothesis was proposed 150 years ago, it was with the expressed intent of destroying the church and Christianity along with it. If a wrench of this kind could be thrown into the machinery of evolution it would go a long way toward turning people back to the only real truth, the Word of God.*

Gibbon's assertion is that evolution theory was developed with the expressed intent of destroying Christianity. This is untrue. In fact, it was proposed as a way to explain the observed facts about the earth and the life on it. Charles Darwin was well aware of the potential criticisms of his theory, as in 1879 he stated that he had never been an atheist in the sense of denying the existence of a god, and that generally 'an Agnostic would be the more correct description of my state of mind'. So how did he see science modifying belief in a god? 'Science has nothing to do with Christ, except insofar as the habit of scientific research makes a man cautious in admitting evidence. For myself, I do not believe that there ever has been any revelation. As for a future life, every man must judge for himself between conflicting vague probabilities.'

However, there was a family of God's creatures that troubled Darwin. This was the parasitoid wasp, *Ichneumonidae*. These insects lay their eggs inside the bodies of their victims, the larvae or pupae of butterflies and moths. After hatching, the ichneumonid larva eats its host alive. Darwin found this parasitic behaviour inconsistent with the theory of a world created by a benevolent god. He wrote in 1860:

*   Loxton and Prothero, op. cit.

I own that I cannot see as plainly as others do, and as I should wish to do, evidence of design and beneficence on all sides of us. There seems to me too much misery in the world. I cannot persuade myself that a beneficent and omnipotent God would have designedly created the *Ichneumonidae* with the express intention of their feeding within the living bodies of Caterpillars, or that a cat should play with mice.*

William Gibbons has made several expeditions in the attempt to prove the existence of the Mokèlé-mbèmbé, sometimes accompanied by a crew from the cryptozoological TV series *Monsterquest*. These programmes feature a dark, spooky style of direction, intercutting simulations of encounters with mysterious beasts with dubious eyewitness accounts and actuality of 'monster hunters' slashing through jungles and panting over mountains. Cable TV shows like this and *Destination Truth* get high ratings and serve to confirm the beliefs of those in the audience who want to believe in the unbelievable. An irony is contained in their titles: *Monsterquest* never finds a monster and *Destination Truth* never arrives at the truth, just as *Finding Bigfoot* never finds Bigfoot.

In March 2009, an episode of *Monsterquest* was filmed in Cameroon with Gibbons which showed a few fuzzy images from a sonar search which were claimed to be a Mokèlé-mbèmbé. Some holes in the ground were supposed to be footprints and then the team dug around a hole in a riverbank, claiming that it was a burrow and that the Mokèlé-mbèmbé was inside. No attempt was made to dig the creature out. It turns out that none of the 'explorers' had any training in zoology. Gibbons is not a zoologist, but holds a degree in religious education from a seminary. Gibbons' companion on the expedition was also a creationist.

---

* In a letter to the American naturalist, Asa Gray.

Should we worry about a bit of cable TV fun? Well, yes. The problem with the creationist cryptozoologists is that they are anti-scientific and seek to overturn all our advances in knowledge since the Enlightenment, in an attempt to justify their narrow belief in the literal truth of Genesis. In his excellent and disturbing study of cryptozoology, Darren Naish makes a strong point:

> While some mystery animal researchers are comfortable with the idea that creationists aim to contribute to cryptozoology, it's important to note that creationism is not consistent with the field, since cryptozoology strives to operate within scientific principles and be partner to mainstream zoology. Indeed, creationists often express their desire to erode and destroy the scientific community and the way science operates as a process, their aim being to move us into an era in which unquestioned faith in a deity is paramount and ideas about deep geological time and evolution are rejected and abandoned in favour of religious dogma. In other words, it should be clear to anyone who cares about science and a scientific view of the world – the view in which advances in medicine, technology, biology, ecology and so on are integral to our way of life and interaction with our biosphere – that the creationist agenda is biased and dangerous. These people are not our friends, and they seek to usurp us.[*]

What can we conclude then about the fabulous Mokèlé-mbèmbé? The author Redmond O'Hanlon returned from his own 1996 failed expedition to find the creature, convinced that witnesses must have mistaken wild elephants crossing rivers with their trunk in the air for a prehistoric dinosaur.

[*] D. Naish, *Hunting Monsters: Cryptozoology and the Reality Behind the Myths* (Arcturus, 2016).

This seems to have the ring of truth. Meanwhile let's wait for a body.

The red-headed Giant of Kandahar

In 2016, a number of websites dedicated to conspiracy theories began claiming that an American Special Forces soldier named Dan serving in Kandahar, Afghanistan in 2002 was killed by a 12-foot-tall sword-wielding red-haired giant from the Old Testament which he had disturbed in a cave. After the soldier was killed, the giant creature was itself shot dead by US forces before being spirited away on a military aircraft. The giant weighed 1,100 lb and stank like rotting corpses or a skunk. This story was promoted by creationists, who claimed the giant was a Nephilim, a race described in the Book of Genesis as offspring of gods and human women who inhabited Canaan at the time of Israelite conquest:

> When people began to multiply on the face of the ground, and daughters were born to them, the sons of God saw that they were fair; and they took wives for themselves of all that they chose. Then the Lord said, 'My spirit shall not abide in mortals forever, for they are flesh; their days shall be one hundred twenty years.' The Nephilim were on the earth in those days – and also afterward – when the sons of God went in to the daughters of humans, who bore children to them. These were the heroes that were of old, warriors of renown.*

These Nephilim are claimed to be giants: 'There we saw the Nephilim; and to ourselves we seemed like grasshoppers, and so we seemed to them.'†

---

* Genesis 6: 1–4, *The Bible, New Revised Standard Version.*

† Numbers 13: 1–2; 21: 27–28, 32–33, *The Bible, New Revised Standard Version.*

The US Department of Defense said they had no record of such an incident. The only soldier with the first name Dan or Daniel who died in Kandahar in 2002 was killed with three others in an accident involving the disposal of explosives.

It turns out that the story appears to have originated with a Mr L.A. Marzulli, a blogger and film-maker who attempts to prove the truth of biblical creatures and prophecies. He posted an episode of his *Watchers* series on YouTube in August 2016 in which he claims to interview a soldier who allegedly witnessed the incident. The expensive use of cartoon animation and footage suggests that there is big money behind this series. Is it likely that 12-foot-tall giants have been living undetected in Afghanistan? No. Does this tale prove the literal truth of the Bible? No, it does not.

Grendel

The epic Old English poem *Beowulf*, written about events during the sixth century, describes a monster far more dreadful than the Giant of Kandahar. The poem is set somewhere in Scandinavia, probably the island of Zealand, at the mead hall of Heorot. This hall is a besieged stronghold of human solidarity set in the poem's desolate landscape of moors and bogs. Outside stalks a monster beyond all horror, and every night he bursts in and eats the kinsmen of Hrothgar, the king of the Danes.

J. R. R. Tolkien was the first academic to take the poem on its own literary merits rather than treat it as an historical document, and in his seminal study of the poem *Beowulf: The Monsters and the Critics* he argued that the theme was mortality: the warrior hero Beowulf defeats the monster Grendel and his mother in the first half, then in old age he himself is killed by a dragon: 'man at war with the hostile world, and his inevitable overthrow in Time'.

The author is unknown but is clearly a skilled and stylish writer. As in Henry James's *Turn of the Screw*, the ghost-monster is never overtly described, leaving the reader to imagine their own particular nightmare. All we know is that Grendel is an unnatural birth, a huge man-like monster whose severed head is so large it has to be carried by four men. In his own translation of the poem, the Nobel laureate poet Seamus Heaney describes how Grendel has been killing and eating the Danes, and so Beowulf, the hero of the Geats, volunteers to help Hrothgar by sleeping in the mead hall and waiting for the beast to appear.

Beowulf and Grendel, locked together, stagger through the dark hall, crashing through mead-benches and scattering gold fittings. With a huge effort, Beowulf tears Grendel's arm off and the monster escapes, dying, into the night. The Danes inspect the severed arm in horror.

Beowulf collects his men and together they track the beast back to his lair by a trail of blood laid across the feculent bog. Grendel dies beneath the murky waters, and so Beowulf and his men return to Heorot. That night, Grendel's mother, enraged by her son's death, comes to the hall and kills and decapitates Æschere, who is Hrothgar's most trusted advisor. Beowulf returns to the lair, swims underwater and attacks Grendel's mother, slicing off her head. Both monsters are now dead.

Later, in old age, Beowulf's kingdom of Geatland (in modern Sweden) is threatened by a dragon. Beowulf manages to kill the creature, but is himself mortally wounded. After his death, he is cremated in a great pyre and buried in a barrow visible from the sea.

There are clues that suggest that *Beowulf* may have been handed down through an oral tradition of illiterate bards and then transcribed by a Christian monk with one foot in a pagan past. If so, one can imagine the listeners of the earlier versions gripped by the descriptions of the monsters, and believing just as implicitly in them as Tibetan children still believe in the stories of the yeti.

Grendel and his mother are trolls, supernatural beings that live in specific natural features such as mountains, bogs and caves. They are ugly, slow-witted and dangerous to humans and generally live together in father-daughter or mother-son pairings. This might suggest they are a cautionary myth warning of the defective offspring of incest. However, trolls turn to stone on exposure to sunlight. In the folktales, two facts give them away to humans: they are unknown to the person meeting them, and they are not Christianised. As in *Beowulf,* these tales emphasised the cleansing of the mead hall of trolls, not just the conflict with them.

In 2011, the Norwegian dark fantasy film *Trollhunter* ended with a clip of the former Norwegian Prime Minister Jens Stoltenberg speaking at a press conference about power lines. His remark about an oil and gas field off the coast of Norway called the Troll Field was edited to make him appear to admit to a belief in the existence of trolls. Apparently, he doesn't. Really.

The Devil's Footprints

On 9 February 1855, residents of Devon in southwest England awoke to an extraordinary sight. In the heavy snow outside their homes, a trail of hoofmarks had appeared overnight, extending over 60 miles. No one had heard a thing. The Devil's Footprints were so named as they seemed to have been made by a pair of cloven hooves. The local newspaper reported:

> It appears on Thursday night last, there was a very heavy snowfall in the neighbourhood of Exeter and the South of Devon. On the following morning the inhabitants of the above towns were surprised at discovering the footmarks of some strange and mysterious animal endowed with the power of ubiquity, as the footprints were to be

seen in all kinds of unaccountable places – on the tops of houses and narrow walls, in gardens and courtyards, enclosed by high walls and palings, as well in open fields.

Over the years, various explanations have been put forward, the most ingenious being that of author Geoffrey Household, who proposed that an experimental balloon released by mistake from Devonport Dockyard had left the mysterious tracks by trailing two U-shaped shackles on the end of its mooring ropes. His evidence for this was one Major Carter, whose grandfather was working at Devonport at the time. Carter claimed that the incident had been suppressed because the balloon had smashed the windows of a number of conservatories and greenhouses.

In the spirit of enquiry, I decided to test this theory, and in 2004 I got together a meteorological balloon filled with helium, some string and a bunch of shackles. Not having any snow, I tried this rig out on the sandy beach on the island of Rum where we had been flying under a rig made of 56 of these balloons. After much experimentation, I found that in fact a single U-shaped shackle left the best impressions, the wind acting on the balloon in a hopping manner, and the tracks climbing up sandy dunes. This seemed a likely enough explanation.

So were the Devil's Footprints made by a balloon, or do we have to create a supernatural being? For advice, I turned to William of Ockham, an English monk who lived between 1288 and 1347, and his famous problem-solving principle, Ockham's razor: *Entia non sunt multiplicanda sine necessitate*, or 'One should not multiply entities beyond necessity.'

Ockham formulates it thus: 'For nothing ought to be posited without a reason given, unless it is self-evident or known by experience or proved by the authority of Sacred Scripture.' In other words, the simplest explanation is the best, because it involves the least number of assumptions. This is sometimes known as the Law of Parsimony. Medics have a version of this: 'When you hear hoof beats in the night, think of horses, not zebras.'

This is not what cryptozoologists do. They discard simple explanations such as bears or wolves, and invent large, hairy primates unknown to science because these support their hopes.

Bear in mind that another rule of logic, 'The exception proves the rule', is often misinterpreted: the presence of a specific exception establishes ('proves') that a general rule exists. So a sign saying 'Yeti footprints prohibited in Base Camp on Tuesdays' (the exception) proves that yeti footprints *are* allowed there on the other days of the week (the rule). But it doesn't prove that yetis exist. Bigfoot enthusiasts often quote the old saw 'Where there's smoke there's fire' in relation to the countless sightings of Bigfoot footprints. This is a logical fallacy: where there's smoke, there's just smoke.

However, it is very hard to prove a negative: that Satan (or yeti) *didn't* make the Devil's Footprints of 1855. Charles Kingsley put it rather well in *The Water-Babies*, a part-satire written in support of Darwin's *On the Origin of Species:*

'But there are no such things as water-babies'. How do you know that? Have you been there to see? And if you had been there to see, and had seen none, that would not prove that there were none . . . And no one has a right to say that no water-babies exist till they have seen no water-babies existing, which is quite a different thing, mind, from not seeing water-babies.[*]

Philosopher Bertrand Russell pointed this out in another way with his space teapot:

If I were to suggest that between the Earth and Mars there is a china teapot revolving about the sun in an elliptical orbit, nobody would be able to disprove my assertion

[*] C. Kingsley, *The Water-Babies: A Fairy Tale for a Land Baby* (Macmillan, 1863).

provided I were careful to add that the teapot is too small to be revealed even by our most powerful telescopes. But if I were to go on to say that, since my assertion cannot be disproved, it is an intolerable presumption on the part of human reason to doubt it, I should rightly be thought to be talking nonsense. If, however, the existence of such a teapot were affirmed in ancient books, taught as the sacred truth every Sunday, and instilled into the minds of children at school, hesitation to believe in its existence would become a mark of eccentricity and entitle the doubter to the attentions of the psychiatrist in an enlightened age or of the Inquisitor in an earlier time.*

Bertrand Russell's teapot is probably just as real as Satan but just as hard to disprove. As it is virtually impossible to prove a negative, Ockham's Razor suggests that the more simple theory (that a balloon made the tracks) trumps the more complex theory (that the devil made them). But how does this apply to the yeti and Bigfoot? Simply this: photographs of tracks are regularly produced by believers as evidence of the existence of a species of ape unknown to science. However, repeated attempts to find corporeal evidence in the form of a corpse, bones or hair have failed. A breeding population sufficiently large to support a species would surely leave traces, even in the remotest Himalayan vastness. So, are the footprints made by hoaxers or known animals; or do we have to invent a new species to make them, one that has managed to stay completely invisible over the last hundred years?

In a way, life is easy for cryptozoologists: they only have to find one live specimen of a cryptid to disprove the scepticism of mainstream scientists. For example, just one black swan,

---

* B. Russell, 'Is There A God?' *Illustrated Magazine*, 1952. Commissioned but not published.

found in Western Australia in 1697, was enough to disprove the assertion that all swans are white.

In the 1980s, local TV news schedules in Wiltshire and Hampshire were filled with reports of crop circles. There were extraordinary claims for them: they were thought by some to be landing areas for UFOs or maybe messages from Gaia about the state of the world. There were believers in the paranormal who claimed crop circles as evidence for their particular obsession. And every year, self-described Croppies still gather at the Barge Inn, Honeystreet, in Wiltshire to view the latest messages. But there was nothing new about them.

In 1678, a woodcut pamphlet had appeared on the streets of England. It told the story of the first reported crop circle. It is hard to read, but goes like this:

> The Mowing-Devil: Or, Strange NEWS out of Hartfordshire. Being a True Relation of a Farmer, who Bargaining with a poor Mower, about the Cutting down Three Half Acres of Oats upon the Mower's asking too much, the Farmer swore, 'That the Devil should Mow it, rather than He.' And lo it fell out, that that very Night, the Crop of Oats shew'd as if it had been all of a Flame, but next Morning appear'd so neatly Mow'd by the Devil, or some Infernal Spirit, that no Mortal Man was able to do the like. Also, How the said Oats lay now in the Field, and the Owner has not Power to fetch them away.

The wood-chiselling journalist presumably wouldn't have sold quite so many pamphlets if he had depicted the annoyed Mower and his mates holding the lanterns he needed to do

The Mowing-Devil:

Or, Strange NEWS out of

Hartford-shire.

Being a True Relation of a Farmer, who Bargaining with a Poor Mower, about the Cutting down Three Half Acres of Oats, upon the Mower's asking too much, the Farmer swore, That the Devil should Mow it, rather than He. And to it fell out, that that very Night, the Crop of Oats shew'd as if it had been all of a Flame; but next Morning appear'd so neatly Mow'd by the Devil, or some Infernal Spirit, that no Mortal Man was able to do the like. Also, How the said Oats ly now in the Field, and the Owner has not Power to fetch them away.

The accompanying wood-cut clearly showed the Devil at work.

his vandalism. Which brings us to the crop circles of the 1980s.

They usually appeared close to roads, in areas of fairly high human population and near other great circles such as Avebury or Stonehenge. This should have been a clue.

Then, in 1991, two artists, Doug Bower and Dave Chorley, came forward and admitted that they had started the whole thing off in 1976. They had been having a few drinks in the Percy Hobbs pub near Winchester and talking about UFOs. A local journalist on the *Warminster Times* had been reporting on strange sightings over the town which he called 'the Warminster Thing'. So Doug and Dave decided to make some UFO landing sites of their own. Using an iron rod as an anchor, a length of rope and a plank of wood, they created increasingly elaborate, swirling designs. A baseball cap fitted with a ring of wire sighted on a lighted cottage window gave them the straight lines for flying saucer runways:*

> David Chorley: 'We did this for two years . . . and nothing came of it. So we decided then, that what we'll be doing is putting them down in sites right under the view of the general public. So near Winchester, in Hampshire in England, there is a hill called Cheesefoot Head with a great view from a height down into a down. So we put one down there, and it was taken up by Mr Pat Delgado, and from then on it took off.

The two men made a circle in front of journalists, who showed it to the famous ufologist Pat Delgado, who declared it authentic. The pair then stepped forwards and claimed authorship. But by then, everyone was making them. A friend of mine filmed a night-time investigation for Channel 4 in the late 1980s and I buttonholed him the next day: 'So what made them?'

'Young farmers,' was the terse reply.

Crop circles

---

* See http://www.telegraph.co.uk/news/earth/7955868/Crop-circle-conundrum.html.

What is interesting about this tale is that the immense effort expended by the hoaxers was only matched by the immense desire felt by the believers to believe. Croppies still come to the Barge Inn from as far as Belgium, the Netherlands and even Japan to worship the season's circles. In other words, there is a priesthood and a congregation. Even the revelation that humans might have made a particular circle fails to quench the Croppies' religious enthusiasm: human circle-makers are merely channels for a greater force, and some formations are made, of course, by divine intervention. It seems that people just need to believe in monsters.

Humans have always explained the inexplicable in their own terms. During the Enlightenment, when clocks were all the rage, the movement of the planets and indeed the universe was explained in terms of clockwork. The English philosopher Samuel Clarke even postulated a divine Clockmaker:

> The Notion of the World's being a great Machine, going on without the Interposition of God, as a Clock continues to go without the Assistance of a Clockmaker; is the Notion of Materialism and Fate, and tends (under pretence of making God a Supra-mundane Intelligence) to exclude Providence and God's Government in reality out of the World.*

In our own time, Sigmund Freud's theories of the unconscious

---

* E. B. Davis, 'Newton's rejection of the "Newtonian world view": the role of divine will in Newton's natural philosophy,' *Science and Christian Belief*, vol. 3, no. 2, 1981, pp. 103–117. Clarke quotation taken from article.

have been used to explain human behaviour. Our skulls contain a warring complex of id, ego and superego. And today the discoveries of quantum physics have opened a Pandora's Box of inexplicable phenomena, stranger than Alice in Wonderland.

Unidentified flying objects

UFOs were seen by people for centuries before man-made aircraft were commonplace. Chinese astronomers recorded what was probably Halley's Comet in 240 BC, and Frank Smythe saw flying saucers on Mount Everest on 1 June 1933. He looked up at the summit and observed:

> It was only 1,000 feet above me, but an aeon of weariness separated me from it. Bastion on bastion and slab on slab, the rocks were piled in tremendous confusion, their light-yellow edges ghost-like against the deep-blue sky. From the crest, a white plume of mist flowed silently away.

Poor Smythe was at his limit after two nights too high in the Death Zone and weakened by too many days at high altitude. Like Somervell and Norton, he was climbing without supplementary oxygen. He was already in an overwrought state, as on his way up the slopes he had found the tattered remnants of the 1924 expedition's highest camp: 'There was something inexpressibly desolate and pathetic in the scene.' Smythe speculated about Mallory and Irvine, the last men to occupy the camp. 'Where were they? Would Everest yield its secret?' Had Mallory and Irvine made it to the summit?

He gave up his own attempt below the point reached by Somervell and Norton and began his descent to the single tent of camp six at 27,400 feet, where Eric Shipton, too sick to climb, lay waiting for him.

As Smythe descended, he had an overpowering sensation that someone was with him. It was so strong that when he stopped, he divided his Kendal mint cake and turned to offer half to his companion.

Shortly afterwards, he noticed two dark, bulbous objects hovering above him. One had 'what looked like squat, under-developed wings, whilst the other had a beak-like protuberance like the spout of a teakettle. They distinctly pulsated . . . as though they possessed some horrible quality of life.'

Smythe was sufficiently collected to do a mental check, looking away and naming each of the peaks around him. Then he looked back. The flying saucers hadn't moved. Cloud came in and when it cleared they had disappeared.

He wrote afterwards: 'Those who have failed on Everest are unanimous in one thing: the relief of not having to go on. The last 1,000 feet of Everest are not for mere flesh and blood.'

UFO sightings have since then provided fertile ground for those who want to believe in little green men who wish to abduct us. And just like the Minnesota Iceman, there are others willing to feed us with hoaxes: like the Roswell alien autopsy, a film of a faked alien with innards made out of sheep's brains, raspberry jam, chicken entrails and knuckle joints. The alleged autopsy was supposed to be a consequence of a UFO crash in 1947 in Roswell, New Mexico. As with the Iceman, the perpe-trator of this particular hoax claimed that his work was a 'reconstruction' of a real event.

CHAPTER ELEVEN

Conserving the yeti. . .space travel is utter bilge. . .Riddle of the Sands. . .Grey Owl. . .mass extinctions. . .the population bomb. . .Malthus. . .how to clone a mammoth. . .the Giant Penguin.

If the yeti *is* discovered, the scientists (and authors) who say it doesn't exist may feel rather foolish. The problem with attempting to suggest that something doesn't exist is that someone will inevitably then produce evidence that it does.

In 1895, Lord Kelvin, a British mathematician and President of the British Royal Society, pronounced: 'Heavier-than-air flying machines are impossible.' This was just eight years before the Wright brothers' first powered flight. On his appointment as Astronomer Royal, Sir Richard Woolley repeated his long-held view that 'space travel is utter bilge'. This was one year before the launch of Sputnik and thirteen years before man stepped on to the Moon. And the *Express* ran the headline 'There Will Be No War in Europe' on 1 September 1939, the day Hitler invaded Poland and the war began.

Consider Norman Angell, author of *The Great Illusion*. Angell argued that war between industrialised nations was futile because conquest did not pay. This was published in 1910, just before the outbreak of the First World War, and republished in 1933, just before the Second (thankfully his publishers have not felt it necessary to produce further editions). Barbara Tuchman in her excellent *The Guns of August* suggests that Angell was reflecting a British belief that there would be no war, and contrasts it with Friedrich von Bernhardi's *Germany and the Next War*, which maintained that war was necessary for Germany and advocated ruthless aggression.

Possibly the first (and best) yachting spy novel ever written, Robert Erskine Childers' *The Riddle of the Sands*,* warned just how unprepared Britain was for war. Two young men on a sailing holiday stumble upon a network of canals and barges behind the Fresian islands and discover preparations for a huge German invasion. Nature followed art and in 1910 two real-life yachtsmen undertook the same journey and gathered information on German installations. They were duly arrested and sentenced to four years' custody (which would have brought them neatly up to 1914, just in time for internment). They were pardoned by the emperor and were employed by the Admiralty on the outbreak of war.

If the yeti *is* discovered to be a real animal, huge efforts will be made to conserve it and its hairy family. (The Bhutanese have already created the Sakteng Wildlife Sanctuary, 'the only reserve in the world created specifically to protect the habitat of the Yeti.') The modern conservation movement was initiated by people like Grey Owl, author of the Canadian classics *The Men of the Last Frontier*, *Pilgrims of the Wild* and *Sajo and her Beaver People*. He believed that humanity has had a disastrous effect on nature and that we all must develop a respect for the natural world. Grey Owl was a native First Nations Canadian who became an apostle of the wild.

Except he wasn't. Grey Owl was actually Archibald Belaney, from Hastings, Sussex. He had emigrated to Canada in 1910

---

* R. E. Childers, *The Riddle of the Sands* (Smith, Elder & Co., 1903).

and had formed a relationship with a young Iroquois woman who taught him to develop from trapper to conservationist. He adopted his fraudulent identity in order to promote his otherwise commendable beliefs and work.

Does it matter that his means were dubious, if his ends were so positive? After all, Grey Owl was only guilty of enhancing his CV, a crime most of us are guilty of. I would contend that it *does* matter, and if we exaggerate stories of, say, yeti footprints, in order to sell copy or secure funding for expeditions, it can only confuse our efforts in finding out the truth about the world.

Nearly everyone wants to believe there are unknown animals out there. I do. Maybe you do. And they *are* out there; as we have seen, humans have only identified around two million of the estimated 10 million living species. However, these unknown species are mostly minuscule or hiding at the bottom of the deepest seas. The chances of an eight-foot-high primate going undiscovered in the woods of North America are vanishingly small. The same goes for the Himalayas, which are more densely populated by observant humans than might be imagined. There probably isn't a dinosaur living undiscovered in the Congo. And as for Loch Ness, just about everything has been done to find the monster short of pouring the entire contents of the loch through a sieve.

We need those unknown species, too. According to a 2017 study in the peer-reviewed journal *Proceedings of the National Academy of Sciences*, the sixth mass extinction in the earth's history is well under way. This paper does not mince its words. The title is 'Biological annihilation via the ongoing sixth mass extinction signalled by vertebrate population losses and declines.'* Biological annihilation? This seems strong language for a sober scientific paper. So, what is going on?

There have been five previous mass extinction events in earth's history that we know about:

---

* See http://www.pnas.org/content/early/2017/07/05/1704949114.

1. **The Ordovician**, 444 million years ago. 86 per cent of species were lost, probably in an ice age. Most life was in the sea in those days. Cause? Probably the uplift of the Appalachians. This caused sea levels to drop, exposing silicate rocks that hoovered carbon dioxide out of the earth's atmosphere. And, as we know, CO_2 makes things nice and warm. With less of it you get an ice age.

2. **The Late Devonian**, 375 million years ago. 75 per cent of species were lost. Cause? Unclear, but maybe algal blooms in the sea caused by nutrients released by the newly evolved land plants.

3. **The Permian**, 250 million years ago. This has been nicknamed The Great Dying, since a disturbing 96 per cent of species died out. All life on earth today is descended from the 4 per cent of species that survived. Cause? Siberian volcanoes released vast amounts of carbon dioxide, causing global temperatures to rocket, the oceans to become acidic and life to become impossible for most species.

4. **Triassic–Jurassic**, 200 million years ago, with 80 per cent of species disappearing. Cause? Bit of a mystery, this one. There were two or three phases of extinctions which have been blamed on everything from asteroid impacts and climate change to eruptions. No one seems to know.

5. **The Cretaceous–Tertiary**, 66 million years ago, with 75 per cent of species lost. This is the famous one that killed off the dinosaurs. But it also saw off many plants and ammonites. Cause? Most scientists think it was an asteroid impacting Mexico and causing a nuclear winter. Effect? The rise of the mammals, one species of which has caused. . .

6. **The Anthropocene** mass extinction event. When? Now. Percentage of species lost is 50 per cent so far, still counting. Still unclear. Cause? Let's find out . . .

'Show me a scientist who claims there is no population problem and I'll show you an idiot.' The speaker is Professor Paul Ehrlich of Stanford University in the USA, who was one of the scientists who contributed to the 'Biological annihilation' paper. His 1968 book *The Population Bomb* still causes controversy. He says now that human civilisation depends totally on plants and animals and by presiding over their extinction we preside over our own. 'The time to act is very short,' he said. 'It will, sadly, take a long time to humanely begin the population shrinkage required if civilisation is to long survive, but much could be done on the consumption front and with "band aids" – wildlife reserves, diversity protection laws – in the meantime.'

Haven't we been here before with Ehrlich? His 1960s book predicted that there would be mass starvation by the 1970s, causing the deaths of hundreds of millions of people, unless high-yielding crops were developed. In this he turned out to be wrong. But it's risky making predictions, especially about the future.

The Population Bomb was half right. In 1968, Ehrlich predicted that a world population of 3.5 billion would double by 2005. In fact, it reached 7 billion in 2011 and the United Nations now expects it to reach 15 billion by the end of the century. What Ehrlich got wrong was the world's ability to feed us. He was writing just at the onset of the Green Revolution, which saw the doubling of yields. However, he did write that new varieties of wheat, rice and corn 'have the potential for at least doubling yields under proper growing conditions'. The problem is that a further doubling looks unlikely, unless sub-Saharan Africa similarly manages to increase production, or technology gives us another doubling with the use of synthetic foodstuffs.

Where Ehrlich lost support was in his suggestions for the reduction of numbers. 'Population control, of course, is the only solution to population growth,' he wrote, suggesting that all men in India with more than three children should be forcibly

259

sterilised: 'Coercion? Perhaps, but coercion in a good cause.' Enthusiastic eugenicists like Himmler might have applauded these sentiments.

The English clergyman Thomas Robert Malthus was the first to point out the population trap in his 1798 *An Essay on the Principle of Population*, a work cited both by Darwin and Wallace as seminal for their theory of natural selection. Malthus noted that when a nation's food production increased, it led to a temporary improvement in living conditions. This, however, was followed by further population growth which again reduced the original per capita production level. Man used abundance to increase his numbers rather than to maintain a high standard of living. So nations would grow in numbers until the poor suffered famine:

> Yet in all societies, even those that are most vicious, the tendency to a virtuous attachment is so strong, that there is a constant effort towards an increase of population. This constant effort as constantly tends to subject the lower classes of the society to distress and to prevent any great permanent amelioration of their condition.[*]

Malthus believed that there were two kinds of checks on population: positive checks such as famine, war and disease which increase the death rate, and negative checks such as abortion, birth control, prostitution, postponement of marriage and celibacy. Not many of these seem appealing. His solutions to this problem are fairly shocking by modern values: he supported the Corn Laws which kept the price of food high and criticised the Poor Laws which gave money to the needy but which increased food price inflation, thus encouraging more children. His views were not popular with Karl Marx or Friedrich Engels, who said that Malthusianism was 'the crudest, most barbarous theory that

---

[*] T. R. Malthus, *An Essay on the Principle of Population* (1798), chap. II.

ever existed, a system of despair which struck down all those beautiful phrases about love thy neighbour and world citizenship'. Lenin said it was typical of the bourgeoisie to blame the working class for the problems of capitalism, and a modern-day Left-leaning writer, George Monbiot, wrote 'Perhaps it's no coincidence that so many post-reproductive white men are obsessed with human population growth, as it's about the only environmental problem of which they can wash their hands.'*

Who's right? Malthus came in for a large amount of abuse, even from one of his editors who claimed falsely that he had exercised population control by hypocritically fathering eleven girls. In fact, the repopulation score was:

Malthus: two daughters, one son.
Marx: four daughters, two sons (and one with his servant, Helene Demuth).
Darwin: four daughters, six sons.
Best beard? Marx, by a whisker over Darwin.

When humans become better educated and better off, they tend to have fewer children. Darwin's Victorian families of ten children are long gone, and Kenyan women who had eight children each a generation ago today have an average of 3.5. This decline is especially noticeable when families move to cities, where extra children are seen as a burden rather than the vital source of agricultural labour that they are back in the country-side. So, the rise of megacities should be welcomed as they actually curb population growth. The real problem is over-consumption by the rich First World countries whose desire for children may be lessened but whose greed for material things is infinite. Improving human technology has so far fed a soaring population, but the costs to the planet are so high that the mass extinction of most other species now seems unavoidable.

* *Guardian*, Thursday, 19 November 2015.

To return to the 'Biological annihilation via the ongoing sixth mass extinction' paper, the authors point out that there is a common misconception that the earth's biota is not immediately threatened, just slowly entering an episode of major biodiversity loss. They demonstrate that in fact there is an extremely high degree of population loss in vertebrates, even in common species of low concern. Dwindling population sizes and range shrinkages amount to a massive anthropogenic erosion of biodiversity and of the ecosystem 'services' essential to civilisation such as clean air and water. This 'biological annihilation' underlines the seriousness for humanity of earth's sixth mass extinction event. In other words, there is a serious problem looming. Anyone watching the BBC's Natural History department's output on television might go away with the idea that the world is crammed with exotic and beautiful animals, but the presenters do not seem able to tell us the true state of affairs. These programmes will be all that is left to remind us of the earth's past glories like the snow leopard and the kingfisher, which will depart like the dodo, the quagga, the Tasmanian tiger, the great auk and the woolly mammoth.

One animal that has not been forced to become extinct is the domestic chicken, even though 60 billion are killed every year. In a strange development, scientists have decided that the humble constituent of Kentucky Fried Chicken will define our own time by its bones. In 2016, the Working Group on the Anthropocene declared the beginning of the new geological epoch. The chair, Professor Jan Zalasiewicz, a geologist at the University of Leicester, declared of the humble Chuckie: 'It has become the world's most common bird. It has been fossilised in thousands of landfill sites and on street corners around the world.'

The chicken was first domesticated in Southeast Asia around 10,000 years ago from the red junglefowl, *Gallus gallus*. This spectacular but scrawny wild bird was tasty and not very good at flying, which made it easy to catch. Now half of the ancestral breeds have been lost, making the domestic chicken even more suitable for the type breed for fossil evidence.

In future, geologists will see chicken bones as the key evidence of the border between the last age, the Holocene, and our new age when humans began to overwhelm the planet. The crucial fossil evidence that will be preserved for future geologists and define our epoch are the bones of our chicken dinners: the KFCene.

There have been objections to the use of bones as a marker. Why not use the presence of plastics (and call it the Plasticene)? Some feel the notion of unilaterally starting another geological epoch, which previously defined rock units, seems rather anthropocentric. After all, the present epoch, the Holocene, only began 11,700 years ago, whereas the previous epoch, the Pleistocene, lasted around 2.5 million years. It makes epochs seem like buses: you wait around for two and a half million years, then two turn up together. Perhaps the Anthropocene is better used as a cultural term, like Neolithic, rather than as a geological one.

Which brings us back to the cryptids. Perhaps there is a reason for the almost needy belief in the existence of monstrous man-beasts in American backwoods, or yetis plodding across moonlit snowfields. In short, do we need to invent mysterious beasts because we need them in some way? And if we need them, could we perhaps *make* them?

Let us be kind to cryptozoologists and assume that the mysterious beasts they crave have become extinct. Could we clone them? Could we make a Bigfoot? Or a Loch Ness monster? Scientists successfully cloned Dolly the sheep in Edinburgh in

1996. She was the first mammal to be cloned from an adult somatic cell, using the process of nuclear transfer. In mammals, somatic cells are the ones that make up all our internal organs, skin, bones, blood and connective tissue, while our mammalian germ cells give rise to spermatozoa and ova which come together during natural fertilisation (sex) to produce a cell called a zygote, which divides and differentiates into the cells of an embryo. Dolly was cloned from a somatic cell from a mammary gland, which proved that a cell taken from another part of the body could successfully recreate a whole individual. Why Dolly? Team member Ian Wilmut said: 'Dolly is derived from a mammary gland cell and we couldn't think of a more impressive pair of glands than Dolly Parton's.'

Since then, pigs, deer, horses and bulls have been cloned, and scientists' thoughts then turned to reviving endangered or extinct species. So far, researchers have cloned a mouflon sheep, a bovine called a gaur in 2001, then a wild cow called a banteng in 2003; and in 2009, scientists from Aragon, northern Spain, announced the cloning of the Pyrenean ibex, a form of wild mountain goat, which was officially declared extinct in 2000. The newborn ibex died shortly after birth due to defects in its lungs, but it is the first time an extinct animal has been cloned. None of the above animals survived into adulthood, but the pace of research is fast, and saving endangered and newly extinct species by resurrecting them from frozen tissue does look as if it is on the cards – eventually.

'Woolly mammoth will be back from extinction within two years, say Harvard scientists,' trumpeted a *Telegraph* headline in February 2017. The *Guardian*, slightly more restrained, had the same story: 'Woolly mammoth on verge of resurrection, scientists reveal.' In both articles, a Professor George Church was quoted as saying: 'Our aim is to produce a hybrid elephant-mammoth embryo. Actually, it would be more like an elephant with a number of mammoth traits.

We're not there yet, but it could happen in a couple of years.'

Professor Church said that his mammoth project had two goals: securing a more hopeful future for the endangered Asian elephant and helping to combat global warming. Woolly mammoths, he claimed, could help prevent tundra permafrost from melting and releasing huge amounts of greenhouse gas into the atmosphere. Permafrost is the thick layer of permanently frozen soil found at high latitudes and it makes up a vast 24 per cent of the Northern Hemisphere's ice-free land mass. This layer stores large amounts of carbon and it is now melting due to the increasing global temperatures. This is released into the atmosphere as carbon dioxide and methane, which are both powerful greenhouse gases. So how will the future herds of 'mammophants' save us from global warming? 'They keep the tundra from thawing by punching through snow and allowing cold air to come in,' Professor Church said. 'In the summer they knock down trees and help the grass grow.'

Will we be riding on the back of a woolly mammoth across the steppes within a couple of years? Not so fast, writes Mary Beth Griggs, a more considered writer, in *Popular Scientist*.* She points out that the weasel word here is 'embryo'. Church's team, the optimistically named 'Woolly Mammoth Revival Project', has been using CRISPR gene-editing technology to put genetic material collected from frozen mammoth corpses into Asian elephant DNA (mammoths are more closely related to the Asian elephant than the African variety).

So far, Professor Church's team has only managed to incorporate traits of the mammoth's ears, fat and hair into the elephant DNA. That means the cloned animal would be a

* See http://www.popsci.com/wooly-mammoth-will-not-be-resurrected-in-two-years#page-2.

fat hairy elephant with little ears, not a 100 per cent genuine mammoth. The team plans to produce an embryo in two years, but it will be a few years more before it will be a viable embryo capable of being placed in the team's claimed artificial womb, grown into a calf and delivered by a scientist. And a few more years before the 'mammophant' can reach adulthood. Then many decades before the necessary thousands of mammophants can trample the bogs of Siberia, by which time these will presumably have melted away. And then what? Matthew Cobb, Professor of Zoology at the University of Manchester, raised the question of the eventual mammoth family: 'The proposed "de-extinction" of mammoths raises a massive ethical issue – the mammoth was not simply a set of genes, it was a social animal, as is the modern Asian elephant. What will happen when the elephant–mammoth hybrid is born? How will it be greeted by elephants?' Possibly with cruel remarks about its bikini-line.

Dr Beth Shapiro, author of *How to Clone a Mammoth*,* said scientists wouldn't be able to achieve a creature which was 100 per cent mammoth, because so far cloning requires living cells. For the same reason, it is unlikely that we will see a Loch Ness monster-like plesiosaur anytime soon. She does see hope for Professor Church's host elephants, though. 'Elephants are an endangered species and what if you could swap out a few genes for mammoth genes, not to bring the mammoth back but to allow them to live in colder climates?' So we might see hairy, cold-adapted elephants on the tundra but not the real mammoth that roamed there 4,000 years ago. In her book, Shapiro, who is an evolutionary biologist, explores how we might revive extinct species but also when we should refrain. She argues that, without restoring the lost ecosystems in which

* B. Shapiro, *How to Clone a Mammoth: The Science of De-extinction* (Princeton University Press, 2015).

266

a resurrected species might feel at home, de-extinction might be too cruel to accept.

Could we clone Bigfoot? As we don't even have a frozen specimen, it would seem unlikely. Working backwards from a large hairy human would seem more possible.

This all seems rather tenuous at present; in fact, the *Telegraph* and *Guardian* stories almost count as fake news. The journalists who covered the mammoth story can hardly be blamed. Who would click on a true story proclaiming: 'Forty-five mammoth genes now in an elephant cell, only 4,000 to go'?

As mass extinctions of species are threatened, it seems appealing to read stories claiming that cloning extinct animals is possible. But it is probably better to stop them becoming extinct in the first place.

Jurassic Park was the 1990 novel by Michael Crichton that brought DNA technology to Conan Doyle's *The Lost World*. As if acknowledging his predecessor, Crichton's 1995 sequel was also titled *The Lost World*. Steven Spielberg's blockbuster films of the two books were enormously successful and propelled the idea of living dinosaurs back into the public mind.

The original novel, though, was more of a cautionary tale about the perils of messing with DNA. A theme park has been created on the fictional island of Isla Nublar, off the west coast of Costa Rica, by a billionaire, John Hammond. His team has managed to recreate Jurassic-era dinosaurs by collecting the dinosaur blood stored in the bodies of ticks and gnats which have been preserved in amber. The DNA in this blood is supplemented by modern-day reptiles, birds and amphibians, and full-sized dinosaurs have been successfully cloned. To control the population, these dinosaurs are all female and they are all deficient in the essential amino acid L-lysine which controls growth. Of course, all this goes wrong, the safeguards fail and before long a velociraptor eggshell is found, proving that reproduction is taking place. A tyrannosaurus attacks the guests and before long dinosaurs are rampaging through the jungles of Costa Rica, eating L-lysine-rich fodder and the odd human.

So far, so good. Spielberg had four consecutive hits on his hands. But what are the real dangers of messing with DNA? Dinosaurs we can deal with, but what about humans? We could face what H. G. Wells' time-traveller found at the end of the world: a divided society inhabited by the genetically engineered children of the ultra-wealthy who are being eaten by the monstrous Morlocks, the spawn of the poor.

The Clearwater Giant Penguin

One pleasant February morning in 1948, a resident of Clearwater, Florida, was taking a stroll along the beach when he saw the tracks of a monster coming out of the water. They were large, 14 inches long and 11 inches wide, with three toes tipped with claws. Whatever had made them had emerged from the Gulf of Mexico and walked north along the sand for two miles before returning to the water. The witness ran home to phone the police.

Later, a young couple reported that they had been harassed by a large sea creature, then a large penguin-like creature was seen swimming at sea by a boat crew. Later still, a sighting of a huge penguin on the Suwannee River was reported from an aircraft. The witness this time was Ivan T. Sanderson, who had come to investigate the creature. He summarised the evidence in his book, *Things and More Things*. First, he investigated the footprints on the beach: 'the tracks invariably followed the gentlest gradients even at the cost of considerable meandering and, secondly, they meticulously avoided all possible snags and obstacles even down to the smallest bushes . . . these are, one and all, typical animal traits'.

Sanderson dismissed the possibility of a hoax: 'If made physically by a man, either with devices strapped to his feet or on stilts, how did he carry a ton on each leg – the absolute minimum that the road engineers said could have made the imprints even in soft ground? He manifestly could not . . . That any man or body of men could know so much about wild animal life as to make the tracks in just the manner that they appear, but that they also should be able to carry this out time and time again at night without anybody seeing them or giving them away . . . is frankly incredible.'

The only possible explanation, Sanderson said, was a 15-foot-high giant penguin which 'would obviously have to be a wanderer in Florida, out of its natural element and perhaps lost'. He named the creature 'Florida Three Toes'.

Tony Signorini wearing cast iron feet used in the 1948 Clearwater "monster" hoax. Although the feet were made with dinosaur tracks in mind, Ivan T. Sanderson interpreted them as belonging to a "giant penguin." Now, after 40 years, the case is solved. (Joe Walles / St. Petersburg Times.)

The Clearwater Giant Penguin

Sanderson died in 1973 so never read the 11 June 1988 issue of the *St Petersburg Times*, in which journalist Jan Kirby uncovered the story. Kirby tracked down Tony Signorini at Clearwater Auto Electric where his partner had been Al Williams, a notorious prankster. Signorini pulled out the real three-toed monster from under a workbench: a pair of cast-iron feet with high-top black sneakers. He strapped the heavy feet on. 'You see, I would just swing my leg back and forth like this and then give a big hop, and the weight of the feet would carry me that far,' Signorini said, explaining the enormous six-foot stride of the creature. 'The shoes were heavy enough to sink down in the sand.'

The pair had based their prank on dinosaur prints but they were happy enough with the Giant Penguin designation, especially when unprompted sightings started coming in. Once again, Ivan Sanderson was implicated in a hoax, but always as the willing believer, never the perpetrator.

It seems that in the world of cryptid fakery there are two kinds of people: the Sharks and the Marks. The Sharks are men like the yeti, Bigfoot and Giant Penguin hoaxers we have met in these pages. The Marks are those of us who want to believe in them.

CHAPTER TWELVE

The Surgeon's knife. . .the Microbe is very small. . .a town like Alice. . . Science vs Arts. . . Science vs Religion.

As you lie in hospital waiting to go under the surgeon's knife, you might be glad that the medic in question has studied a bit of science. Soon you will be grateful for the science of anaesthesia, as you won't be screaming past a bullet clenched between your teeth. Your chances of recovery will be improved by advances in antibiotics. And yet there seems to be a general loathing of scientists by the Bigfoot-believer and Creationist fraternities.

The reason for this is fairly clear: scientists seem to just love to rain on their parade. Not only do they deny the existence of Bigfoot, yetis and monsters; they seem to relish their intellectual superiority while doing it. 'Show me the body,' they say, when you just *know* he exists.

This suggests a misunderstanding about the nature of the scientific process, which is simply the testing of hypotheses. A scientist will have an idea that seems to explain some observation about nature, and then it is seen if the idea withstands critical scrutiny. Science is not about proving things true, it's about proving them false. Darwin's *On the Origin of Species* did not set out to destroy Christianity; it sought to disprove prevailing assumptions about evolution. Scientists are generally open-minded but sceptical. The Minnesota Iceman hoax showed how easily Bernard Heuvelmans allowed himself to be duped by a fairground shyster, all because he *wanted* to believe in the Iceman. He failed to follow quantum physicist Richard Feynman's dictum: 'The first principle is that you must not fool yourself, and you are the easiest person to fool.' We have to trust scientists to find the truth about our obsessions. However:

> The Microbe is so very small
> You cannot make him out at all,
> But many sanguine people hope
> To see him through a microscope.*

Authors who deal with technical or scientific subjects often fail to get full recognition in our society. Nevil Shute, who wrote *On the Beach* and *A Town Like Alice*, springs to mind. The reason for this is not far to seek, and is important to our understanding of the whole phenomenon of belief in monsters.

C. P. Snow, a chemist and novelist, delivered a lecture about the relationship between scientists and the literary elite. In 'The Two Cultures and the Scientific Revolution', he lamented the fact that Victorian schooling had over-emphasised the humanities in the form of Latin and Greek at the expense of scientific education. This led to the British political and administrative elites being deprived of vital preparation for managing the scientific world:

> A good many times I have been present at gatherings of people who, by the standards of the traditional culture, are thought highly educated and who have with considerable

* H. Belloc, 'The Microbe'

gusto been expressing their incredulity at the illiteracy of scientists. Once or twice I have been provoked and have asked the company how many of them could describe the Second Law of Thermodynamics. The response was cold: it was also negative. Yet I was asking something which is about the scientific equivalent of: 'Have you read a work of Shakespeare's?'

I now believe that if I had asked an even simpler question – such as, 'What do you mean by mass, or acceleration?' which is the scientific equivalent of saying, 'Can you read?' – not more than one in ten of the highly educated would have felt that I was speaking the same language. So the great edifice of modern physics goes up, and the majority of the cleverest people in the western world have about as much insight into it as their Neolithic ancestors would have had.[*]

Snow's point is even more relevant today as we head for a new world dominated by digital technology. Around 60 per cent of British students opt for arts and humanities courses while 40 per cent go for science, maths and technology. It was the divide between the disciplines that concerned Snow, the trend to compartmentalise knowledge. A study[†] showed that, the more renowned a scientist, the more likely they were to be actively engaged in the arts. Einstein had an opinion on this: 'The greatest scientists are artists as well.' You need a head and a heart.

A lack of scientific understanding among journalists or the public at large should concern anyone trying to determine whether a previously undiscovered Jurassic creature is likely to live in Loch Ness, or a Bigfoot in the forests of North America.

[*] C. P. Snow, 'The Two Cultures and the Scientific Revolution,' Rede Lecture, 7 May 1959.

[†] R. Root-Bernstein, L. Allen, et al., 'Arts Foster Scientific Success,' *Journal of Psychology of Science and Technology*, vol. 1, no. 2 (Springer, 2008).

Our mystery beasts have demonstrated various kinds of human fallibility. I believe Eric Shipton's yeti footprint was a deliberate hoax, done partly as a prank, partly to encourage interest in another Mount Everest expedition, partly through dislike of the Establishment. Bigfoot reveals a deep human need to believe in a mysterious man-like beast in an over-technological society. The crucial Loch Ness monster sighting was influenced by the popular fiction of living dinosaurs, then fuelled by the tourism industry. Mokèlé-mbèmbé was seized on by creationists as a way of disproving the theory of evolution. *Beowulf* spoke to our deepest human fear of monsters, and the Giant Penguin proved that people will believe the most ludicrous propositions. And that leads us on to the problem of distinguishing between truth and lies.

Animal Farm was about animals who talked, and not just the two-legged ones. The author, George Orwell, wrote that political language is 'designed to make lies sound truthful and murder respectable, and to give an appearance of solidity to pure wind'. We have seen a few lies and more than a little pure wind in our search for cryptobeasts.

Nineteen-sixty-one was the year of US President John F. Kennedy's inauguration, and the apogee of yeti and Bigfoot mania. It was also the year that Ivan T. Sanderson published his *Abominable Snowmen*, a book filled with exaggeration, supposition and hoaxed animals. In the same year, the American social historian Daniel J. Boorstin wrote *The Image*, his prophetic theory of pseudo-events. He looked back at the 50 years of technological progress, from the daguerreotype to colour television, which had led to an explosion of news reporting. When real stories ran out, and in the absence of real news such as wars, earthquakes or assassinations, news was invented. Pseudo-events such as PR stunts, movie premieres (or even fake animals) provided copy. When real heroes failed, celebrities were created to replace them; people remarkable only for being well known. Politicians, in particular, bought into this artificial world. According to Boorstin:

> Until recently, we have been justified in believing Abraham Lincoln's familiar maxim: 'You may fool all the people some of the time; you can even fool some of the people all the time; but you can't fool all of the people all the time.' This has been the foundation belief of American democracy. Lincoln's appealing slogan rests on two elementary assumptions. First, that there is a clear and visible distinction between sham and reality, between the lies a demagogue would have us believe and the truths which are there all the time. Second, that the people tend to prefer reality to sham, that if offered a choice between a simple truth and a contrived image, they will prefer the truth.
>
> Neither of these any longer fits the facts. Not because people are less intelligent or more dishonest. Rather because great unforeseen changes – the great forward strides of American civilization – have blurred the edges of reality. The pseudo-events which flood our consciousness are neither true nor false in the old familiar senses. The very same advances which have made them possible have also made the images – however planned, contrived, or distorted – more vivid, more attractive, more impressive, and more persuasive than reality itself.*

Remember, this was over half a century ago. As a result of the vivid reporting of contrived or pseudo-events such as PR releases or anniversaries, Boorstin claimed that Americans had

* D. J. Boorstin, *The Image: A Guide to Pseudo-events in America* (Vintage Books, 1992).

begun to live in a synthetic world where illusion replaced reality:

> The American citizen thus lives in a world where fantasy is more real than reality, where the image has more dignity than its original. We hardly dare face our bewilderment, because our ambiguous experience is so pleasantly iridescent, and the solace of belief in contrived reality is so thoroughly real. We have become eager accessories to the great hoaxes of the age. These are the hoaxes we play on ourselves. Pseudo-events from their very nature tend to be more interesting and more attractive than spontaneous events. Therefore in American public life today pseudo-events tend to drive all other kinds of events out of our consciousness or at least to overshadow them. Earnest, well-informed citizens seldom notice that their experience of spontaneous events is buried by pseudo-events. Yet nowadays, the more industriously they work at 'informing' themselves the more this tends to be true . . . Our seeming ability to satisfy our exaggerated expectations makes us forget that they are exaggerated.

Boorstin didn't reckon on the invention of the Internet, which has led us faster towards an entirely synthetic world where objective truth has little importance. Not since the days of fairies and hobgoblins has society been so beset by tall tales and myths. Everyone can be their own news editor and everyone can manufacture their own celebrity using faked pictures on Instagram and exaggerated exploits on Facebook.

'Post-truth' was the *Oxford Dictionary* international word of 2016, the year in which the UK voted to leave the European

Union and Donald Trump was elected US president. It describes a situation 'in which objective facts are less influential in shaping public opinion than appeals to emotion and personal belief'.

Trump's butler at the time, Anthony Senecal, was reading his employer's book *The Art of the Deal* when he came upon the passage in which Trump relates that the ceramic tiles in the nursery at Mar-a-Lago had been personally made by Walt Disney. Impressed, he asked the soon-to-be-president if it was really true. 'Who cares?' came the response. Bullshit is not new; it has been around as long as humans have been organised into tribes. But it is different from lying; it's much worse. Here's why.

'One of the most salient features of our culture is that there is so much bullshit.' In his philosophical study of the subject,* Harry G. Frankfurt distinguishes between the liar and the bullshitter, who 'does not reject the authority of the truth, as the liar does, and oppose himself to it. He pays no attention to it at all. By virtue of this, bullshit is a greater enemy of truth than lies are.'

Both liars and bullshitters are trying to gain an advantage. But liars are aware of truth and their lie is a conscience act of deception. That is why their discomfort can sometimes be detected by their 'tells'. But the bullshitter has a complete disregard for the truth; his bullshit may be true or it may not. Frankfurt thinks that this indifference to the way things really are is the essence of bullshit. Since bullshitters ignore truth instead of acknowledging and subverting it, bullshit is therefore a greater enemy of truth than lies.

What our story of the Western yeti, Bigfoot, Mokèlé-mbèmbé and the Loch Ness monster shows us is that tall-storytellers, bullshitters and outright liars have always sought to convince the gullible that monsters exist when the truth is that they don't. This is nothing new. Religious charlatans through the ages have sought to convince the gullible that eternal life is

---

* H. G. Frankfurt, *On Bullshit* (Princeton University Press, 2005).

possible and that dried hands and scalps have magical powers. It probably isn't, and they probably don't.

In June 2017, Facebook CEO Mark Zuckerberg compared his website Facebook to a religion, being able to offer a sense of community and filling the gap left by falling church membership. He announced that the social networking site had hit the two billion user mark, with one in every four humans on the planet now using Facebook every month. With 100 million users active in what Zuckerberg called 'meaningful communities' within Groups on Facebook, he told the world of his ambition to raise that number to a billion. He said: 'If we can do this, it will not only turn around the whole decline in community membership we've seen for decades, it will start to strengthen our social fabric and bring the world closer together.' Comparing Facebook to a church, he spoke about the need for 'great leaders' in such a community, saying: 'A church doesn't just come together. It has a pastor who cares for the well-being of their congregation, makes sure they have food and shelter . . . People who go to church are more likely to volunteer and give to charity – not just because they're religious, but because they're part of a community.'

This begs a few questions. If Facebook is a religion, what does it believe in? Who are its great leaders? If Zuckerberg ran for the US presidency, he would almost certainly win with his unprecedented grasp of his followers' hearts and minds. Who is controlling the content presented on Facebook as news and with what objective? The answers are unclear, but many social commentators are uncomfortable about the way social media is developing, particularly in the realm of fake news, or lies, as they used to be called.

Our Western society seems to have arrived at a high point in bullshit. How did we get here? In his study of Post-truth,*

* M. d'Ancona, *Post-Truth: The New War on Truth and How to Fight Back* (Ebury, 2017).

The Spectator editor Matthew d'Ancona blames Sigmund Freud. In psychoanalysis, claims d'Ancona, the imperative is to treat the patients irrespective of the truth of their delusions. The spread of this therapeutic culture into the real world means that real-life decisions are being made on the basis of emotions. 'Sharing your innermost feelings, shaping your life-drama, speaking from the heart: these pursuits are increasingly in competition with traditional forensic values.' So if we *feel* a Facebook story is true, it is. Everything is equally true on the Internet; the images and assertions on the screen have the same authority as a printed page in a book.

D'Ancona goes on to implicate French postmodernists who argued there was no such thing as truth and objectivity, only power and interests. He cites Jean-François Lyotard, who pointed out the increasing public scepticism towards grand, large-scale theories and philosophies of the world, such as the progress of history, the knowability of everything by science, and the possibility of absolute freedom.* Lyotard argues that no one seemed to agree on what was real and everyone has their own perspective and story. And the democratising effect of the Internet has helped by giving us a disdain for experts. Fake news stories that agree with our prejudices are easy to believe.

What can we do about it? D'Ancona says we must fight. 'This is not a battle between liberals and conservatives. This is a battle between two ways of perceiving the world, two fundamentally different approaches to reality. Are you content for the central values of the Enlightenment, of free societies and of democratic discourse, to be trashed by charlatans – or not?'

---

* J.-F. Lyotard, *The Postmodern Condition: A Report on Knowledge* (Manchester University Press, 1984).

I used to work as a TV producer on the BBC business investment programme *Dragons' Den* in which entrepreneurs attempt to convince sceptical investors that their particular product is worth the money presented on the studio table in an open briefcase (the money was fake). In the course of the first four shows, I became increasingly aware that the pitches being made on both sides were often largely invention. When performing due diligence, it became obvious to me that ideas were often not original nor were the claimed benefits possible. Sometimes the millionaires were not quite what they seemed, either. It was a bullshit-slinging match. As a result, very few real investments were made. The presenter of the show, Evan Davis, has written a book called *Post-Truth: Why We Have Reached Peak Bullshit and What We Can Do About It** (surely a title with more capital letters in it than is entirely necessary). Davis has met a few politicians in his role as BBC *Newsnight* presenter and feels that our Western societies have become 'characterised by a pervasive tendency of those in authority to overstate their case. They bombard us with messages that are disconnected from reality as we see it. In the Soviet case it was the reality that was shameful; in ours, it is the communicators.' But we are to blame, Evans argues; we lap it up, and the more we lap it up, the more it flows; the less attention we pay to facts, the more non-facts will be deployed.

Davis's next point is relevant to our yeti/Bigfoot phenomenon. He recalls the Nobel Prize-winner Daniel Kahneman who distinguished between two human systems of thinking when suddenly presented with evidence such as monstrous

---

* E. Davis, *Post-Truth: Why We Have Reached Peak Bullshit and What We Can Do About It* (Little, Brown, 2017).

280

footprints.* System One's reaction is fast, non-rational, emotional and intuitive: 'Am I in danger? Do I want to believe in this monster? Give me a quick escape strategy.' System Two is Sherlock Holmes's calm, rational, logical approach: 'What are the facts? Here is a likely truth.' Kahneman shows how bullshitters and liars appeal to the System One part of our brains, and that System Two might be more deliberate and rational, but is lazy and tires easily. So it often accepts the easy answers offered by System One.

In his *Post-Truth: How Bullshit Conquered The World*,† Wikileaks employee James Ball explains how the rise of the Internet has changed everything for traditional media such as newspapers. They have suffered from falling advertising revenue, which leads to fewer reporters being hired. This in turn leads to a lack of resources to undertake investigative reporting, which leads to the regurgitation of politicians' statements instead of digging into the truth of what they're saying. Ball explains how fake news sites have taken this new business model to its logical conclusion. Instead of checking stories, just make them up. The result is that the impressionable news consumer gives no more weight to the BBC, the *Guardian* or the *New York Times* than to someone's Facebook status or a click-bait site. But does any of this really matter?

The site Infowars claimed during the US presidential election run-up in 2016 that the Democratic party was hosting a child sex-slave ring out of Comet Ping Pong, a pizza restaurant in Washington. As a result of reading this, 28-year-old Edgar Maddison Welch carried an assault rifle into the establishment and pointed it at an employee, who fled. The man then discharged the weapon several times. He claimed he was attempting to find and rescue child sex slaves who he believed were being held in the basement, a belief based on his reading

* D. Kahneman, *Thinking, Fast and Slow* (Penguin, 2012).

† J. Ball, *Post-Truth: How Bullshit Conquered the World* (Biteback Publishing, 2017).

281

of the false story circulating online. The police disagreed and Welch was indicted by a federal grand jury in December 2016. In jail, Welch texted to friends: 'Raiding a pedo ring, possibly sacraficing [*sic*] the lives of a few for the lives of many.' He added: 'I'm sorry bro', but I'm tired of turning the channel and hoping someone does something and being thankful it's not my family. One day it will be our families. The world is too afraid to act and I'm too stubborn not to.' The conspiracy theorist, Alex Jones, who runs Infowars, apologised. The story 'was based upon what we now believe was an incorrect narrative'. An incorrect narrative? Or a lie?

'Alternative facts' is the immortal phrase used by US Counsellor to the President, Kellyanne Conway, during an interview in January 2017, in which she defended White House Press Secretary Sean Spicer's untrue statement about the attendance numbers of Donald Trump's inauguration as president of the United States. When pressed during the interview with Chuck Todd to explain why Spicer 'uttered a provable falsehood', Conway said that Spicer was giving 'alternative facts'. Todd replied, 'Look, alternative facts are not facts. They're falsehoods.'

What can we do? James Ball suggests a number of small strategies: support traditional media, don't share articles on social media without checking their veracity, learn how statistics work, treat the stories we believe as sceptically as those we don't and try not to succumb to conspiratorial thinking.

Evan Davis thinks we may have now reached peak bullshit, because the professional persuaders have got carried away by their message and forgotten about the quality of the product they want us to buy: 'In short, they've become deluded by their own skill and deluded by their own science and have taken bullshit way beyond the optimal level.' This is a curious choice of words. Optimal level? Is there an optimal level for lies? As a high-profile friend of mine once said to me in relation to his exploits: 'You're OK, as long as you don't believe your own bullshit.'

There is a deeper, more disturbing, truth here. Since the neoliberal economic ideas of Friedrich Hayek and Milton Friedman were embraced by Ronald Reagan and Margaret Thatcher, our Western societies have believed that competition is the only legitimate organising principle for human activity. We seem to have forgotten the central values of the Enlightenment: critical thinking, progress, individual liberty and tolerance. For Hayek, the market didn't just facilitate trade in services and goods; it revealed the truth about human affairs by being a kind of consciousness itself. The market has become a vast Mind which constantly reveals truth in the only form it understands: monetary price. It knows the price of everything but the value of nothing. Each of us is now a consumer, an economic unit whose price is only revealed by what we can sell of ourselves on the market. However, Hayek didn't know that the Internet was coming. Truth is now the aggregation of recursive clicks on Google, a vast number of users acting as a market. The more clicks on a news story, the more the consumers want it and therefore the truer it is.

Fake news is nothing new, as I learned in the course of my Mallory search, and fakery was relevant to my search for the truth about the yeti and Bigfoot. I started both my quests hoping they were true, but in both cases I had to revise my opinion as I discovered more evidence. There were the assertions: 'Mallory succeeded in climbing to the summit of Everest,' and 'There is a large ape-like creature unknown to science that lives in the wilds.' Both legends were enduring in the face of a large amount of evidence to the contrary. Both legends are difficult to disprove: the impossibility of proving a negative. Both legends are still firmly believed by the sort of people who dislike hearing facts that contradict their opinion. In fact, the 'Backfire Effect' means that contradiction often consolidates these prejudices.

Reinhold Messner had a problem when his lectures solving the yeti question failed to sell in great numbers: 'A lot of people said, "I'm not coming for a bear." I would have much more success if it had been the other way round – if I'd claimed that it is some big human-like creature. But this is not the answer.'

Like Messner, I believe that the sightings of the yeti are of bears, not apes. Finding the truth is difficult because of the Sherpa bear-myths which have always described the animal in human terms, and the rise of the Westerners' yeti, which is more to do with an appetite for sensational stories. The printed press were the first to feed this with the embroidered stories we have seen, and since then TV and the Internet have been the main source.

This is a pattern that repeats itself over and over again up to the present: a report of a footprint leads to fabricated stories of 'wild men'. Further evidence such as DNA always points to a bear being involved. We now call this fake news. I believe these stories are fabricated by climbers, journalists and TV producers. Who benefits? The climbers get funding for their next trip, the journalists sell more copy and the TV commissioners sell more advertising.

What's not to like about fake news? Only this: it's not true. Does that matter? Yes, and here's why: in the debate around Britain's referendum to leave or stay in the European Union, the Leavers' side of Boris Johnson, Michael Gove and Nigel Farage told a number of lies during the campaign, including a whopper so big that it had to be painted on the side of a large red bus:

We send the EU £350 million a week. Let's fund our NHS instead. Vote Leave.

The Leavers continued using the slogan despite Sir Andrew Dilnot, chair of the UK Statistics Authority, saying it was misleading and undermined trust in official statistics. They also persisted with it after the Institute of Fiscal Studies called the claim 'absurd'. The facts are these: Britain had negotiated a discount, paying £285 million a week. It was also untrue that those saved fees would be channelled straight into health services. However, the Remainers were helpless in the face of these untruths. It was the defeat of a complex truth by a simple lie. The consequence of this and other lies was that the country narrowly voted to exit the EU, a decision that will probably inflict profound damage to the nation's economy and social fabric. In any sensible country in the past, politicians who committed an act of treachery so heinous would have had their names blackened forever. As Jonathan Swift wrote:

> . . . so the greatest Liar has his Believers; and it often happens, that if a Lie be believ'd only for an Hour, it has done its Work, and there is no farther occasion for it. Falsehood flies, and the Truth comes limping after it; so that when Men come to be undeceiv'd, it is too late; the Jest is over, and the Tale has had its Effect.*

Fake news also drove the citizens of the United States to elect a showman as president. Repeated lies become truth by repetition. As the Bellman said during the *Hunting of the Snark*: 'I have said it thrice: What I tell you three times is true.'

So truth really does matter, even the truth about the yeti.

The future of monsters

People needed monsters in the past. Water kelpies kept children away from dangerous bodies of water, yetis warned of bears, and trolls were perhaps a warning about the defective offspring of father–daughter or brother–sister matings. 'Once upon a time, it was of great survival value to be worried about everything that could go wrong,' says Johan Norberg, a

---

* J. Swift, *The Examiner*, 1710.

Swedish historian whose book *Progress: Ten Reasons to Look Forward to the Future* explains why we are natural-born pessimists. In our cave-dwelling past, it was an advantage if our attention was drawn by our fears since they might indicate a risk to our own survival. If we always assumed there was a monster behind the next rock, we would usually be wrong but would be more likely to survive and reproduce, passing on our fearful nature. In modern times, writers like Ivan T. Sanderson, newspapers, television and the Internet can invent monsters and our stone-age credulity will accept the deceit. As the Red Queen said to Alice in *Through the Looking Glass*: 'Why, sometimes I've believed as many as six impossible things before breakfast.'

In the present, Bigfoot provides an outlet for men of a traditional type to exercise their tracking, wilderness and firearms skills in a bland nation of shopping malls. What of the future? Mary Shelley's *Frankenstein* warned of the dangers of unrestrained science. We are unlikely to see a cloned plesiosaur pasturing in the swamps of Africa. But soon, humanity will enter a virtual world where anything is possible. Historian Yuval Noah Harari warns in his book *Homo Deus** that intelligence and consciousness are coming apart and we may soon live in a totally digital world. Monsters like Grendel might be generated that will lurk outside until you pay your taxes or give your blood. Horrors beyond our wildest imagining could be waiting for us in the strange new world of artificial intelligence.

I leave the last words to the extinct Bill Tilman: 'When the dust of conflict had settled the Abominable Snowman survived to pursue his evasive, mysterious, terrifying existence, unruffled as the snow he treads, unmoved as the mountains in which he dwells, uncaught, unspecified, but not unhonoured.'

---

* Y. N. Harari, *Homo Deus: A Brief History of Tomorrow* (Harvill Secker, 2017).

Bibliography

Anderson, John, *High Mountains and Cold Seas* (Gollancz, 1980).

Ball, James, *Post-Truth: How Bullshit Conquered the World* (Biteback Publishing, 2017).

Bettelheim, Bruno, *The Uses of Enchantment* (Thames & Hudson, 1977).

Bonington, Chris, *Annapurna South Face* (Cassell, 1971).

Boorstin, Daniel J., *The Image: A Guide to Pseudo-events in America* (1962).

Bowman, William Ernest, *The Ascent of Rum Doodle* (Arrow, 1956).

Childers, Robert Erskine, *The Riddle of the Sands* (Smith, Elder & Co., 1903).

Coburn, Broughton, *The Vast Unknown: America's First Ascent of Everest* (Crown, 2013).

Coleman, Loren, *Tom Slick and the Search for the Yeti* (Faber & Faber, 1989).

Coleridge, Samuel Taylor, 'Constancy to an Ideal Object,' *The Collected Works of Samuel Taylor Coleridge* (Princeton University Press, 1981).

Colinvaux, Paul, *Why Big Fierce Animals Are Rare: An Ecologist's Perspective* (Allen & Unwin, 1978).

Conan Doyle, Arthur, *The Adventure of the Dancing Men* (Dover, 2003).

Cronin, Edward W., *The Arun: A Natural History of the World's Deepest Valley* (Houghton Mifflin, 1979).

D'Ancona, Matthew, *Post-Truth: The New War on Truth and How to Fight Back* (Ebury, 2017).

Daegling, David J., *Bigfoot Exposed: An Anthropologist Examines America's Enduring Legend* (Altamira Press, 2004).

Davis, Evan, *Post-Truth: Why We Have Reached Peak Bullshit and What We Can Do About It* (Little, Brown, 2017).

Fleming, Ian, *Casino Royale* (Jonathan Cape, 1953).

Fletcher Prouty, Leroy, *The Secret Team: The CIA and its Allies in Control of the United States and the World* (Ballantine Books, 1974).

Frankfurt, Harry G., *On Bullshit* (Princeton University Press, 2005).

Fraser, Nick, *The Importance of Being Eton* (Short Books, 2006).

Gerrie, Matthew P., Maryanne Garry and Elizabeth F. Loftus, *Psychology and Law: An Empirical Perspective* (Guilford Press, 2005).

Gould, Rupert, *Loch Ness Monster* (Geoffrey Bles, 1934).

Grosso, Michael, *The Man Who Could Fly: St Joseph of Cupertino and the Mystery of Levitation* (Rowman & Littlefield, 2015).

Hale, Christopher, *Himmler's Crusade: The True Story of the 1938 Nazi Expedition to Tibet* (Bantam Press, 2003).

Harari, Yuval Noah, *Homo Deus: A Brief History of Tomorrow* (Harvill Secker, 2017).

Harkness, Ruth, *The Lady and the Panda: An Adventure* (Carrick & Evans, 1938).

Heaney, Seamus, *Beowulf* (Faber & Faber, 1999).

Heuvelmans, Bernard, 'Notice on a specimen preserved in ice of an unknown form of living hominid: Homo pongoides', *Bulletin of the Royal Belgian Institute of Natural Sciences*, February 1969.

Hillary, Edmund and Desmond Doig, *High in the Thin Cold Air* (Doubleday, 1962).

Howard-Bury, Charles, George Leigh-Mallory and Richmond Wollaston, *Mount Everest: The Reconnaissance, 1921* (Blumenfeld Press, 2009).

Hoyland, Graham, *Last Hours on Everest* (William Collins, 2013).

Hoyland, Graham, *Walking Through Spring* (William Collins, 2016).

Hunt, John, *The Ascent of Everest* (Hodder & Stoughton, 1953).

Izzard, Ralph, *Abominable Snowman Adventure* (Hodder & Stoughton, 1955).

Jackson, John, 'The Elusive Snowman', *Alpine Journal*, 1999.

Jackson, John, *More Than Mountains* (Harrap, 1955).

Kahneman, Daniel, *Thinking, Fast and Slow* (Penguin, 2012).

Kingsley, Charles, *The Water-Babies: A Fairy Tale for a Land Baby* (Macmillan, 1863).

Knight, William Henry, *Diary of a Pedestrian in Cashmere and Thibet* (Cosimo, 2005).

Kohli, Mohan and Kenneth Conboy, *Spies in the Himalayas* (University Press of Kansas, 2003).

Lan, Tianying, Stephanie Gill, Eva Bellemain, Richard Bischof, Muhammad Ali Nawaz and Charlotte Lindqvist, 'Evolutionary history of enigmatic bears in the Tibetan Plateau–Himalaya region and the identity of the yeti', *Proceedings of the Royal Society B*, 29 November 2017.

Lobsang Rampa, Dr Tuesday, *The Third Eye* (Secker & Warburg, 1956).

Loxton, Daniel and Donald R. Prothero, *Abominable Science! Origins of the Yeti, Nessie, and Other Famous Cryptids* (Columbia University Press, 2013).

Lydekker, P. Z. S., 'The Blue Bear of Tibet', *Journal of the Asiatic Society Bengal, 1897*.

Lyotard, Jean-François, *The Postmodern Condition: A Report on Knowledge* (Manchester University Press, 1984).

Malthus, Thomas Robert, *An Essay on the Principle of Population* (1798).

Martin, David and Alastair Boyd, *Nessie: The Surgeon's Photograph Exposed* (Thorne, 1999).

McCoy, Alfred W., *The Politics of Heroin in Southeast Asia* (Harper & Row, 1972).

Meier-Hüsing, Peter, *Nazis in Tibet: Das Rätsel um die SS-Expedition Ernst Schäfer* (Theiss, 2017).

Messner, Reinhold, *My Quest for the Yeti* (St Martin's Press, 2000).

Montgomery Hyde, H., *Room 3603* (The Lyons Press, 2001).

Mummery, Albert Frederick, *My Climbs in the Alps and Caucasus* (Nabu Press, 2014).

Naish, Darren, *Hunting Monsters: Cryptozoology and the Reality Behind the Myths* (Arcturus, 2016).

Napier, John, *Bigfoot: The Yeti and Sasquatch in Myth and Reality* (E. P. Dutton, 1973).

Newton, Michael, *'Almas/Almasti' Encyclopedia of Cryptozoology: A Global Guide* (McFarland & Company, 2005).

Perrin, Jim, *Shipton and Tilman: The Great Decade of Himalayan Exploration* (Arrow Books, 2013).

Perrin, Jim, *The Villain: The Life of Don Whillans* (Hutchinson, 2005).

Preston, Christine, *The Rise of Man in the Gardens of Sumeria: A Biography of L. A. Waddell* (Sussex Academic Press, 2009).

Pringle, Heather, *The Master Plan: Himmler's Scholars and the Holocaust* (Hachette Books, 2006).

Rawicz, Sławomir, *The Long Walk: The True Story of a Trek to Freedom* (Constable, 1956).

Rodway, George, and Ian R. Mitchell, *Prelude to Everest: Alexander Kellas, Himalayan Mountaineer* (Luath Press, 2011).

Russell, Bertrand, 'Is There a God?' *Illustrated Magazine*, 1952.

Russell, Miles, *Piltdown Man: The Secret Life of Charles Dawson* (The History Press, 2003).

Russell, Miles, *The Piltdown Man Hoax: Case Closed* (The History Press, 2012).

Schäfer, Ernst, *Dach der Erde* (Verlag Paul Parey, 1938).

Scott, Sir Peter and Robert H. Rines, 'Naming the Loch Ness Monster', *Nature*, 11 December 1975.

Shapiro, Beth, *How to Clone a Mammoth: The Science of De-extinction* (Princeton University Press, 2015).

Shermer, Michael, 'Show Me the Body', *Scientific American*, May 2003.

Shields, Sharma, *The Sasquatch Hunter's Almanac* (Holt McDougal, 2015).

Shipton, Eric, *Blank on the Map* (Hodder & Stoughton, 1938).

Shipton, Eric, *The Mount Everest Reconnaissance Expedition 1951* (Hodder & Stoughton, 1953).

Smith, Robert D., *Comparative Miracles* (B. Herder, 1965).

Smythe, Frank, *Behold the Mountains: Climbing with a Colour Camera* (Chanticleer Press, 1949).

Smythe, Frank, *Kamet Conquered* (Gollancz, 1932).

Smythe, Frank, *The Valley of the Flowers* (Hodder & Stoughton, 1938).

Smythe, Tony, *My Father, Frank: Unresting Spirit of Everest* (Baton Wicks Publications, 2013).

Snaith, Stanley, *At Grips with Everest* (The Percy Press, 1937).

Snow, Charles Percy, 'The Two Cultures and the Scientific Revolution,' Rede Lecture, 7 May 1959.

Somervell, Howard, *After Everest* (Hodder & Stoughton, 1936).

Stephenson, William, *The Secret History of British Intelligence in the Americas, 1940–1945* (Fromm, 1999).

Stoner, Charles, *The Sherpa and the Snowman* (Hollis & Carter, 1955).

Sturrock, Donald, *Storyteller: The Life of Roald Dahl* (Harper Press, 2010).

Sykes, Bryan, *The Nature of the Beast: The First Scientific Evidence on the Survival of Apemen into Modern Times* (Coronet, 2015).

Thompson, Harry, *Tintin: Hergé and his Creation* (Hodder & Stoughton, 1991).

Tibballs, Geoff, *The World's Greatest Hoaxes* (Barnes & Noble, 2006).

Tilman, H. W. 'Bill', *China to Chitral*.

Tilman, H. W. 'Bill', *Mischief in Greenland*.

Tilman, H. W. 'Bill', *Mount Everest 1938* (Cambridge University Press, 1948).

Tilman, H. W. 'Bill', *Two Mountains and a River* (Vertebrate Digital, 2016).

Tombazi, N. A., *Account of a Photographic Expedition to the Southern Glaciers of Kangchenjunga in the Sikkim Himalaya* (Bombay, 1925).

Verne, Jules, *Journey to the Centre of the Earth* (Griffith and Farran, 1863).

Waddell, Laurence Austine, *Among the Himalayas* (Andesite Press, 2015).

Ward, Michael, 'Everest 1951: The footprints attributed to the Yeti – myth and reality,' *Wilderness & Environmental Medicine*, 1997.

Acknowledgements

No one reads the acknowledgements, but here goes anyway. A book like this relies heavily on the sources, and I read around 100 books for this slim volume. So I am eternally grateful to my climbing friend, surgeon and bookbinder Mark Lambert for his steady supply of rare mountaineering books. Next, I must thank Daniel Loxton and Donald Prothero for their excellent scientific appreciation of the subject of cryptids listed in the bibliography. Thanks to Steve Berry for suggesting the ridiculous idea of a yeti-hunt in Bhutan in the first place, to Sonam for spotting the footprints and to Harry Marshall of Icon Films for supporting us. Finally, thanks to my editor Myles Archibald for entertaining the idea of a book about mythical beasts and then advising me during my calls from the vast landscapes of the Himalayas and the endless white sands of the Outer Hebrides.

Picture Credits

Page viii courtesy of Pedja Jovanovik

Illustrations on pages 5, 7 © Hergé/Moulins/
  Éditions Casterman S.A.

Page 70 © Topical Press Agency/Hulton Archive/
  Getty Images

Page 76 © Chronicle/Alamy

Page 93 © John Mock/Lonely Planet Images/Getty Images

Page 94 by Lotte Jacobi © University of New Hampshire/
  Gado/Getty Images

Pages 109, 128 © ZUMA Press, Inc./Alamy

Page 140 © Anindya Mukherjee (Raja)

Page 141 © Gina Waggott

Page 251 © David Goddard/Getty Images

Index

Page references in *italics* indicate
images.
GH indicates Graham Hoyland.

306